dog spelled backwards

dog
spelled
backwards

soulful writing

by literary dog lovers

mordecai siegal

St. Martin's Press ⚬ New York

www.stmartins.com

See pages 281–282 for copyright acknowledgments.

Photographs by Mordecai Siegal. Copyright © 2007 by Mordecai Siegal.

Book design by Abby Kagan
Dog illustration by Leslie Evans

Library of Congress Cataloging-in-Publication Data

Dog spelled backwards : soulful writing by literary dog lovers / [edited by] Mordecai Siegal.—1st ed.
    p. cm.
    ISBN-13: 978-0-312-28179-3
    ISBN-10: 0-312-28179-X
    1. Dogs—Literary collections. 2. American literature. 3. English literature. I. Siegal, Mordecai.

PS509.D6D64 2007
810.8'03629772—dc22   2007014403

First Edition: August 2007

10   9   8   7   6   5   4   3   2   1

for roger caras, my friend, my mentor

contents

acknowledgments   xiii

introduction   xv

part one: genesis of the dog-eared heart

Halfway to Heaven: The Story of the St. Bernard,
     Ruth Adams Knight   3

The Coming of Riquet, Anatole France   15

John Scott's Affectionate Pup, Ellis Parker Butler   30

Memoirs of a Yellow Dog, O. Henry   33

From *A Midsummer Night's Dream,* William Shakespeare   39

A Tribute to the Dog, George Graham Vest   40

part two: brave and sacred hearts

Bum: A Brooklyn Dog, Sarah Noble Ives   45

My Buddy, Murray Weinstock   58

For the Love of a Man, Jack London   60

Stop Kicking My Dog Around, Anonymous   74

part three: a breed apart

Remarkable Dog, Mark Twain   77

Gulliver the Great, Walter A. Dyer   80

Old Dog Tray, Stephen Collins Foster 94
The Westminster Kennel Club, Charles S. Pelham-Clinton 96
Four on the Floor, Mordecai Siegal 103

part four: poetry in motion

Elizabeth Barrett Browning and a Spaniel Named Flush,
  Mordecai Siegal 107
To Flush, My Dog, Elizabeth Barrett Browning 111
Flush or Faunus, Elizabeth Barrett Browning 117
From *Flush: A Biography*: The Back Bedroom,
  Virginia Woolf 117
To My Dog, John Galsworthy 121
From *A Midsummer Night's Dream*, William Shakespeare 122

part five: the world according to dogs

The Bar Sinister, Richard Harding Davis 127
Angel on a Leash, Murray Weinstock 159
Three's Company, Steve Dale 160
When I Get to Heaven: Questions from an Anxious Dog,
  Anonymous 165
Old Blue, Anonymous 167

part six: love unleashed

Garm—A Hostage, Rudyard Kipling 171
The Power of the Dog, Rudyard Kipling 188
The Checkers Affair: A Cocker Spaniel, a Speech,
  and the Political Survival of Richard M. Nixon,
  Mordecai Siegal 190
Another Speech, Another Dog, Mordecai Siegal 197
Dog Names of the Great and Not So Great,
  Mordecai Siegal 199

part seven: god is coming, look busy

The Soul of Caliban, Emma-Lindsay Squier 203

The Barking Dog, Zen Master Hsu Yun 217

For Ashley Whippet: A Testimonial, Mordecai Siegal 218

A Dog's Best Friend, Anonymous 221

A Prayer for Animals, Albert Schweitzer 222

part eight: litter-ature

From *Peter Pan*: Peter Breaks Through, and The Shadow,
  J. M. Barrie 225

That Spot, Jack London 235

Underdog, Mordecai Siegal 246

Dandy: The Story of a Dog, W. H. Hudson 246

part nine: heavenly days

The Bonding, Roger Caras 255

Going Home, Stephen and Patti Thompson 259

To My Dog, John Galsworthy 261

Enter Tarzan, Mordecai Siegal 262

Erica's Song, Arlene Klein 271

From *Old Dogs, Old Friends: Enjoying Your Older Dog*:
  Memories Are Forever, and Grow Old with Me,
  Bonnie Wilcox, D.V.M., and Chris Walkowicz 273

Copyright Acknowledgments 281

acknowledgments

Much time and effort go into the making of a book, and often many hands besides those of the author help roll the creative dough, shape it, and fill it like a succulent pie with a lot of the delectable goodies. That was certainly the case with *Dog Spelled Backwards*. Unlike anything I have done before, it has been an adventure, a walk through a literary amusement park, unmapped, with no directions. Thank God for the invaluable help, the ideas, and the stimulus from friends and professionals who really do know something and came through at critical times. Recognizing them for their generous and invaluable help is why these pages exist.

It all began with the magnificent library of the American Kennel Club (*shhh!*), where resides an incredible collection of dog books and periodicals. I owe a great deal to AKC librarian Barbara Kolk, M.L.S., and her staff for their generous help and cooperation. Ms. Kolk is the silent engine of that very quiet but dynamic canine asset.

In the beginning, there were empty folders and blank pages, but they were soon filled with a flood of possibilities, thanks to the initial research efforts of Suzannah Schiff-Holiday, digging up clippings, quotes, songs, writings, and so much more from the many, many libraries of upstate New York. Most valuable was her enthusiasm for this canine literary pie at the stepping-off place, which is when I needed it the most.

And *thank you* is so inadequate an expression for the mental energy and professional views so generously given by my friend and fellow author Carol Lea Benjamin. The influence of her very thoughtful suggestions along with her zest for the basic concept is evident throughout the book.

Valerie Feldner Volinski, formerly of *The New Yorker* and *TV Guide* among many other publications, was an early cheerleader for this book and helped on many occasions with her keen-eyed scrutiny of the contents, especially of my own writing contributions. Her opinions were essential along with her friendship.

To my good friend David Frei, director of communications at the Westminster Kennel Club, for providing fascinating materials and information from the archives of that distinguished dog club. There's only one.

Many thanks to George Berger, former publisher of American Kennel Club Publications, for his willingness to help.

With maximum gratitude to Chuan Zhi Shakya, Abbot, Zen Buddihist Order of Hsu Yun; Stephen and Patti Thompson; Arlene Klein; Jill B. Caras; Chris Walkowicz; Bonnie Wilcox; Harry Paine; Steve Dale; Murray Weinstock; Cel Hope; and Charlotte Reed.

It is no trade secret that few books ever see the light of day unless a literary agent begins the process. So to my literary representative, Mel Berger of the William Morris Agency, thank you for your vision and all the efforts you make on my behalf. A quarter of a century: so far, so good.

It has been a privilege working with my editor at St. Martin's Press, Elizabeth Beier, who acquired this project and then with unbelievable patience, not to mention sharp eyes, made the book better than it would have been. Of course I cannot ignore the fine work of her editorial assistant, Michelle Richter, who has such a gentle disposition for one doing such heavy lifting. It's been a rewarding experience. Biscuits and popsicles to our book designer extraordinaire, Abby Kagan, and illustrator, Leslie Evans, who created the interior of this book as a warm, attractive place to visit, whether you're human, canine, or *dog spelled backwards*.

introduction

There is a legend among dog lovers that God was so pleased with his four-legged, tail-wagging, tongue-panting creation because of his courage and faithfulness and extremely pleasing ways that he decided to name him after himself, but for the sake of modesty, he did it indirectly. Hence, the name dog, which if spelled backwards . . . well, that's the legend, and I have yet to meet a dog lover that would argue with it.

Most dog owners are sentimental, spiritual, deeply caring about their four-legged family member, and some even believe their dogs have a divine presence in the hereafter. I once did a eulogy for a friend of mine and I quoted something he once said about his dog. My friend Danny said, "I don't care where I end up after I'm gone, as long as I have Amanda with me."

Those of us who live in the dog culture, who love and lavish attention on our pampered pets, know just how necessary they have become to our inner condition. We no longer keep a dog, but, rather, share a life. *Doghouse* is no longer a pejorative term. It is where canines and humans live with mutual feelings and needs. Dogs are deeply loved companions and friends who offer unshakable loyalty and wholly reliable relationships that become as meaningful as any that we can nurture. Dogs that share the pleasures of a hectic family or a one-dog, one-person life are as necessary as security blankets and as much a part of the household as an adopted child. The value of a dog is immeasurable when it shatters the silence of a lonely existence. Dogs make us feel alive and part of nature and, to many, part of a spiritual mosaic. In a special sense, dogs are forever. Children and other people sense it and feel it instantly. Dogs plunge deep into the human heart and there they stay for a lifetime.

It is important to understand that most of the fifty million dog owners in North America do not merely endow their dogs with human qualities but also connect with them in emotional terms, which can be very close to a spiritual mind-set. *Dog Spelled Backwards* is not about religion and dogs. It is about imagined or actual experiences that have inspired the creation of memorable writing from well-known and lesser-known dog lovers, from historically significant writers and several contemporary writers. Offered herein is a smorgasbord of literary bits and pieces, short stories, poems, quotes, sayings, prayers, and song lyrics, served up buffet style. They all declare the emotional and inspirational attachment that we feel for our dogs. It is a compilation of dog writing that I hope will inspire reflection. Stop anyone on the street walking his dog and ask how he feels about his friend on the other end of the leash, or better yet, ask what role his dog plays in his life. You will be amazed at the answers.

If you gently hold your dog's face within your hands or embrace him in your arms and experience the rhythm of his breathing, the beat of his great heart, and the warmth of his presence, you will discover all the sweet comfort and hope that can be had in a world that often confuses and upsets the best of us. Dogs can slow down a racing pulse or drive away despair or feelings of burning anger. They can transform wounding thoughts into soothing feelings of peacefulness and love. A dog can be a guide and a healer and a good friend to those whose spirits are down or in need of repair. Dogs are certainly fun, but they are much more than that; they are a reassuring comfort and at the same time friends and companions. Is that inspirational? Of course it is. Is that spiritual? Yes, a thousand times yes. A dog by your side suggests a generous gift from a revered source of existence.

Dog Spelled Backwards implies something quite wonderful about these creatures that share our lives with something beyond a game of fetch, long walks, or one-sided conversations. These children of nature, who never judge, never criticize, and who love with no questions asked are an organic part of our lives, like the thick bough of a tree. You never hear of a dog asking to see *your* papers, do you? The uncomplicated way in which dogs respond to us is irresistible because they are so direct and honestly glad to be with us, making us wonder who is depending on whom and whose dependency is greater.

You may refer to this connection as spiritual or inspirational, or as something indefinable, improving our lives and making us better than we are; or you may simply call it love. It doesn't matter what you call it. What matters is that it braids our lives together, attaching us to intangibles that stir the heart and make us wonder about a better place and a higher power. The creation of the dog cannot be an accident; it has to be a generous, merciful gift from the heavens for those with the good sense to accept it. Poets and writers of every generation and from every culture, from O. Henry to Roger Caras, have often expressed this idea. It is an important thing to know, and the works presented here are an appreciation of that inspirational, sometimes spiritual, connection between dogs and those who love them.

The writing is as varied as the dogs themselves. Within these pages is a shared intimacy from a diverse assortment of authors and a wide range of their expression. The one thing binding them together is the notion that the canine experience is deep and meaningful, connecting us to nature and whatever we feel lies beyond. In this book can be found humor and irony and even some sadness, all expressing the significance of the canine presence in the human environment, from Stephen Foster to Elizabeth Barrett Browning to Mark Twain right on up to Virginia Woolf and contemporary writers such as Steve Dale, Bonnie Wilcox, Chris Walkowicz, and myself. These various creations are from writers who were inspired by the connection they have experienced with dogs that trotted in and out of their lives. They also reveal dogs that touched their hearts with a laugh-provoking dash or by poignantly laying a head on a lap, not to mention a soulful look or a gentle touch of the paw. There are even dogs that narrate their own stories. Whether a supporting character or a central figure, the dogs in literature and history usually symbolize virtues that are too often lacking in ourselves. The dog exemplifies undying love, devotion, fidelity, courage, intelligence, good judgment, and just plain goodness. By endowing the canine with these qualities, authors have faulted humans for failing to live up to the high standards set by their four-legged friends.

Embedded in all this writing is the conclusion that dogs may be something like furry angels. All that's missing are the wings and the feathers.

part one

genesis of the dog-eared heart

I care not for a man's religion whose dog
and cat are not the better for it.
—Abraham Lincoln

halfway to heaven

the story of the st. bernard

ruth adams knight

Halfway to Heaven is about the St. Bernard Hospice at the Mons Iovis pass between Italy and Switzerland and the legendary monk Canon Joseph and the great St. Bernard Barry der Menschenretter (lifesaver).

Ruth Adams Knight (1894–1974) began her long career as a journalist writing news and feature stories for the *Toledo Times*. Eventually, she wrote for radio, and in 1936, she began writing for various network programs. She wrote numerous books for adults and teenagers, including *Halfway to Heaven* and *A Friend in the Dark: The Story of a Seeing Eye Dog*.

XIV

. . . The startling thing was that Barry never failed him. The list of his rescues grew long. Barry worked alone, he worked with other dogs, he worked with any monk on a rescue mission. But most beautifully of all he worked with Canon Joseph. On the trail, through the grim passages, it made no difference to Barry. He knew the valley as wild animals know their own haunts. Storms never frightened him, he ran with the wind, snow was his natural element. If there was life under a wide expanse of snow he detected it and found the lost one. Many a traveler made his way to the Hospice by clutching Barry's tail and stumbling along behind him.

For all his heroism he was a gay and friendly dog. But he owed allegiance to one man only, and that man was Canon Joseph.

A Canon and on his way to be a priest. A young man commended by the new Prior, and the right hand of Father Henri, who still was Abbé. Canon Joseph, who went down both sides of the mountain now on errands of business and of mercy, who had come to know the way to Martigny as well now as the familiar path to Aosta, and who loved and was loved by many in both directions. No longer did Joseph feel he was Italian and an alien in Helvetia. Often he forgot he was not Swiss as he was sure the Swiss forgot he was Italian. Switzerland he had come to love and the Swiss people. It was a magnificently beautiful country, and a bold free country. It would not tolerate domination for long. But Italy still held his roots. Here on the frontiers of both he was happy, regarding no land as his own, since a monk's kingdom must be the Kingdom of Heaven.

Below him on one side was a deep, narrow crevasse; on the other side was the ice wall. One misstep was all that was needed to send them both plunging into eternity.

And with the years Joseph had grown almost as valiant as Barry. His single ancient fear had never been completely conquered. He knew that without Barry he would be much less a man. But no other thing challenged him. He would work here and work hard as long as he was able. And he would be able as long as Barry was, he assured himself. Afterward he would serve as a priest, or be assigned to Martigny. And there by some special dispensation Barry must be with him always.

"He is brave and selfless, that one," the new Prior observed to Father Henri, watching Joseph go with Barry down the slope one day.

"He fears one thing only. His heart clings to the dog. It is an ancient love. If something should happen there—" The Abbé's gesture was one of helplessness.

"It is hard to censure him for it. Canon Joseph is loved by everyone, except perhaps—"

The two men looked at one another.

"Canon Emil wished to be Keeper," the Abbé said. "These disappointments require self-discipline. There is rivalry too between the dogs."

But most of this Joseph had trained himself to disregard. As Keeper he was busy every moment, absorbed. When Barry was on a mission without him, when the thunder roared and the wind swept down from the peaks, he still clenched his hands in apprehension and his heart seemed a stone in his breast, but that was still Joseph's secret from almost everyone. If the Abbé remembered and understood no word was said.

Winter, summer, winter, summer. Barry's list of rescued grew to twenty-seven. No dog had done so much. The lifesaver, they began to call him, as Joseph had dreamed they would. Barry the rescuer.

"I must go with him always," Canon Joseph told himself. "When I am with him the fear vanishes, no matter how bad the storm. It is only when he faces the Alps alone that I am terrified for him."

And for many months they went side by side.

It had been a day of snowfall, one in which the danger of slides built to great proportions. It seemed wise to send out several dogs to reconnoiter. If a traveler was found who could not follow the dogs back, an animal always came to the Hospice to summon the monks. Barry was not to be one of the group tonight, Joseph decided, and defended his decision because Barry had already made a trip that morning.

He opened the door of the kennels and ordered all the dogs into the enclosure. They advanced eagerly, Barry at their head. Then abruptly, as though at a sharp command, they retreated. They actually leaped back into the kennel. Barry alone hesitated. He caught Canon Joseph's sleeve in his teeth and dragged him into the kennel with him. Joseph shouted but the exclamation of rebuke had hardly reached his lips before he understood.

Snow that had drifted all day suddenly came roaring down the mountain in a gigantic slide. It crashed along the side of the monastery and down the slope. There was the sound of rending timber. Everything which had been in the enclosure it carried with it.

"But how do they know?" one of the novices asked, coming to help clear away the debris. "How could the dogs tell the avalanche was coming?"

How could anyone have known, unless he could read the mind of God? But if Barry had not known, both he and Canon Joseph would have been lying under tons of ice and snow, far down the valley.

As it was, the dogs still had to go out. Canon Joseph selected them, made them ready. Canon Emil stood watching. Then abruptly, without waiting for orders, he swung open the kennel door. The dogs shot out and away. But not as Joseph had planned. For with them, leading them, went Barry the lifesaver.

It happened so swiftly, so unexpectedly there was no time to call him back. He vanished into the growing darkness.

Had Canon Emil deliberately let Barry go? Joseph could not ask him. There was nothing to do about it now.

"I will not grow anxious until midnight," Canon Joseph thought.

Since it was a night of real danger several of the Brothers waited with him for the dogs to return. Within a couple of hours one came back followed by a half-dead soldier. Obviously a deserter, but he was fed and warmed and put to bed. After a while one more came in with a workman. And the last two of the dogs returned leading a young couple, hysterical with fear and grief.

It was an avalanche, the woman was crying. She caught at Canon Joseph's robe. "*Oh save my baby, my little girl!* I had her in my arms. When the slide came it swept us away. I lost my hold.

When I was conscious again I was alone in the snow. Finally my husband found me. We searched and searched. But the snow fell too fast and the wind blew. When at last the dogs came we followed them for help. Oh save her. *Save her!*"

Canon Joseph organized a party immediately.

After a time they became separated. Alone, Joseph searched for endless hours. Never had he faced a worse storm. He could see only in glimpses. But he persisted, walking on and calling until it seemed to him hope no longer was in him. That not only would he not find the child, but that Barry too must be gone. He had prayed for a long time, but now it seemed to him words would no longer come.

He himself felt drowsy, overwhelmed. He had been exhausted when he started out and he knew this gradual slipping away was a danger signal. But he could not fight it. He thought vaguely, "I am a young man still. I have much to do," but waves of blackness swept over him. He stumbled to his knees and could not rise again. His head fell lower and lower. . . .

Beside her stood Barry. He was covered with snow, an icy image of a dog. But an active one. He was trying to rouse the child by pulling and tugging at her clothing and by licking her face.

Was this then the end? He knew himself going. There was nothing more he could do. Sinking, he clung to consciousness. He tried to pray. . . .

"Our Father—in Heaven—Thy will be done—" Suddenly a thought came simple and clear. God's will must be done, always. There was no other power. What more was there to say then? He lay still, at peace.

There was a lull in the wind. He heard a sound. It was not loud, but it was distinct and familiar. It echoed from somewhere beyond and below him.

An instinct told him he might be near the edge of the canyon. Painfully he inched his way forward. He was. He peered down. On a ledge below him lay the little lost girl.

Beside her stood Barry. He was covered with snow, an icy image of a dog. But an active one. He was trying to rouse the child by pulling and tugging at her clothing and by licking her face. She seemed to stir. Then Canon Joseph heard her cry and as he watched she sat up and threw her arms about the great animal's neck.

It was what Barry wanted, what he had been working for. He turned his body so that his head was beside hers and began an attempt to get her on his back. At first it appeared hopeless. But finally the child seemed to understand and she began to try too. And finally she did lie there, her head on his great head, her small body extended along his back, her arms clasped tightly about his neck.

The fog in the Canon's mind cleared. He was alert now, hypnotized, hardly breathing with excitement and with hope. Slowly, carefully, Barry worked his way along the ledge carrying his precious burden. Below him on one side was a deep, narrow crevasse; on the other side was the ice wall. One misstep was all that was needed to send them both plunging into eternity.

But Barry made no misstep. His great paws went down cautiously. And they were at the end of the ledge. A scramble, and they were out of the canyon and on the solid snow.

Only then did Joseph speak to him. The big dog brought his burden to him and Joseph lifted the child in his own arms. Joy gave him strength as he strode toward the Hospice. Joy and a new understanding. Ahead of them Barry rushed proudly.

The Hospice windows showed gray and the child was warm and safely asleep as were her exhausted parents when at last the Abbé came, sent by the Prior to commend Canon Joseph and to give him permission to take one hour from duty for sleep, a concession made only on rare occasions.

"Canon Emil released Barry deliberately," he said. "When we thought you were lost Emil came to me and confessed."

"It is of no matter. Emil's enmity can never reach me again," Joseph said and knew he spoke the truth.

"You and Barry should be happy and satisfied," the Abbé said.

Canon Joseph's eyes met his and in them was a look the Abbé remembered well, the frank look of boyish innocence. The dark head nodded wearily.

"Barry finds his joy in service, as we all do." A smile flickered. "And Father Henri, this is childish, but I can say it to you, for it is a thing we spoke of on a night long ago. I shall not face fear again. Tonight at last I have come to *feel* faith." His face shone. "It is as you said, very simple. It is but to say—and *know*—'Thy will be done.' "

XV

The years were all the same. They were the beads on a rosary. Joseph told them over and over, remembering their rich rewards, amazed as they slipped through his fingers.

Life at the Hospice was timeless, it was now and it was forever. In this spot existence became caught and held in eternity, Joseph sometimes thought. Yet he realized he had grown older and that Barry, whose span of life was so much shorter than his own, was no longer a young dog. He was a famous and heroic one. He was Barry der Menschenretter, and the count of the lives he had saved mounted steadily—*thirty, thirty-five, forty. . . .*

It was inconceivable, yet it was true. One day life here must be over for both of them. Father Joseph would go, to the valley, to Martigny, and Barry would go with him. They would have many duties there, but their days of rescue would be finished. Neither of them could be called ancient, but twelve years of service on the heights was the limit of what could be endured.

And then their last winter at the Hospice came.

Father Joseph felt no regrets. He accepted it as he had come to accept the entire pattern of his life, recognizing its inevitability.

Both of them felt the cold intensely now. The resistance which they had built up during the early years was dissipated and the chill pierced them through and through. A few more weeks and the Hospice would know them no more except as visitors. Only in the fair weather would they still climb the heights together, a link between the Hospice itself and the authority below.

But though spring was approaching there was no sign of it now at the Pass. The terrific gales were blowing. And with the ardor with which he had so long met the challenge of the storm Father Joseph felt his spirit respond to it. There came a night when he would not even ask for volunteers. Tonight, he decided, would belong to him and to Barry. They would go into the storm as they had so many times before, to search for the lost ones.

> . . . but there was a chance the good monks of St. Bernard might be searching for travelers, might manage a rescue. If he could make them hear him. He shouted but faintly, and then his voice was gone.
>
> He lay in the snow to die.

Father Joseph took his cloak and lantern and made his way to the kennel. He did not need to call; at the sound of the lock opening Barry was beside him, eager and ready. Side by side they passed through the great outer door, and were at once in the heart of the tumult.

They moved down the slope, the chain collar Barry wore to protect him from wild animals clanking in the stillness. Snow blew about them and blinded them, the same snow they had battled so long. Its sting was a familiar pain. Father Joseph pulled his hood low; he felt his way with his staff; the light of his lantern glowed dimly. Ahead the fawn patches of Barry's coat showed dark against the snow.

They were away from the Hospice now, Barry pressing on steadily, not too fast, not too slow, accommodating his pace to his master as he had done a thousand times before. The snow was deeply drifted, the way steep and all landmarks obliterated. But Barry would find the trail. Guided by an instinctive knowledge deeper than any human intelligence, Barry was unfailing, invincible.

They had walked for an hour when Father Joseph recognized they had reached a danger spot. Here snow piled in a deep valley and travelers frequently became lost. Barry was pushing on fast now and Father Joseph raised his lantern and peered. At first he saw nothing.

Then below him in the snow he made out a black, huddled object.

"God be thanked," Father Joseph said, as he always said it when one who otherwise would have been lost was rescued. "Thank God we were guided here."

Barry began running, Barry the lifesaver, speeding to the rescue. In the snow a man stirred.

A soldier on leave had been foolish enough to think he could go over the Pass and visit his mother in Martigny. He had started out valiantly but the storm had closed in on him. The drifts were deep, he had missed the way. He had floundered and, floundering, become exhausted. When he realized he could go no farther he was frightened, but the numbing cold dulled his senses. He tried to call. There seemed no one to answer but there was a chance the good monks of St. Bernard might be searching for travelers, might manage a rescue. If he could make them hear him. He shouted but faintly, and then his voice was gone.

He lay in the snow to die.

He dreamed then and in his dreams he was a child again, tending sheep on his father's hillside. He cared for them lovingly and watchfully, for there were many wolves and he had to keep constant guard. He sat on the hillside, relaxed but alert. And when without warning a great beast sprang out of the darkness at him, he was magnificently ready. The knife he carried in his belt fitted his hand, he held it strongly. He had never killed a wolf but he would certainly kill this one. He saw its glowing eyes, its great mouth open, its dripping fangs, felt its hot breath, and the knife plunged. . . .

There was a cry, long, tortured, mortal. It was no wolf cry. He struggled up.

In an anguished flash Father Joseph coming up saw what had happened. He saw the blood on the white fur, and the eyes that looked at him in wondering suffering, and the drooping head. And in the last moment before Barry der Menschenretter fell he saw him move to guide the man who had killed him in the direction of the Hospice of St. Bernard.

XVI

It was summer and the gentians and the rhododendrons were in bloom again.

The way up from Martigny had been a path of beauty. Even the wild scenery in the stretch beyond Bourg St. Pierre was sunwashed slate and the sky was the blue of the Madonna.

If I had a test for goodness in a man, he thought, I would base it on a man's relationship to his dog.

What was grief? Father Joseph wondered. He bore it with what equanimity he could but it was always with him. There was a strange and peculiar bond between a man and a dog which lay perhaps in the complete trust which an animal bestowed upon his master. A dog loves you completely, Father Joseph thought, and in that love he is vulnerable, open to your action in love or enmity. And when he is gone nothing replaces him in your affections.

If I had a test for goodness in a man, he thought, I would base it on a man's relationship to his dog.

A dog was after all an animal, they had said to him, trying to console him. What did that mean? A dog was love, faithfulness, devotion, courage, self-sacrifice. Were not these qualities God-given? Were they not attributes of Heaven?

He looked again at the golden day. If Barry were here he would be running far ahead and then returning, he would be leaping and scrambling and in his fashion praising God.

But Barry was dead. Something in Joseph, perhaps the joy of the eager boy who had felt Barry's first puppy kiss, had died too on that stormy night.

Father Joseph strode on. He rounded a curve and with his eyes lifted to the Hospice almost ran into a young girl. She was standing in the pathway, lovely and wide-eyed, and in her arms she held a great sheaf of flowers.

"They told me at the Hospice you were expected, that you would be coming up the path soon," she said. "I came to meet you. Father Emil said you would be glad to see me. Father Emil loves you. I knew from the way he spoke."

He and Emil were true brothers now, grievances forgotten.

Joseph greeted her courteously, without recognition. "You don't remember, do you?" she said. "But I owe you and Barry my life. You rescued me from a ledge and cared for me at the Hospice."

But she had been a little child. How the years flew.

"It was Barry who rescued you," he said. "Barry. But Barry is dead."

"I know," she said simply. "I heard. That's why I came today. To bring flowers to put on his grave and thank him again. But they tell me he isn't buried here. That he was taken away, to Martigny. So I have brought my flowers to you."

He thanked her.

"Perhaps you would put them on the altar in the chapel," she said. "I should like to think of them there, in the Hospice. I like to think of Barry too—what a wonderful life he had."

The girl didn't seem to think it mattered at all he was dead.

"It was a great tragedy, about his being killed," she went on. "But after I got through crying I saw what a good thing it was. No pain, no waiting around, old and lonely and helpless, not able to do the one thing he lived for. Dying right in the act of saving someone's life, the one thing he lived for. I was very happy for him."

The sun shone around her head like a nimbus and she was smiling. What a lovely, wise girl. She had spoken of Barry as though he were not dead because he was not dead. She had made Joseph see it. In her and in all the others, in forty persons who breathed and moved on earth because of him, Barry still lived. And he would continue to live, through them and their children and their children's children, and through all those who would retell his story down the years. Barry the hero dog, whose strength had been the strength of love, and so unfailing, eternal.

"Father Emil told me from now on one dog, the best at the Hospice, always will be named Barry."

Father Joseph nodded.

The girl was still holding out the bouquet. She was smiling. He took it and smiled back at her, and knew his grief was gone forever.

Standing there, his robe blowing in the wind, the sun shining on his dark hair, he lifted his eyes to the snow peaks above him. And happily he felt that he had climbed a little way at least up one of the hills of Heaven which as a small boy those rich unbelievable years ago he had started out to ascend.

All things bright and beautiful,
All creatures great and small,
All things wise and wonderful,
The Lord God made them all.
—Cecil Francis Alexander

• • •

In the beginning, God created man, but seeing him so
feeble, He gave him the dog.
—Toussenel

the coming of riquet

anatole france

Anatole France (1844–1924) is the nom de plume for Jacques-Anatole-François Thibault, who was born in Paris, France. He was awarded the Nobel Prize for Literature in 1921. His life was devoted to his output of literature, which was prolific, including poems, stories, novels, and social commentaries. His work was acclaimed throughout Europe for being typically French, imbued with irony and skepticism but always urbane and sophisticated. His work was very popular and he achieved great fame throughout his lifetime. The French Academy inducted him as a member in 1896. "The Coming of Riquet" is a story that depicts the furtive plots and maneuvers of people living in a provincial town in France. It is from one of the four novels known collectively as *Contemporary History*. They consist of: *The Elm Tree on the Mall* (1897); *The Wicker-Work Woman* (1897); *The Amethyst Ring* (1899); and *Monsieur Bergeret in Paris* (1901). He loved dogs.

What's that?" asked M. Bergeret.

It was a little dog of doubtful breed, having something of the terrier in him, and a well-set head, a short, smooth coat of a dark tan color, and a tiny little stump of a tail. His body retrained its puppy-like softness, and he went sniffling at the carpet.

"Angélique," said M. Bergeret, "take this animal back to its owner."

"It has no owner, Monsieur."

M. Bergeret looked silently at the little creature, who had come to examine his slippers, and was giving little sniffs of approval.

"The dog," said M. Bergeret, "is a religious animal. In his savage state he worships the moon and the lights that float upon the waters. These are his gods, to whom he appeals at night with long-drawn howls. In the domesticated state he seeks by his caresses to conciliate those powerful genii who dispense the good things of this world—to wit, men."

M. Bergeret was a philogist, which perhaps explains why at this juncture he asked a vain question.

"What is he called?"

"Monsieur," replied Angélique, "he has no name."

M. Bergeret seemed put out at this answer: he looked at the dog sadly, with a disheartened air.

Then the little animal placed its two front paws on M. Bergeret's slipper, and holding it thus, began innocently to nibble at it. With a sudden access of compassion M. Bergeret took the tiny nameless creature upon his knee. The dog looked at him intently, and M. Bergeret was pleased at his confiding expression.

"What beautiful eyes!" he cried.

The dog's eyes were indeed beautiful, the pupils of a golden-flecked chestnut set in warm white. And his gaze spoke of simple, mysterious thoughts, common alike to the thoughtful beasts and simple men of the earth.

Tired, perhaps, with the intellectual effort he had made for the purpose of entering into communication with a human being, he closed his beautiful eyes, and, yawning widely, revealed his pink mouth, his curled-up tongue, and his array of dazzling teeth.

M. Bergeret put his hand into the dog's mouth, and allowed him to lick it, at which old Angélique gave a smile of relief.

"A more affectionate little creature doesn't breathe," she said.

"The dog," said M. Bergeret, "is a religious animal. In his savage state he worships the moon and the lights that float upon the waters. These are his gods, to whom he appeals at night with long-drawn howls. In the domesticated state he seeks by his caresses to conciliate those powerful genii who dispense the good things of this world—to wit, men. He worships and honors men by the accomplishment of the rites passed down to him by his ancestors: he licks their hands, jumps against their legs, and when they show signs of anger towards him he approaches them crawling on his belly as a sign of humility, to appease their wrath."

"All dogs are not the friends of man," remarked Angélique. "Some of them bite the hand that feeds them."

"Those are the ungodly, blasphemous dogs," returned M. Bergeret . . .

"All dogs are not the friends of man," remarked Angélique. "Some of them bite the hand that feeds them."

"Those are the ungodly, blasphemous dogs," returned M. Bergeret, "insensate creatures like Ajax, the son of Telamon, who wounded the hand of the golden Aphrodite. These sacrilegious creatures die a dreadful death, or lead wandering and miserable lives. They are not to be confounded with those dogs who, espousing the quarrel of their own particular god, wage war upon his enemy, the neighboring god. They are heroes. Such, for example, is the dog of Lafolie, the butcher, who fixed his sharp teeth into the leg of the tramp Pied-d'Alouette. For it is a fact that dogs fight among themselves like men, and Turk, with his snub nose, serves his god Lafolie against the robber gods, in the same way that Israel helped Jehovah to destroy Chamos and Moloch."

The puppy, however, having decided that M. Bergeret's remarks were the reverse of interesting, curled up his feet and stretched out his head, ready to go to sleep upon the knees that harbored him.

"Where did you find him?" asked M. Bergeret.

"Well, Monsieur, it was M. Dellion's *chef* gave him to me."

"With the result," continued M. Bergeret, "that we now have this soul to care for."

"What soul?" asked Angélique.

"This canine soul. An animal is, properly speaking, a soul; I do not say an immortal soul. And yet, when I come to consider the positions this poor little beast and I myself occupy in the scheme of things, I recognize in both exactly the same right to immortality."

After considerable hesitation, old Angélique, with a painful effort that made her upper lip curl up and reveal her two remaining teeth, said:

"If Monsieur does not want a dog, I will return him to M. Dellion's *chef*; but you may safely keep him, I assure you. You won't see or hear him."

She had hardly finished her sentence when the puppy, hearing a heavy van rolling down the street, sat bolt upright on M. Bergeret's knees, and began to bark both loud and long, so that the window-panes resounded with the noise.

M. Bergeret smiled.

"He's a watch-dog," said Angélique, by way of excuse. "They are by far the most faithful."

"Have you given him anything to eat?" asked M. Bergeret.

"Of course," returned Angélique.

"What does he eat?"

"Monsieur must be aware that dogs eat bread and meat."

Somewhat piqued, M. Bergeret retorted that in her eagerness she might very likely have taken him away from his mother before he was old enough to leave her, upon which he was lifted up again and re-examined, only to make sure of the fact that he was at least six months old.

M. Bergeret put him down on the carpet, and regarded him with interest.

"Isn't he pretty?" said the servant.

"No, he is not pretty," replied M. Bergeret. "But he is engaging, and has beautiful eyes. That is what people used to say about me," added the professor, "when I was three times as old, and not half as intelligent. Since then I have no doubt acquired an outlook upon the universe which he will never attain. But, in comparison with the Absolute, I may say that my knowledge equals his in the smallness of its extent. Like his, it is a geometrical point in the

infinite." Then, addressing the little creature who was sniffing the
waste-paper basket, he went on: "Smell it out, sniff it well, take
from the outside world all the knowledge that can reach your simple brain through the medium of that black truffle-like nose of
yours. And what though I at the same time observe, and compare,
and study? We shall never know, neither the one nor the other of
us, why we have been put into this world, and what we are doing in
it. What are we here for, eh?"

As he had spoken rather loudly, the puppy looked at him anx-
iously, and M. Bergeret, returning to the thought which had first
filled his mind, said to the servant:

"We must give him a name."

With her hands folded in front of her she replied laughingly
that that would not be a difficult matter.

Upon which M. Bergeret made the private reflection that to the
simple all things are simple, but that clear-sighted souls, who look
upon things from many and diverse aspects, invisible to the vulgar
mind, experience the greatest difficulty in coming to a decision
about even the most trivial matters. And he cudgelled his brains,
trying to hit upon a name for the little living thing that was busily
engaged in nibbling the fringe of the carpet.

"All the names of dogs," thought he, "preserved in the ancient
treatises of the huntsmen of old, such as Fouilloux, and in the verses
of the sylvan poets such as La Fontain-Finaud, Miraut, Briffaut,
Ravaud, and such-like names, are given to sporting dogs, who are
the aristocracy of the kennel, the chivalry of the canine race. The
dog Ulysses called Argos, and he was a hunter too, so Homer tells
us. 'In his youth he hunted the little hares of Ithaca, but now he was
old and hunted no more.' What we require is something quite different. The names given by old maids to their lap-dogs would be
more suitable, were they not usually pretentious and absurd. Azor,
for instance, is ridiculous!"

So M. Begeret ruminated, calling to memory many a dog
name, without being able to decide, however, on one that pleased

him. He would have liked to invent a name, but lacked the imagination.

"What day is it?" he asked at last.

"The ninth," replied Angélique. "Thursday, the ninth."

"Well, then!" said M. Bergeret, "can't we call the dog Thursday, like Robinson Crusoe who called his man Friday, for the same reason?"

"As Monsieur pleases," said Angélique. "But it isn't very pretty."

"Very well," said M. Bergeret, "find a name for the creature yourself, for, after all, you brought him here."

"Oh, no," said the servant. "I couldn't find a name for him; I'm not clever enough. When I saw him lying on the straw in the kitchen, I called him Riquet, and he came up and played about under my skirts."

"You called him Riquet, did you?" cried M. Bergeret. "Why didn't you say so before? Riquet he is and Riquet he shall remain; that's settled. Now be off with you, and take Riquet with you. I want to work."

"Monsieur," returned Angélique, "I am going to leave the puppy with you; I will come for him when I get back from market."

"You could quite well take him to market with you," retorted M. Bergeret.

"Monsieur, I am going to church as well."

It was quite true that she really was going to church at Saint-Exupère, to ask for a Mass to be said for the repose of her husband's soul. She did that regularly once a year, not that she had even been informed of the decease of Borniche, who had never communicated with her since his desertion, but it was a settled thing in the good woman's mind that Borniche was dead. She had therefore no fear of his coming to rob her of the little she had, and did her best to fix things up to his advantage in the other world, so long as he left her in peace in this one.

"Eh!" ejaculated M. Bergeret. "Shut him up in the kitchen or some other convenient place, and do not wor—"

He did not finish his sentence, for Angélique had vanished, purposely pretending not to hear, that she might leave Riquet with his master. She wanted them to grow used to one another, and she also wanted to give poor, friendless M. Bergeret a companion. Having closed the door behind her, she went along the corridor and down the steps.

M. Bergeret set to work again and plunged head foremost into his *Virgilius nauticus*. He loved the work; it rested his thoughts, and became a kind of game that suited him, for he played it all by himself. On the table beside him were several boxes filled with pegs, which he fixed into little squares of cardboard to represent the fleet of Aeneas. Now where he was thus occupied he felt something like tiny fists tapping at his legs. Riquet whom he had quite forgotten, was standing on his hind legs patting his master's knees, and wagging his little stump of a tail. When he tired of this, he let his paws slide down the trouser leg, then got up and began his coaxing over again. And M. Bergeret, turning away from the printed lore before him, saw two brown eyes gazing up at him lovingly.

"What gives a human beauty to the gaze of this dog," he thought, "is probably that it varies unceasingly, being by turns bright and vivacious, or serious and sorrowful; because through these eyes his little dumb soul finds expression for thought that lacks nothing in depth nor sequence. My father was very found of cats, and, consequently, I liked them too. He used to declare that cats are the wise man's best companions, for they respect his studious hours. Bajazet, his Persian cat, would sit at night for hours at a stretch, motionless and majestic, perched on a corner of his table. I still remember the agate eyes of Bajazet, but those jewel-like orbs concealed all thought, that owl-like stare was cold, and hard, and wicked. How much do I prefer the melting gaze of the dog!"

Riquet, however, was agitating his paws in frantic fashion, and M. Bergeret, who was anxious to return to his philological amusements, said kindly, but shortly:

"Lie down, Riquet!"

Upon which Riquet went and thrust his nose against the door through which Angélique had passed out. And there he remained, uttering from time to time plaintive, meek little cries. After a while he began to scratch, making a gentle rasping noise on the polished floor with his nails. Then the whining began again followed by more scratching. Disturbed by these sounds, M. Bergeret sternly bade him keep still.

Riquet peered at him sorrowfully with his brown eyes, then, sitting down, he looked at M. Bergeret again, rose, returned to the door, sniffed underneath it, and wailed afresh.

"Do you want to go out?" asked M. Bergeret.

Putting down his pen, he went to the door, which he held a few inches open. After making sure that he was running no risk of hurting himself on the way out, Riquet slipped through the doorway and marched off with a composure that was scarcely polite. On returning to his table, M. Bergeret, sensitive man that he was, pondered over the dog's action. He said to himself:

"I was on the point of reproaching the animal for going without saying either good-bye or thank you, and expecting him to apologize for leaving me. It was the beautiful human expression of his eyes that made me so foolish. I was beginning to look upon him as one of my own kind."

And M. Bergeret carefully consulted a great number of texts, in order to throw a light upon the word which he could not understand, and which he had to explain. He was almost on the point of grasping the solution, or, at any rate, he had caught a glimpse of it, when he heard a noise like the rattling of chains at his door, a noise which, although not alarming, struck him as curious. The disturbance was presently accompanied by a shrill whining, and M. Bergeret, interrupted in his philological investigations, immediately concluded that these importunate wails must emanate from Riquet.

As a matter of fact, after having looked vainly all over the house for Angélique, Riquet had been seized with a desire to see M. Bergeret again. Solitude was as painful to him as human society was dear. In order to put an end to the noise, and also because

What I want you to understand is that if you desire to live with me, you will have to drop your mongrel manners and behave like a *scholar*, in other words, to remain silent and quiet, to respect work . . .

he had a secret desire to see Riquet again, M. Bergeret got up from his arm-chair and opened the door, and Riquet re-entered the study with the same coolness with which he had quitted it, but as soon as he saw the door close behind him he assumed a melancholy expression, and began to wander up and down the room like a soul in torment.

He had a sudden way of appearing to find something of interest beneath the chairs and tables, and would sniff long and noisily; then he would walk aimlessly about or sit down in a corner with an air of great humility, like the beggars who are to be seen in church porches. Finally he began to bark at a cast of Hermes which stood upon the mantel-shelf, whereupon M. Bergeret addressed him in words full of just reproach.

"Riquet! such vain agitation, such sniffing and barking were better suited to a stable than to the study of a professor, and they lead one to suppose that your ancestors lived with horses whose straw litters they shared. I do not reproach you with that. It is only natural you should have inherited their habits, manners, and tendencies as well as their close-cropped coat, their sausage-like body, and their long, thin nose. I do not speak of your beautiful eyes, for there are few men, few dogs even, who can open such beauties to the light of day. But, leaving all that aside, you are a mongrel, my friend, a mongrel from your short, bandy legs to your head. Again I am far from despising you for that. What I want you to understand is that if you desire to live with me, you will have to drop your mongrel manners and behave like a *scholar*, in other words, to remain silent and quiet, to respect work, after the manner of Bajazet, who of a night would sit for four hours without stirring, and watch my father's pen skimming over the paper. He was a silent and tactful creature. How different is your own character, my friend! Since you came into this chamber of study your hoarse voice your unseemly snufflings and your whines, that sound like steam whistles, have constantly confused my thoughts and interrupted my reflections. And now you have made me lose the drift of an important passage in Servius, referring to the construction of one of the ships of Aeneas. Know then, Riquet, my friend, that this is the house of silence and the abode of meditation, and that if you are anxious to stay here you must become literary. Be quiet!"

Thus spoke M. Bergeret. Riquet, who had listened to him with mute astonishment, approached his master, and with suppliant gesture placed a timid paw upon the knee, which he seemed to revere in a fashion that savored of long ago. Then a kind thought struck M. Bergeret. He picked him up by the scruff of his neck, and put him upon the cushions of the ample easy chair in which he was sitting. Turning himself round three times, Riquet lay down, and then remained perfectly still and silent. He was quite happy. M. Bergeret was grateful to him, and as he ran through Servius he occasionally stroked the close-cropped coat, which, without being soft, was smooth and very pleasant to the touch. Riquet fell into a gentle doze, and communicated to his master the generous warmth of his body, the subtle, gentle heat of a living, breathing thing. And from that moment M. Bergeret found more pleasure in his *Virgilius nauticus.*

From floor to ceiling his study was lined with deal shelves, bearing books arranged in methodical order. . . . The books of archaeology and art found a resting-place on the highest shelves, not by any means out of contempt, but because they were not so often used.

Now, while M. Bergeret worked at his *Virgilius nauticus* and shared his chair with Riquet, he found, as chance would have it, that it was necessary to consult Ottfried Müller's little *Manual,* which happened to be on one of the topmost shelves.

There was no need of one of those tall ladders on wheels topped by railings and a shelf, to enable him to reach the book; there were ladders of this description in the town library, and they had been used by all the great book-lovers of the eighteenth and nineteenth centuries; indeed, several of the latter had fallen from them, and thus died honorable deaths, in the manner spoken of in the pamphlet entitled: *Des bibliophiles qui moururent en tombant de leur échelle.* No, indeed! M. Bergeret had no need of anything of the sort. A small pair of folding steps would have served his purpose excellently well, and he had once seen some in the shop of Clérambaut, the cabinet-maker, in the Rue de Josde. They folded up, and looked just the thing, with their bevelled uprights each pierced with a trefoil as a grip for the hand. M. Bergeret would have given anything to possess them, but the state of his finances, which were somewhat involved, forced him to abandon the idea. No one knew better than he did that financial ills are not mortal, but, for all that, he had no steps in his study.

In place of such a pair of steps he used an old cane-bottomed chair, the back of which had been broken, leaving only two horns or antennae, which had shown themselves to be more dangerous than useful. So they had been cut to the level of the seat, and the chair had become a stool. There were two reasons why this tool was ill-fitted to the use to which M. Bergeret was wont to put it. In the first place the woven-cane seat had grown slack with long use, and now contained a large hollow, making one's foothold precarious. In the second place the stool was too low, and it was hardly possible when standing upon it to reach the books on the highest shelf, even with the finger-tips. What generally happened was that in the endeavor to grasp one book, several others fell out; and it depended upon their being bound or paper-covered whether they lay with broken corners, or sprawled with leaves spread like a fan or a concertina.

Now, with the intention of getting down the *Manual* of Ott-fried Müller, M. Bergeret quitted the chair he was sharing with Ri-quet, who, rolled into a ball with his head tight pressed to his body, lay in warm comfort, opening one voluptuous eye, which he re-closed as quickly. Then M. Bergeret drew the stool from the dark corner where it was hidden and placed it where it was re-quired, hoisted himself upon it, and managed, by making his arm as long as possible, and straining upon tiptoe, to touch, first with one, then with two fingers, the back of a book which he judged to be the one he was needing. As for the thumb, it remained below the shelf and rendered no assistance whatever. M. Bergeret, who found it therefore exceedingly difficult to draw out the book, made the reflection that the reason why the hand is a precious imple-ment is on account of the position of the thumb, and that no being could rise to be an artist who had four feet and no hands.

"It is to the hand," he reflected, "that men owe their power of becoming engineers, painters, writers, and manipulators of all kinds of things. If they had not a thumb as well as their other fin-gers, they would be as incapable as I am at this moment, and they could never have changed the face of the earth as they have done. Beyond a doubt it is the shape of the hand that has assured to man the conquest of the world."

Then, almost simultaneously, M. Bergeret remembered that monkeys, who possess four hands, have not, for all that, created the arts, nor disposed that earth to their use, and he erased from his mind the theory upon which he had just embarked. However he did the best he could with his four fingers. It must be known that Ottfried Müller's *Manual* is composed of three volumes and an atlas. M. Bergeret wanted volume one. He pulled out first the second volume, then the atlas, then volume three, and finally the book that he required. At last he held it in his hands. All that now remained for him to do was to descend, and this he was about to do when the cane seat gave way beneath his foot, which passed through it. He lost his balance and fell to the ground, not as heavily as might have been feared, for he broke his fall by grasping at one of the uprights of the bookshelf.

He was on the ground, however, full of astonishment, and wearing on one leg the broken chair; his whole body was permeated and as though constricted by a pain that spread all over it, and that presently settled itself more particularly in the region of the left elbow and hip upon which he had fallen. But, as his anatomy was not seriously damaged, he gathered his wits together; he had got so far as to realize that he must draw his right leg out of the stool in which it had so unfortunately become entangled, and that he must be careful to raise himself up on his right side, which was unhurt. He was even trying to put this into execution when he felt a warm breath upon his cheek, and turning his eyes, which fright and pain had for the moment fixed, he saw close to his cheek Riquet's little face.

At the sound of the fall Riquet had jumped down from the chair and run to his unfortunate master; he was now standing near him in a state of great excitement; then he commenced to run round him. First he came near out of sympathy, then he retreated out of fear of some mysterious danger. He understood perfectly well that a misfortune had taken place, but he was neither thoughtful nor clever enough to discover what it was; hence his anxiety. His fidelity drew him to his suffering friend, and his prudence stopped him on the very brink of the fatal spot. Encouraged at length by the calm and silence which eventually reigned, he licked M. Bergeret's neck and looked at him with eyes of fear and of love. The fallen master smiled, and the dog licked the end of his nose. It was a great comfort to M. Bergeret, who freed his right leg, stood erect, and limped good-humoredly back to his chair.

Riquet was there before him. All that could be seen of his eyes was a gleam between the narrow slit of the half-closed lids. He seemed to have forgotten all about the adventure that a moment before had so stirred them both. The little creature lived in the present, with no thought of time that had run its course; not that he was wanting in memory, inasmuch as he could remember, not his own past alone, but the faraway past of his ancestors, and his little head was a rich storehouse of useful knowledge; but he took no pleasure in remembrance, and memory was not for him, as it was for M. Bergeret, a divine muse.

Gently stroking the short, smooth coat of his companion, M. Bergeret addressed him in the following affectionate terms:

"Dog! at the price of the repose which is dear to your heart, you came to me when I was dismayed and brought low. You did not laugh, as any young person of my own species would have done. It is true that however joyous or terrible nature may appear to you at times, she never inspires you with a sense of the ridiculous. And it is for that very reason, because of your innocent gravity, that you are the surest friend a man can have. In the first instance I inspired confidence and admiration in you, and now you show me pity.

"Dog! when we first met on the highway of life, we came from the two poles of creation; we belong to different species. I refer to this with no desire to take advantage of it, but rather with a strong sense of universal brotherhood. We have hardly been acquainted two hours, and my hand has never yet fed you. What can be the meaning of the obscure love for me that has sprung up in your little heart? The sympathy you bestow on me is a charming mystery, and I accept it. Sleep, friend, in the place that you have chosen!"

Having thus spoken, M. Bergeret turned over the leaves of Ottfried Müller's *Manual,* which with marvelous instinct he had kept in his hand both during and after his fall. He turned over the pages, and could not find what he sought.

Every moment, however, seemed to increase the pain he was feeling.

"I believe," he thought, "that the whole of my left side is bruised and my hip swollen. I have a suspicion that my right leg is grazed all over and my left elbow aches and burns, but shall I cavil at pain that has led me to the discovery of a friend?"

His reflections were running thus when old Angélique, breathless and perspiring, entered the study. She first opened the door, and then she knocked, for she never permitted herself to enter without knocking. If she had not done so before she opened the door, she did it after, for she had good manners, and knew what was expected of her. She went in therefore, knocked, and said:

"Monsieur, I have come to relieve you of the dog."

M. Bergeret heard these words with decided annoyance. He had not as yet inquired into his claims to Riquet, and now realized that he had none. The thought that Madame Borniche might take the animal away from him filled him with sadness, yet, after all, Riquet did belong to her. Affecting indifference, he replied:

"He's asleep; let him sleep!"

"Where is he? I don't see him," remarked old Angélique.

"Here he is," answered M. Bergeret. "In my chair."

With her two hands clasped over her portly figure, old Angélique smiled, and, in a tone of gentle mockery, ventured:

"I wonder what pleasure the creature can find in sleeping there behind Monsieur!"

"That," retorted M. Bergeret, "is his business."

Then, as he was of inquiring mind, he immediately sought of Riquet his reasons for the selection of his resting-place, and lighting on them, replied with his accustomed candor:

"I keep him warm, and my presence affords a sense of security; my comrade is a chilly and homely little animal." Then he added: "Do you know, Angélique? I will go out presently and buy him a collar."

Acquiring a dog may be the only opportunity
a human ever has to choose a relative.
—Mordecai Siegal

• • •

Of all the things I miss from my veterinary practice,
puppy breath is one of the most fond memories!
—Dr. Tom Cat

john scott's affectionate pup

ellis parker butler

Ellis Parker Butler was one of the best-known and most-loved American writers, during the forty years in which his work was published, starting in 1893. He is credited for having written over 2,200 stories, poems, essays, and full-length books, of which there were thirty. What is even more remarkable is that he was only a part-time writer; his full-time job was as a banker. He founded the Authors' League of America and took an active part in the New York City literary scene. During his lifetime, his contemporaries were Mark Twain, F. Scott Fitzgerald, Don Marquis, Will Rogers, and Edgar Rice Burroughs, among many others. He was the most published writer of the so-called pulp fiction era and much of his work was cherished by a loyal readership. His most successful and enduring work was titled "Pigs is Pigs," the sardonic story of a typical bureaucrat, a railroad stationmaster who insisted on levying a livestock rate on the shipment of two pet guinea pigs, classifying them as actual pigs. Due to their quarantining at the station throughout the dispute, they began to multiply profusely. The story made Butler famous throughout the world for the rest of his life and is identified as his signature work. "John Scott's Affectionate Pup" was published in the March 18, 1911, issue of *Judge* magazine.

One of the most touching things in nature is the affection of a dog for its master. Authors have wept over this before now. Indeed, in some cases, canine affection would make a cube of billiard chalk weep.

John Scott has an affectionate dog. It is a young dog, but joyful, and he keeps it in the cellar at night. The dog and the furnace are great friends, probably because contrasted natures agree well; the dog's nature is warm, and the furnace's nature is cold. But the pup simply adores John Scott.

A few nights ago, John Scott left the banquet of the Petonic Club at one o'clock in the morning, when his wife had told him positively to be home at ten-thirty. She had told him, also, to drink but one cocktail. That was all the cocktails he drank, but in the bright lexicon of banquets there are other drinks. The carefree yet dignified manner in which John Scott wended his homeward way gave proof that he had studied the lexicon.

He was not intoxicated. He could still lift his feet as he walked, but when he had lifted a foot he waved it in the air a moment before he decided just where to set it down, and it did not always hit the exact spot he had selected. But his brain was clear as a bell. He remembered that he must put coal in the furnace before he went to bed.

When he opened the cellar door the pup was asleep on his bed in a box, but by the time John Scott had descended the cellar stairs the pup and its affectionate nature were wide awake. The pup gave one little bark of joy and rushed across the cellar like a rubber shoe fired out of a cannon, and stopped itself by making a flying tackle with its teeth on the hem of one of the legs of John Scott's dress trousers. John Scott swayed, put out a hand, and sat down on the floor, and the pup affectionately climbed into his lap and, putting two coal-dusty paws on John Scott's shirt bosom, kissed him.

This evidence of canine affection was too much for John Scott. He compared it with the reception he would probably receive from Mrs. Scott, and he was so affected that he hugged the pup to his bosom and wept. Then he placed the pup carefully on the cellar floor and stood up. The pup immediately got between his feet, threw him twice as he walked to the coal bin, and, when he bent down to pick up the coal scoop, grabbed the tail of his dress coat in a death grip.

Mr. Scott divested himself of the pup by taking off his coat and hanging it on a nail—the one the poker hangs on. All indications pointed to a permanent suspension of the pup. The pup hung to the coattail and the coat hung on the nail, and Mr. Scott turned to the coal bin. He raised the scoop, ready to plunge it into the coal, but as he did so he paused. The pup was standing on the coal, just where the scoop was about to scoop up coal. At intervals the pup would dash down and worry the heel of Mr. Scott's dress trousers, but whenever the scoop approached the coal the pup got in front of it. Sometimes Mr. Scott scooped up the pup, and sometimes he missed the pup, the coal, and the bin; but whenever he got coal he got the pup, too. If, by chance, he got coal in the scoop without any pup, the pup showed its canine affection by jumping into the scoop. Then the coal and the pup would slide off the scoop onto the floor.

Not for worlds would John Scott have shoveled the affectionate pup into the furnace, but he saw that he was likely to do so any minute if he continued to fool with the scoop. There was but one way to get the coal into the furnace without cremating the pup. So John Scott proceeded in that way. He sat on the coal and held the pup in his lap and threw the coal, piece by piece, at the furnace door.

And this was the only basis for Mrs. John Scott's unjust suspicion that John Scott had taken more than one cocktail at the Petonic Club banquet. She came to the head of the cellar stairs to see what was bombarding the tin sides of the furnace, and she saw John Scott sitting on the coal in his shirt sleeves, weeping over the affection of the pup, and throwing coal at the furnace with his left hand, while the pup nestled inside his dress waistcoat and kissed his face. And she accused him of having taken more than one cocktail!

But a woman never knows how the affection of a canine affects a tenderhearted Petonic Club banqueter. The love of a dog for its master will touch the heart of the strongest man.

Women and cats will do as they please, and men and dogs should relax and get used to the idea.
—*Robart A. Heinlein*

• • •

To err is human, to forgive, canine.
—*Anonymous*

memoirs of a yellow dog

o. henry

O. Henry (William Sydney Porter, 1862–1910) was one of America's most prolific writers, with six hundred short stories published in at least ten collections during his lifetime. Between 1903 and 1906, the *New York World* hired him to submit an original short story every week. During this time he coined the epithet "Baghdad on the Subway" for New York City, referring to the teeming underside of urban life.

"Memoirs of a Yellow Dog" appears in the short story collection *The Four Million*, referring to New York City's population of the time. Obviously, O. Henry's scope was much larger. "Memoirs of a Yellow Dog" appeared in this collection in 1906 and is about a dog's life in the steamy tenements of New York City at the turn of the twentieth century. The narrator of the story is a sweet, innocent dog that is grateful for the bond that develops between himself and the wimpish husband of his mistress, from whom they escape together from their dissatisfied lives. By the end of the tale, both dog and man become traveling companions, sharing a special spiritual bond.

I don't suppose it will knock any of you people off your perch to read a contribution from an animal. Mr. Kipling and a good many others have demonstrated the fact that animals can express themselves in remunerative English, and no magazine goes to press nowadays without an animal story in it, except the old-style monthlies that are still running pictures of Bryan and the Mont Pelee horror.

But you needn't look for any stuck-up literature in my piece, such as Bearoo, the bear, and Snakoo, the snake, and Tammanoo, the tiger, talk in the jungle books. A yellow dog that's spent most of his life in a cheap New York flat, sleeping in a corner on an old sateen underskirt (the one she spilled port wine on at the Lady Longshoremen's banquet), mustn't be expected to perform any tricks with the art of speech.

I was born a yellow pup; date, locality, pedigree and weight unknown. The first thing I can recollect, an old woman had me in a basket at Broadway and Twenty-third trying to sell me to a fat lady. Old Mother Hubbard was boosting me to beat the band as a genuine Pomeranian-Hambletonian-Red Irish-Cochin-China-Stoke-Pogis fox terrier. The fat lady chased a V around among the samples of gros grain flannelette in her shopping bag till she cornered it, and gave up. From that moment I was a pet—mamma's own wootsey squidlums. Say, gentle reader, did you ever have a 200-pound woman breathing a flavour of Camembert cheese and Peau d'Espagne pick you up and wallop her nose all over you, remarking all the time in an Emma Eames tone of voice: "Oh, oo's um oodlum, doodlum, woodlum, toodlum, bitsy-witsy skoodlums?"

From a pedigreed yellow pup I grew up to be an anonymous yellow cur looking like a cross between an Angora cat and a box of lemons. But my mistress never tumbled. She thought that the two primeval pups that Noah chased into the ark were but a collateral branch of my ancestors. It took two policemen to keep her from entering me at the Madison Square Garden for the Siberian bloodhound prize.

I'll tell you about that flat. The house was the ordinary thing in New York, paved with Parian marble in the entrance hall and cobblestones above the first floor. Our flat was three fl—well, not flights—climbs up. My mistress rented it unfurnished, and put in the regular things—antique upholstered parlour set, oil chromo of geishas in a Harlem tea house, rubber plant and husband.

By Sirius! there was a biped I felt sorry for. He was a little man with sandy hair and whiskers a good deal like mine. Henpecked?—well, toucans and flamingoes and pelicans all had their bills in him. He wiped the dishes and listened to my mistress tell about the cheap, ragged things the lady with the squirrel-skin coat on the second floor hung out on her line to dry. And every evening she made him take me out on the end of a string for a walk.

If men knew how women pass the time when they are alone they'd never marry. Laura Lean Jibbey, peanut brittle, a little almond cream on the neck muscles, dishes unwashed, half an hour's talk with the iceman, reading a package of old letters, a couple of pickles and two bottles of malt extract, one hour peeking through a hole in the window shade into the flat across the air-shaft—that's about all there is to it. Twenty minutes before time for him to come home from work she straightens up the house, fixes her rat so it won't show, and gets out a lot of sewing for a ten-minute bluff. I led a dog's life in that flat. 'Most all day I lay there in my corner watching that fat woman kill time. I slept sometimes and had pipe dreams about

"You old flea-headed woodchuck-chaser," I said to him—"you moon-baying, rabbit-pointing, egg-stealing old beagle, can't you see that I don't want to leave you? Can't you see that we're both Pups in the Wood . . ."

being out chasing cats into basements and growling at old ladies
with black mittens, as a dog was intended to do. Then she would
pounce upon me with a lot of that drivelling poodle palaver and
kiss me on the nose—but what could I do? A dog can't chew cloves.

I began to feel sorry for Hubby, dog my cats if I didn't. We
looked so much alike that people noticed it when we went out; so
we shook the streets that Morgan's cab drives down, and took to
climbing the piles of last December's snow on the streets where
cheap people live.

One evening when we were thus promenading, and I was trying
to look like a prize St. Bernard, and the old man was trying to look
like he wouldn't have murdered the first organ-grinder he heard
play Mendelssohn's wedding march, I looked up at him and said,
in my way:

"What are you looking so sour about, you oakum trimmed
lobster? She don't kiss you. You don't have to sit on her lap and listen to talk that would make the book of a musical comedy sound
like the maxims of Epicetus. You ought to be thankful you're not a
dog. Brace up, Benedick, and bid the blues begone."

That matrimonial mishap looked down at me with almost canine intelligence in his face.

"Why, doggie," says he, "good doggie. You almost look like
you could speak. What is it, doggie—cats?"

Cats! Could speak!

But, of course, he couldn't understand. Humans were denied
the speech of animals.

In the flat across the hall from us lived a lady with a black-and-
tan terrier. Her husband strung it and took it out every evening,
but he always came home cheerful and whistling. One day I touched
noses with the black-and-tan in the hall, and I struck him for an
elucidation.

"See here, Wiggle-and-Skip," I says, "you know that it ain't the
nature of a real man to play dry nurse to a dog in public. I never
saw one leashed to a bow-wow yet that didn't look like he'd like to

lick every other man that looked at him. But your boss comes in every day as perky and set up as an amateur prestidigitator doing the egg trick. How does he do it? Don't tell me he likes it."

"Him?" says the black-and-tan. "Why, he uses Nature's Own Remedy. He gets spifflicated. At first when we go out he's as shy as the man on the steamer who would rather play pedro when they make 'em all jackpots. By the time we've been in eight saloons he don't care whether the thing on the end of his line is a dog or a catfish. I've lost two inches of my tail trying to sidestep those swinging doors."

The pointer I got from that terrier—vaudeville please copy—set me to thinking.

One evening about 6 o'clock my mistress ordered him to get busy and do the ozone act for Lovey. I have concealed it until now, but that is what she called me. The black-and-tan was called "Tweetness." I consider that I have the bulge on him as far as you could chase a rabbit. Still "Lovey" is something of a nomenclatural tin can on the tail of one's self-respect.

At a quiet place on a safe street I tightened the line of my custodian in front of an attractive, refined saloon. I made a dead-ahead scramble for the doors, whining like a dog in the press despatches that lets the family know that little Alice is bogged while gathering lilies in the brook.

"Why, darn my eyes," said the old man, with a grin; "darn my eyes if the saffron-coloured son of a seltzer lemonade ain't asking me in to take a drink. Lemme see—how long's it been since I saved shoe leather by keeping one foot on the foot-rest? I believe I'll—"

I knew I had him. Hot Scotches he took sitting at a table. For an hour he kept the Campbells coming. I sat by his side rapping for the waiter with my tail, and eating free lunch such as mamma in her flat never equalled with her homemade truck bought at a delicatessen store eight minutes before papa comes home.

When the products of Scotland were all exhausted except the rye bread the old man unwound me from the table leg and played me outside like a fisherman plays a salmon. Out there he took off my collar and threw it into the street.

"Poor doggie," says he; "good doggie. She shan't kiss you any-more. 'S darned shame. Good doggie, go away and get run over by a street car and be happy."

I refused to leave. I leaped and frisked around the old man's legs happy as a pug on a rug.

"You old flea-headed woodchuck-chaser," I said to him—"you moon-baying, rabbit-pointing, egg-stealing old beagle, can't you see that I don't want to leave you? Can't you see that we're both Pups in the Wood and the missis is the cruel uncle af-ter you with the dish towel and me with the flea liniment and a pink bow to tie on my tail. Why not cut that all out and be pards forever more?"

Maybe you'll say he didn't understand—maybe he didn't. But he kind of got a grip on the Hot Scotches, and stood still for a minute, thinking.

"Doggie," says he, finally, "we don't live more than a dozen lives on this earth, and very few of us live to be more than 300. If I ever see that flat any more I'm flat, and if you do you're flatter; and that's no flattery. I'm offering 60 to 1 that Westward Ho wins out by the length of a dachshund."

There was no string, but I frolicked along with my master to the Twenty-third street ferry. And the cats on the route saw reason to give thanks that prehensile claws had been given them.

On the Jersey side my master said to a stranger who stood eat-ing a currant bun:

"Me and my doggie, we are bound for the Rocky Mountains."

But what pleased me most was when my old man pulled both of my ears until I howled, and said:

"You common, monkey-headed, rat-tailed, sulphur-coloured son of a doormat, do you know what I'm going to call you?"

I thought of "Lovey," and I whined dolefully.

"I'm going to call you 'Pete,'" says my master; and if I'd had five tails I couldn't have done enough wagging to do justice to the occasion.

a midsummer night's dream, from act v, scene 1

william shakespeare

PROLOGUE
. . . And through Wall's chink, poor souls, they are content
To whisper, at the which let no man wonder.
This man, with lantern, dog, and bush of thorn,
Presenteth Moonshine. . . .

MOONSHINE
All that I have to say is to tell you that the lantorn is the moon; I,
the man in the moon; this thorn-bush, my thorn-bush; and this
dog, my dog.

Whoever said you can't buy happiness forgot about little puppies.
—Gene Hill

• • •

What are the two best words in the English language?
Free puppies.
—Elizabeth Beier

Dogs are not our whole life, but they make our lives whole.
—*Roger Caras*

a tribute to the dog

george graham vest

This tribute is from an address to a jury in 1870 by George Graham Vest. His client had been suing a man for two hundred dollars for killing his dog; the jury deliberated for two minutes before awarding five hundred dollars damages to the plaintiff. It is one of the classics of canine literature.

The best friend a man has in this world may turn against him and become his enemy. His son or daughter that he has reared with loving care may prove ungrateful. Those who are nearest and dearest to us, those whom we trust with our happiness and our good name, may become traitors to their faith. The money that a man has he may lose. It flies away from him, perhaps when he needs it most. The people who are prone to fall on their knees to do honor when success is with you may be the first ones to throw the stone of malice when failure settles its cloud upon our heads.

The one absolutely unselfish friend that a man can have in this selfish world, the one that never deserts him, the one that never proves ungrateful or treacherous, is his dog. A man's dog stands by him in prosperity and in poverty, in health and in sickness. He will sleep on the cold ground, where the wintry winds blow and the snow drives fiercely, if only he may be near his master's side. He will kiss the hand that has no food to offer; he will lick the wounds, and sores that come with the roughness of the world. He guards the sleep of his pauper master as if he were a prince. When all other friends desert he alone remains. When riches take wings and reputation falls to pieces, he is as constant in his love as the sun in its journeys through the heavens.

If fortunes drive the master forth an outcast in the world, friendless and homeless, the faithful dog asks for no higher privilege than that of accompanying him, to guard him against danger, to fight against his enemies. And when the last scene of all comes and death takes his master in its embrace and his body is laid away in the cold ground, no matter if all other friends pursue the way, there by the graveside will be found the noble dog, his head between his paws and his eyes sad, but open in alert watchfulness, faithful and true, even in death.

A dog has the soul of a philosopher.
—*Plato*

part two

brave and sacred hearts

Never judge a dog's pedigree by the kind of books he chews.
—Anonymous

bum

a brooklyn dog

sarah noble Ives

This story is from the collection *Dog Heroes of Many Lands,* by Sarah
Noble Ives. She was born in Grosse Ile, Michigan, in 1864. Among
her various literary accomplishments were her published regional his-
tories. She was also a successful illustrator of children's books. *Dog
Heroes of Many Lands* was published in 1922 and includes inspiring
and amusing dog stories from many countries. Included in the collec-
tion are "Tige the Goatherd: A Dog of the Sierra Nevadas"; "Zip: A
Dog of the Northland"; "Sirrah: A Dog of the Ettrick Hills"; "Darky: A
New Zealand Dog"; "Byron: A Dog of Scotland"; "Brakje: A Kafir
Dog"; "Ask Him: An Indian Dog"; "Tom: A Dog of the Eastern States";
"Bruce: A Fire Dog of New York"; and the story reprinted here, "Bum:
A Brooklyn Dog." Sarah Noble Ives lived in Pasadena, California, at
the time of her death in 1944.

Got any references?"

"No. D' I look like havin' references?"

"Not any to speak of, I'll admit." The owner of the Bergen
Street Stables looked over the derelict specimen of humanity with
amused contempt. The long, lanky form had the air of not having
been well constructed in the first place; a suit of clothes, once dark
blue—now faded to an indescribable greenish brown—ill covered
him, so shrunken was the poor shoddy of its material. Frayed
edges and unmended holes betokened the lack of personal care
and the lack of any one to care for him; the coat-collar, turned up

and buttoned to the throat, hid what the worn sleeves betrayed by
their skimped length, that there was need of the garment to which
one attaches collars and cuffs. Dried mud caked his boots between
the holes and decked the man's trousers, thinning out to splashes
on the coat-tails. He was hollow-cheeked and hollow-eyed, and his
whole being was a threnody of hard luck. It was almost a sacrilege
to call him a man; but "God made him," so he passed for one.

"Where did you work last?"

"On the Pennsylvania Road."

"Hum! President, I suppose, or maybe only a conductor in a
palace-car."

"Quit yer kiddin'. I was diggin' on the road-bed wit' the Da-
gos."

"And you got fired?"

"What if I did? You git fired for nothin' nowadays. I wasn't a
union man, and they found I had another man's ticket."

"Yes, yes, I know. There isn't much humanity in any kind of
corporation nowadays. That's nothing, being fired. Anybody's li-
able to lose his place. But there's something else. Done time,
haven't you?"

"What business is that of yours?" The young man gave the
elder a sharp sidelong glance.

"Oh, nothing, nothing. I should say it was about two years
ago, judging from the condition of your clothes. That's the regular
cut they give them when they let them out. I've seen others. And
you haven't got all of the lock-step out of your system yet. I saw
you as you turned in. Quite a Sherlock Holmes, I am. Now, see
here; I'd rather like to know what you did. It wasn't murder, or you
wouldn't be out with that suit on, but while there are some things
a man can live down, there are others that if he does once he does
again—and worse. What was it you went up for?"

"Burglary, if you gotta know. When a feller's hard up and can't
find nothin' to do, he's gotta do what he kin. I s'pose it's no use
now to ask you for a job." The man coughed and turned away.

"Hm!" The stable-owner rubbed his hand carefully over his beard, terminating with a roll of the fingers toward the tip. "How old are you?"

"Twenty-three."

"Hm! Well, maybe it isn't in the grain yet. A man that steals for a business is hard to cure; but if it 's a case of being hard up, maybe there's a chance. Now see here, boy." Mr. Devin straightened up and looked directly into the young fellow's eyes. "It's plain to see that you haven't had much of the upper crust, or the filling. Maybe it's your own fault, and maybe it isn't. But you're young, and perhaps if you can get off your uppers you'll make good yet. I'm going to give you a chance; not a big one, but a chance. If you can dig on a railroad bed, you can clean out stables. I need a stable-boy. But mind you, no drink, and no smoking. Cut those out. I can't have my horses neglected nor my stables set on fire. As for stealing, try the straight thing and see how it works. What's your name?"

"Gallagher. Thomas Gallagher. Say, Mr. Devin, you're white, you are, and you won't be sorry."

"Forget it," said Devin. "Here's a quarter. Run and get yourself a cup of coffee and a sandwich before you begin. Got a place to stay?"

"No."

"Well, sleep in the stables if you like. I have to keep some one here, and the other men all have families. Wait. Got any money?"

"Just this here quarter."

"Well, I'll give you part of your week's wages in advance to tide you over. Curran here'll show you what to do."

Gruff, generous Mr. Devin turned back to his book-balancing in the little coop of an office, and Gallagher, with a tear trembling on his eyelid,—he was not so far from boyhood as to be above human emotion,—went about his new duties.

"He trusted me. I'll show him."

And Gallagher did show him. Never had Mark Devin so little cause for complaint in his under stable-hand. He cleaned the stalls, he fetched and carried, and even when the other men imposed on him, he did not resent it. "I'll make good," he said.

November was passing by, and Thanksgiving was near. Already Gallagher had made a rough attempt at mending up the old suit for work. With his scanty savings he had acquired a sweater and a decent pair of trousers, and aspired, with his next week's surplus, to a shirt. He was planning even still further grandeur.

"By New Year's I guess I'll be able to get me a good warm coat. This sweater'll have to do till then. Lucky I don't have to pay room-rent." He glanced down the street after Curran, who had just driven out with a dray. "Looks like snow in them clouds. Oh, well, snow's nothin' when you've got a job and a place to sleep. Kinder cozy in this here stable, too."

Snow it did. That great storm of November 25 is not yet forgotten. A real blizzard it was, with wind howling, snow flying, drifts piling, traffic stopped. The next morning Devin could not get over from his home on Myrtle Avenue. One of the stable-men who lived near—Curran it was—floundered in, breathless and spent with his struggle.

"Some storm!" he said to Gallagher. "You're lucky to be here without coming." He removed his coat and cap and shook off the snow that hung, wet and thick, to the rough wool. "There won't be any business this day. Devin'll play a losin' game. No team could haul anything half a block. What, you going out? You're a fool to try."

"Got to get my breakfast, now you're here," said Gallagher.

"Sho! I'd give you part of my lunch, if I had enough to last. You will have to get something, I suppose, and enough to last all day, so you won't have to go out again. There isn't a restaurant open, though. You'll have to go about three blocks. There's a little soup factory over on Atlantic Avenue that'll be boiling the pot, I guess. The folks live there. That's the only place you can be sure of."

Gallagher buttoned up his sweater to the last notch, and swung out, letting the wind help him. He covered the three blocks, despite the difficulties of travel. With a hot breakfast to hearten him he started back, but found that making progress against the gale was quite another thing. Pulling down his cap to cover his ears, and with his bundle of lunch under his arm, he started. But even while he had been sitting in the little eating- house, new drifts had whirled in on the side-street eddies, and the way he had come was choked and impassable.

"I'll try it on the next cross-strect," he said to himself. "There is a warehouse there with a covered walk."

Battling, pushing, stumbling, falling, rising again and struggling on, he fought his way along. Just one block more, and he would be back in the stables.

Heavens! What a blast that was! Gallagher was turning the corner that led back to Bergen Street when the wind, rushing down between the buildings, caught him, knocked the breath out of him, and plastered him flat against a brick wall.

"Jiminy! Just saved my cap that time. This beats anything."

He pried himself loose from the wall, only to be hurled into a snow-bank. Blinded, dizzy, and breathing in dry gasps, he righted himself. "What's that?"

Out of the other side of the drift came a wail, a pitiful, sobbing whimper.

"Some poor cur lost in it," said Gallagher. "Well, I got to save myself."

Again the cry, heart-breaking and almost human in its pathos.

"That's trouble, no mistake. Guess I'll have to turn life-saver. Hi, there! Coming, if I can git to you."

For an answer, a yelp, faint but imploring.

"Coming, coming there!"

Gallagher waited behind the drift for a lull, and then made a plunge around to the other side. Gritting his teeth he burrowed in toward the place of wailing and pulled out the wailer, a small dog, with nothing to recommend him but the agony in his eyes.

"There, you pore little feller. I'll save you. Stop cryin' now. You and me is the same breed, I guess. There!"

He stuffed the animal under his sweater, bent his head to the wind, and staggered on. Now he was down, and he and his burden were floundering helplessly, almost hopelessly. Now he was up again. His breath came quick and hard, and his lungs felt as if their power was burning to the last flicker. Things began to go black. Then, with a final lurch, and still holding the dog, he fell heavily against the stable door.

Curran opened it and pulled him in, picked him up, and set him on an overturned half-bushel measure against the wall; and while the boy slowly recovered his breath, the man took a good look at the specimen of canine infirmity that Gallagher had dropped on the floor.

"Where'd you get it?"

"Snowdrift," said Gallagher, when he could speak.

"What d' you call it?"

"Dog, I reckon."

"Pretty bum specimen. Worth saving, do you think?"

"I had to. It yelped."

"Yes, I s'pose so, just as we preserve idiots and crazy folks— because we can't kill 'em. What'll you do with him?"

"Keep him. Think Devin'll let me?"

"I dunno. He doesn't look useful, and you can't call him an ornymint."

Certainly he was not an ornament: of no race at all, although with an imagination you might guess that some ancestor at some time had been a fox-terrier. He was, or had been at birth, white, with black spots on his head and sides; he was so thin that every bone showed, so empty that his ribs almost knocked together; his surface displayed almost every species of eruption and evidence of assault and battery that could be collected together in so small an area—he had them all from the mange to a broken tooth, the latter evidently the result of application of boot.

"Well, now you've got the pretty little thing, what's your next move?"

"First thing, I'll thaw him out." Gallagher dropped on his knees beside the dog and began rubbing the cold-stiffened limbs.

"Here's a horse-blanket to lay him on," said Curran, who began to awake to an unusual good-Samaritan feeling. "Say, as soon as you get him so's he can wiggle, I've got some coffee in my tin, and I can heat a bit on the office stove. You keep rubbing."

Curran bustled off, and in a minute he was back. "Here, You hold his jaws open and I'll pour it down."

The dog opened his eyes as the warm liquid went down his throat.

"That'll surprise his interior, I'm thinking. There, see! He's coming to. What do you think of that?"

The dog struggled and tried weakly to get on his emaciated legs, cowering at the same time, as if he expected a blow.

"See that, now," said Gallagher. "He's been kicked around so much that he doesn't recognize friends when he meets up with them."

"He's the limit for looks. Here, give him another nip of that—er—beveridge."

"Do you think Devin'd object if I took him into the office where it's warm?"

"Devin ain't here, and he won't be while this storm lasts, so he won't know. Better thaw him out a bit more first, though. Too hot for a frozen dog in there. Then after a bit I'll give him a piece of cold mutton I got with my lunch."

"I brought something, too, from the restaurant," said Gallagher. "I guess we can manage to fill him up, and keep him."

"Well, you take the risks yourself. He's your—dog. What you goin' to call him? A bum-looking beast like that ought to be proud of any old name."

"I'll just call him that," said Gallagher; "Bum. He's a bum-looking dog, and I'm bum myself. Here, you Bum, you jest lay still inside this blanket. I'm goin' to git the frost-bite out'n you and some grub into you."

"And I'd advise, first thing, that you give him a bath and get the mange off him. I've got some soap to do the trick. I'll bring in a pail of water and heat it on the office stove, and we'll roll him up in the blanket till he dries off. A bath'll be the most surprisin' thing yet. 'Likely the first he ever had."

The dog took the rough but kindly treatment in a dazed fashion, not understanding it in the least. But he did come around under it all and in a vague way began to realize that no harm was intended him. There being no business that day, the two men, after their regular work of tending the horses, spent their spare hours putting heart into this new-comer. He was fed, scrubbed, rubbed down, and dried, while the storm howled in baffled fury outside. By nightfall he was on his legs, following timidly at Gallagher's heels, cringing when spoken to, but sneaking up, in spite of his fear, for the kind touch of this new and extraordinary master. He even managed to coax a bit of wag into that broken tail of his, which never before had had any occasion for such demonstration.

That night, after all the stable-work was done and Curran had gone home to his family around the block, Gallagher took Bum with him to his little cubby in the hay-loft, and together they lay in mutual warmth and happiness, the derelict man with the hollow chest and the derelict dog with the grateful heart. And the storm hissed and shrieked under the eaves and around the window-casement in vain.

Whatever Mr. Devin thought when he came in bright and early the next morning, he did not disclose. He only said, as Curran had:

"Where did you get—that?"

"In a drift," said Gallagher. Then, with a new note in his voice, he asked:

"Kin I keep him?"

"Hm! He's not a beauty, and he won't bring trade. Just now he isn't much of an advertisement for the business. Oh, yes, keep him if you want to, but fatten him up as soon as you can."

So Bum became an attaché of the Bergen Street Stables. Beautiful he could never be, and never did he lose that habit of cringing when spoken to suddenly, but in spite of it, his confidence in humankind grew apace, and his devotion to Gallagher was almost abject. At his heels he followed from early morn till dewy eve. Gallagher picked a restaurant where dogs were favored, and many a bone came his way from the slipshod waiter. Whatever Gallagher could afford for himself he shared, with Bum, not minding that his purchase of warmer clothing had to be put off a little farther. December was a mild month that year, and Gallagher made up for the chilliness of his exterior by the warmth about his heart. He began to whistle about his chores, though now and then he would be interrupted by a fit of coughing. The dog grew in plumpness, if not in grace, but Gallagher himself did not.

Christmas Eve, and a cold, clear sunset, with a rising wind. The people doing their last bits of shopping drew their furs closer as they stepped out into the street and joined the gay hurrying throng. Mr. Devin, about eight of the clock, came into the stables for a last look. He glanced at the thermometer that hung outside and saw that it registered ten below zero and was still falling. Curran and the other men had gone home, and he stopped to glance over his accounts and to smile at the balance to his credit. He smiled again, as he looked at an armful of bundles that were to go home with him, and be added to the piles under the bulging stockings: yes, and for the wonderful Christmas-tree, waiting in the darkened room, around whose doors five merry children had been tip-toeing all day. Christmas was a great institution for the kids. And he and mother, too, were as excited as the rest when Jenny or Rob laid on their altars some gift of their own contriving.

Devin had been prospered this year; yes. He looked into the glow of the little office stove. Already the red was dying out, and a chill crept through the office walls.

The sound of a hollow cough came from the stables without. "Gallagher!"

Gallagher came in with Bum at his heels. "It is cold to-night. Be sure and give the horses good, thick beds, and blanket them well. Will you be all right yourself?"

"Yes, sir. I've plenty of bed covers, and I kin git an extry horse-blanket, if need be."

Devin looked sharply at the thin face.

"You don't look any too spry. Bum here is growing to be the handsomer man of the two. Aren't you well?"

"I'm all right," said Gallagher with a little shrug. "Jest a nasty little cough. It's nothin'. Next week pay-day I'll be able—"

"See here, haven't you got warm underwear?"

"Haven't needed it. As I say, next week I'll—"

"Now, now, I didn't think of that! This Christmas Eve business started me to remember that I haven't paid you very big wages while I was trying you out. Why, yes, a fellow's got to live, and even bones for Bum must cost something. See here, you come up to my house tomorrow at two o'clock, and we'll give you a Christmas dinner that'll make your eyeballs jingle. And I've some old under-wear you can have; and I'm going to raise your wages; you've done mighty well. Good night, and a merry Christmas."

"Merry Christmas, sir. Mr. Devin, you've been white all through to me, and I'm not forgettin' it."

"All right, all right. You've proved my theory. A man needn't al-ways stay in the gutter because he fell in once, or because he was born there either. I take it you never had much of a chance."

"I was born on the East Side, sir, in New York. I guess I've been pretty tough."

Devin pressed the lad's hand and was gone out into the cold street, whose pavement rang like ice under steel runners. "I haven't done my whole duty by that boy," he said to himself. "He's got no one to look after him, and he needs mothering. Mary'd love to do it, God bless her!"

The streets rang with happy laughter. How bright the little shops were! Devin swung aboard the cross-town car for Myrtle Avenue, and, his mind went back to his armful of bundles and the cheery apartment where his wife and children waited for him.

After Devin had gone Gallagher opened his palm and stood staring at a crisp five-dollar bill. Devin certainly was good; the lad—he was only that—had never known anything like this before. And to-morrow there was to be a great dinner, and he was invited! He put the bill carefully away in an old wallet and locked the stable door. Then he saw to it that the horses were well provided for against the growing cold. He shivered as he turned to go upstairs to his loft, and his face was drawn and blue. "I'm lucky to have this place to sleep," he said, "but it's an awful cold night. Bum, you and I got to snuggle up mighty close or we'll get nipped."

The night grew colder and colder. Gallagher tried in vain to coax the sluggish blood in his veins to a faster beat; the frost seemed to burrow into him, blankets or no blankets. He was grateful for the warmth of Bum against his body, but how cold his feet and hands were!

Hours went by. The stars burned clear and cold, high above the thin, keen air, but they did not comfort; sleep did not come to Gallagher.

One of the horses grew restless. "Likely his blanket's off; I'll go down and see." Gallagher wrapped the covers around Bum and stole down the stairs. Yes, old Bayberry was uncovered. He fastened the blanket more securely, and piled straw deep around the horses' legs. Somehow it seemed less cold here than in the chilly loft. What harm if he sat for a bit on that pile of straw, with a blanket around his shoulders? For a moment, anyhow. So weary he was with the lack of sleep that to climb the stairway just now seemed impossible. Just a minute, and then back to Bum. How queer and dry his lungs felt. His cough racked him, and he lay back exhausted.

He was growing sleepy now; the cold did not seem to bite so

fiercely. He wrapped the horse-blanket tighter around him, and nodded. . . . Sleep was coming . . . how good it was to sleep and sleep and not feel the cold. . . . The Christmas bells were ringing now; they made a pretty sound. It was Christmas morning, and at two o'clock he was to have a grand dinner. . . .

A milk-cart went creaking down the street, with the driver clapping his arms around him to quicken the circulation. The milk-cans clattered and the frost sang on the tires. Bum stirred in his blankets and nosed around for Gallagher, but he was gone. He listened; no sound. He bounded out and down the stair. Yes, there was Gallagher, his Gallagher. Running to him, he poked his nose into the hand that always caressed him, but Gallagher did not move. The dog licked the white, pinched face upturned on the straw.

There was a quiver of the eyelids. "Good old Bum!" murmured Gallagher, and then the eyes closed again.

The dawn was coming in through the stable windows. It was not usual for Gallagher to be asleep down here, and so fast asleep. It was not all right. Bum must find help. He ran to the office; no one was there. He threw his weight on the street door; it was fastened. Nothing left but to call for help. Bum barked and barked. Then he ran back to Gallagher. He did not stir. Bum returned to the door, sat down, and howled long and impotently. No answer. Again he barked and howled his misery and fear. Raging back and forth he kept up his desperate appeal.

The children in the tenement opposite the stables opened their eyes as the gold began to creep up in the east. "Merry Christmas!" they shouted. "Let's look in our stockings. My! but it's cold. There's a dog barking somewhere; I bet he's shiverin'."

The elders stirred in their warm beds. "I wonder what's the matter with that bothersome dog? He's spoiled my nap."

"Merry Christmas!" shouted the children. Sure enough, and the flapjacks must be baked. Mrs. Kittery shivered and began to dress hurriedly.

Still the barking and howling, more frantic and insistent. "Where is that brute of a dog?" said Pat Kittery. "Sounds as if he was over in Devin's stables."

"I believe something's wrong," said Mrs. Kittery from the kitchen, where she was mixing the batter. "Why don't you go over and see? That Gallagher stays there nights."

Kittery put his nose out the window. "Br-r-r-r!" he said, and put on his overcoat and cap. He went down the stair, crossed the street, and knocked at the stable door. The barking and howling became more frantic than ever.

"What's the matter in there?"

"Oo-oo-oo-oo!" wailed Bum.

"The door is locked. I'll have to go around the block and get Curran. Wait there, you. I'm coming back."

Curran and Kittery entered the stables. A little half-crazed dog jumped on them, and then darted away toward the corner of the stable. The men did not follow immediately. He ran back, renewed his pleading, and was gone again.

And then they followed him. When they reached the pile of straw, Bum was crouched on Gallagher's chest, moaning and licking the cold cheek.

Curran stooped and placed his ear close to the white face.

"There's life there yet. We'll bring him around. Bum, you saved your pal; he'd have been gone soon. We ain't been as decent as you, or he'd have been better fitted to be here this cold night. I'll telephone Devin."

When Mr. Devin came Gallagher was just able to smile weakly despite the pain in his chilled limbs.

"We are going to fix you up all right, boy, and then for a merry Christmas dinner, and a few other changes. Bum, you go to the party too, and you deserve the best bit of breast on the turkey."

"Good old Bum!" said Gallagher.

• • •

Properly trained, a man can be a dog's best friend.
—Corey Ford

my buddy

music and lyrics by murray weinstock

"My Buddy" is an original song from the CD *Tails of the City*, which are songs from a dog's point of view, sung by Murray Weinstock, with music ensemble. Visit www.dogtunes.com for more information.

He's my buddy, he's my pal
Man's best friend, and I'll tell you how
When I'm down or feeling blue
Buddy's at my side to see me through

Never had a friend like this
Unconditional sloppy kiss
Got no problems that can't be licked
How can anybody resist?

He's my buddy, yes I love that buddy
Oh, I love my buddy, how I love that dog

Went for a walk, the other night
The streets were crazy, and just not right
Don't know what my buddy heard,
But he looked up and he said these words:

"I'll protect you, 'cause you're my guy."
These words he said just made me cry
Now I feel safe, and I don't know why
Buddy's only sixteen inches high

He's my buddy, yes I love that buddy . . .

He's got his leash wrapped 'round his snout
Easy read, it's time to go out
There's nothing in this world that I wouldn't do
'Cause Buddy makes me happy through and through.

When Buddy goes, there'll be no other,
Little soul and little brother
When it's time for him to take that ride,
We'll be buddies forever, deep inside.

He's my buddy, yes I love that buddy
Oh, I love my buddy, how I love that dog

• • •

Oddball: Still up! [A bomb blows up the bridge.] No it ain't.
Woof, woof, woof! That's my dog impression. Arf, arf arf.
That's my other dog impression.
—From Kelly's Heroes

for the love of a man

jack london

During the course of his life, Jack London (1876–1916) wrote over fifty books, including novels, stories, and journalism and essay collections. Among his most enduring and beloved fiction are the novels *The Call of the Wild, White Fang,* and *The Sea-Wolf.* His love for dogs and his belief in them as superior, heroic, mystical creatures are apparent in his most popular books, most notably *The Call of the Wild,* from which the chapter reprinted here is taken. London was twenty-seven when he reached international fame as the author of *The Call of the Wild,* published in 1903. His fiction is set in California, the Yukon, the South Pacific, or at sea. His journalism reflects an involvement with those areas, as well as his interest in Japan and its impact on the rest of the world. London predicted war between the United States and Japan after reporting the armed conflict between Russia and Japan at the turn of the twentieth century. He set the mold as a writer who had an adventurous, insightful, and even heroic life. Clearly, he influenced Ernest Hemingway and generations of young writers who followed, whether knowingly or not. In addition to writing fiction, he was a prolific journalist, greatly admired for his travels and exploits and as someone who rose from poverty to international success. He died in 1916 at the age of forty.

. . . When John Thornton froze his feet in the previous December, his partners had made him comfortable and left him to get well, going on themselves up the river to get out a raft of sawlogs for Dawson. He was still limping slightly at the time he rescued Buck, but with the continued warm weather even the slight limp left him. And here, lying by the river bank through the long spring days, watching the running water, listening lazily to the songs of birds and the hum of nature, Buck slowly won back his strength.

This man had saved his life, which was something; but, further, he was the ideal master. Other men saw to the welfare of their dogs from a sense of duty and business expediency; he saw to the welfare of his as if they were his own children, because he could not help it. And he saw further. He never forgot a kindly greeting or a cheering word, and to sit down for a long talk with them ("gas" he called it) was as much his delight as theirs. He had a way of taking Buck's head roughly between his hands, and resting his own head upon Buck's, of shaking him back and forth, the while calling him ill names that to Buck were love names. Buck knew no greater joy than that rough embrace and the sound of murmured oaths, and at each jerk back and forth it seemed that his heart would be shaken out of his body, so great was its ecstasy. And when, released, he sprang to his feet, his mouth laughing, his eyes eloquent, his throat vibrant with unuttered sound, and in that fashion remained without movement, John Thornton would reverently exclaim, "God! you can all but speak!"

Buck had a trick of love expression that was akin to hurt. He would often seize Thornton's hand in his mouth and close so fiercely that the flesh bore the impress of his teeth for some time afterward. And as Buck understood the oaths to be love words, so the man understood this feigned bite for a caress.

For the most part, however, Buck's love was expressed in adoration. While he went wild with

Mercy did not exist in the primordial life. It was misunderstood for fear, and such misunderstandings made for death. Kill or be killed, eat or be eaten, was the law; and this mandate, down out of the depths of Time, he obeyed.

happiness when Thornton touched him or spoke to him, he did not seek these tokens. Unlike Skeet, who was wont to shove her nose under Thornton's hand and nudge and nudge till petted, or Nig, who would stalk up and rest his great head on Thornton's knee, Buck was content to adore at a distance. He would lie by the hour, eager, alert, at Thornton's feet, looking up into his face, dwelling upon it, studying it, following with keenest interest each fleeting expression, every movement or change of feature. Or, as chance might have it, he would lie farther away, to the side or rear, watching the outlines of the man and the occasional movements of his body. And often, such was the communion in which they lived, the strength of Buck's gaze would draw John Thornton's head around, and he would return the gaze, without speech, his heart shining out of his eyes as Buck's heart shone out.

For a long time after his rescue, Buck did not like Thornton to get out of his sight. From the moment he left the tent to when he entered it again, Buck would follow at his heels. His transient masters since he had come into the Northland had bred in him a fear that no master could be permanent. He was afraid that Thornton would pass out of his life as Perrault and Francois and the Scotch half-breed had passed out. Even in the night, in his dreams, he was haunted by this fear. At such times he would shake off sleep and creep through the chill to the flap of the tent, where he would stand and listen to the sound of his master's breathing.

But in spite of this great love he bore John Thornton, which seemed to bespeak the soft civilizing influence, the strain of the primitive, which the Northland had aroused in him, remained alive and active. Faithfulness and devotion, things born of fire and roof, were his; yet he retained his wildness and wiliness. He was a thing of the wild, come in from the wild to sit by John Thornton's fire, rather than a dog of the soft Southland stamped with the marks of generations of civilization. Because of his very great love, he could not steal from this man, but from any other man, in any other camp, he did not hesitate an instant; while the cunning with which he stole enabled him to escape detection.

His face and body were scored by the teeth of many dogs, and he fought as fiercely as ever and more shrewdly. Skeet and Nig were too good-natured for quarrelling—besides, they belonged to John Thornton; but the strange dog, no matter what the breed or valor, swiftly acknowledged Buck's supremacy or found himself struggling for life with a terrible antagonist. And Buck was merciless. He had learned well the law of club and fang, and he never forewent an advantage or drew back from a foe he had started on the way to Death. He had lessoned from Spitz, and from the chief fighting dogs of the police and mail, and knew there was no middle course. He must master or be mastered; while to show mercy was a weakness. Mercy did not exist in the primordial life. It was misunderstood for fear, and such misunderstandings made for death. Kill or be killed, eat or be eaten, was the law; and this mandate, down out of the depths of Time, he obeyed.

He was older than the days he had seen and the breaths he had drawn. He linked the past with the present, and the eternity behind him throbbed through him in a mighty rhythm to which he swayed as the tides and seasons swayed. He sat by John Thornton's fire, a broad-breasted dog, white-fanged and long-furred; but behind him were the shades of all manner of dogs, half-wolves and wild wolves, urgent and prompting, tasting the savor of the meat he ate, thirsting for the water he drank, scenting the wind with him, listening with him and telling him the sounds made by the wild life in the forest; dictating his moods, directing his actions, lying down to sleep with him when he lay down, and dreaming with him and beyond him and becoming themselves the stuff of his dreams.

So peremptorily did these shades beckon him, that each day mankind and the claims of mankind slipped farther from him. Deep in the forest a call was sounding, and as often as he heard this call, mysteriously thrilling and luring, he felt compelled to turn his back upon the fire and the beaten earth around it, and to plunge into the forest, and on and on, he knew not where or why; nor did he wonder where or why, the call sounding imperiously, deep in the forest. But as often as he gained the soft unbroken earth and the green shade, the love for John Thornton drew him back to the fire again.

Thornton alone held him. The rest of mankind was as nothing. Chance travellers might praise or pet him; but he was cold under it all, and from a too demonstrative man he would get up and walk away. When Thornton's partners, Hans and Pete, arrived on the long-expected raft, Buck refused to notice them till he learned they were close to Thornton; after that he tolerated them in a passive sort of way, accepting favors from them as though he favored them by accepting. They were of the same large type as Thornton, living close to the earth, thinking simply and seeing clearly; and ere they swung the raft into the big eddy by the saw-mill at Dawson, they understood Buck and his ways, and did not insist upon an intimacy such as obtained with Skeet and Nig.

For Thornton, however, his love seemed to grow and grow. He, alone among men, could put a pack upon Buck's back in the summer travelling. Nothing was too great for Buck to do, when Thornton commanded. One day (they had grub-staked themselves from the proceeds of the raft and left Dawson for the head-waters of the Tanana) the men and dogs were sitting on the crest of a cliff which fell away, straight down, to naked bed-rock three hundred feet below. John Thornton was sitting near the edge, Buck at his shoulder. A thoughtless whim seized Thornton, and he drew the attention of Hans and Pete to the experiment he had in mind. "Jump, Buck!" he commanded, sweeping his arm out and over the chasm. The next instant he was grappling with Buck on the extreme edge, while Hans and Pete were dragging them back into safety.

"It's uncanny," Pete said, after it was over and they had caught their speech.

Thornton shook his head. "No, it is splendid, and it is terrible, too. Do you know, it sometimes makes me afraid."

"I'm not hankering to be the man that lays hands on you while he's around," Pete announced conclusively, nodding his head toward Buck.

"Py Jingo!" was Hans's contribution. "Not mineself either."

It was at Circle City, ere the year was out, that Pete's apprehensions were realized. "Black" Burton, a man evil tempered and malicious, had been picking a quarrel with a tenderfoot at the bar, when Thornton stepped good-naturedly between. Buck, as was his custom, was lying in a corner, head on paws, watching his master's every action. Burton struck out, without warning, straight from the shoulder. Thornton was sent spinning, and saved himself from falling only by clutching the rail of the bar.

Those who were looking on heard what was neither bark nor yelp, but a something which is best described as a roar, and they saw Buck's body rise up in the air as he left the floor for Burton's throat. The man saved his life by instinctively throwing out his arm, but was hurled backward to the floor with Buck on top of him. Buck loosed his teeth from the flesh of the arm and drove in again for the throat. This time the man succeeded only in partly blocking, and his throat was torn open. Then the crowd was upon Buck, and he was driven off; but while a surgeon checked the bleeding, he prowled up and down, growling furiously, attempting to rush in, and being forced back by an array of hostile clubs. A "miners' meeting," called on the spot, decided that the dog had sufficient provocation, and Buck was discharged. But his reputation was made, and from that day his name spread through every camp in Alaska.

Later on, in the fall of the year, he saved John Thornton's life in quite another fashion. The

When he felt him grasp his tail, Buck headed for the bank, swimming with all his splendid strength. But the progress shoreward was slow; the progress down-stream amazingly rapid. From below came the fatal roaring where the wild current went wilder and was rent in shreds and spray by the rocks which thrust through like the teeth of an enormous comb.

three partners were lining a long and narrow poling boat down a bad stretch of rapids on the Forty-Mile Creek. Hans and Pete moved along the bank, snubbing with a thin Manila rope from tree to tree, while Thornton remained in the boat, helping its descent by means of a pole, and shouting directions to the shore. Buck, on the bank, worried and anxious, kept abreast of the boat, his eyes never off his master.

At a particularly bad spot, where a ledge of barely submerged rocks jutted out into the river, Hans cast off the rope, and, while Thornton poled the boat out into the stream, ran down the bank with the end in his hand to snub the boat when it had cleared the ledge. This it did, and was flying down-stream in a current as swift as a mill-race, when Hans checked it with the rope and checked too suddenly. The boat flirted over and snubbed in to the bank bottom up, while Thornton, flung sheer out of it, was carried downstream toward the worst part of the rapids, a stretch of wild water in which no swimmer could live.

Buck had sprung in on the instant; and at the end of three hundred yards, amid a mad swirl of water, he overhauled Thornton. When he felt him grasp his tail, Buck headed for the bank, swimming with all his splendid strength. But the progress shoreward was slow; the progress down-stream amazingly rapid. From below came the fatal roaring where the wild current went wilder and was rent in shreds and spray by the rocks which thrust through like the teeth of an enormous comb. The suck of the water as it took the beginning of the last steep pitch was frightful, and Thornton knew that the shore was impossible. He scraped furiously over a rock, bruised across a second, and struck a third with crushing force. He clutched its slippery top with both hands, releasing Buck, and above the roar of the churning water shouted: "Go, Buck! Go!"

Buck could not hold his own, and swept on downstream, struggling desperately, but unable to win back. When he heard Thornton's command repeated, he partly reared out of the water, throwing his head high, as though for a last look, then turned obediently toward the bank. He swam powerfully and was dragged ashore by Pete and Hans at the very point where swimming ceased to be possible and destruction began.

They knew that the time a man could cling to a slippery rock in the face of that driving current was a matter of minutes, and they ran as fast as they could up the bank to a point far above where Thornton was hanging on. They attached the line with which they had been snubbing the boat to Buck's neck and shoulders, being careful that it should neither strangle him nor impede his swimming, and launched him into the stream. He struck out boldly, but not straight enough into the stream. He discovered the mistake too late, when Thornton was abreast of him and a bare half-dozen strokes away while he was being carried helplessly past.

Hans promptly snubbed with the rope, as though Buck were a boat. The rope thus tightening on him in the sweep of the current, he was jerked under the surface, and under the surface he remained till his body struck against the bank and he was hauled out. He was half drowned, and Hans and Pete threw themselves upon him, pounding the breath into him and the water out of him. He staggered to his feet and fell down. The faint sound of Thornton's voice came to them, and though they could not make out the words of it, they knew that he was in his extremity. His master's voice acted on Buck like an electric shock. He sprang to his feet and ran up the bank ahead of the men to the point of his previous departure.

Again the rope was attached and he was launched, and again he struck out, but this time straight into the stream. He had miscalculated once, but he would not be guilty of it a second time. Hans paid out the rope, permitting no slack, while Pete kept it clear of coils. Buck held on till he was on a line straight above Thornton; then he turned, and with the speed of an express train headed down upon him. Thornton saw him coming, and, as Buck struck him like a battering ram, with the whole force of the current behind him, he reached up and closed with both arms around the shaggy neck. Hans snubbed the rope around the tree, and Buck and Thornton were jerked under the water. Strangling, suffocating, sometimes one uppermost and sometimes the other, dragging over the jagged bottom, smashing against rocks and snags, they veered in to the bank.

Thornton came to, belly downward and being violently propelled back and forth across a drift log by Hans and Pete. His first glance was for Buck, over whose limp and apparently lifeless body Nig was setting up a howl, while Skeet was licking the wet face and closed eyes. Thornton was himself bruised and battered, and he went carefully over Buck's body, when he had been brought around, finding three broken ribs.

"That settles it," he announced. "We camp right here." And camp they did, till Buck's ribs knitted and he was able to travel.

That winter, at Dawson, Buck performed another exploit, not so heroic perhaps, but one that puts his name many notches higher on the totem-pole of Alaskan fame. This exploit was particularly gratifying to the three men; for they stood in need of the outfit which it furnished, and were enabled to make a long-desired trip into the virgin East, where miners had not yet appeared. It was brought about by a conversation in the Eldorado Saloon, in which men waxed boastful of their favorite dogs. Buck, because of his record, was the target for these men, and Thornton was driven stoutly to defend him. At the end of half an hour one man stated that his dog could start a sled with five hundred pounds and walk off with it; a second bragged six hundred for his dog; and a third, seven hundred.

"Pooh! Pooh!" said John Thornton. "Buck can start a thousand pounds."

"And break it out, and walk off with it for a hundred yards?" demanded Matthewson, a Bonanza king, he of the seven hundred vaunt.

"And break it out, and walk off with it for a hundred yards," John Thornton said cooly.

"Well," Matthewson said, slowly and deliberately, so that all could hear, "I've got a thousand dollars that says he can't. And there it is." So saying, he slammed a sack of gold dust of the size of a bologna sausage down upon the bar.

Nobody spoke. Thornton's bluff, if bluff it was, had been called. He could feel a flush of warm blood creeping up his face. His tongue had tricked him. He did not know whether Buck could start a thousand pounds. Half a ton! The enormousness of it appalled him. He had great faith in Buck's strength and had often thought him capable of starting such a load; but never, as now, had he faced the possibility of it, the eyes of a dozen men fixed upon him, silent and waiting. Further, he had no thousand dollars; nor had Hans or Pete.

"I've got a sled standing outside now, with twenty fiftypound sacks of flour on it," Matthewson went on with brutal directness; "so don't let that hinder you."

The team of ten dogs was unhitched, and Buck, with his own harness, was put into the sled. He had caught the contagion of the excitement, and he felt that in some way he must do a great thing for John Thornton. Murmurs of admiration at his splendid appearance went up. He was in perfect condition, without an ounce of superfluous flesh . . .

Thornton did not reply. He did not know what to say. He glanced from face to face in the absent way of a man who has lost the power of thought and is seeking somewhere to find the thing that will start it going again. The face of Jim O'Brien, a Mastodon King and old-time comrade, caught his eyes. It was a cue to him, seeming to rouse him to do what he would never have dreamed of doing.

"Can you lend me a thousand?" he asked, almost in a whisper.

"Sure," answered O'Brien, thumping down a plethoric sack by the side of Matthewson's. "Though it's little faith I'm having, John, that the beast can do the trick."

The Eldorado emptied its occupants into the street to see the test. The tables were deserted, and the dealers and gamekeepers came forth to see the outcome of the wager and to lay odds. Several hundred men, furred and mittened, banked around the sled within easy distance. Matthewson's sled, loaded with a thousand pounds of flour, had been standing for a couple of hours, and in the intense cold (it was sixty below zero) the runners had frozen fast to the hard-packed snow. Men offered odds of two to one that Buck could not budge the sled. A quibble arose concerning the phrase "break out." O'Brien contended it was Thornton's privilege to knock the runners loose, leaving Buck to "break it out" from a dead standstill. Matthewson insisted that the phrase included breaking the runners from the frozen grip of the snow. A majority of the men who had witnessed the making of the bet decided in his favor, whereat the odds went up to three to one against Buck.

There were no takers. Not a man believed him capable of the feat. Thornton had been hurried into the wager, heavy with doubt; and now that he looked at the sled itself, the concrete fact, with the regular team of ten dogs curled up in the snow before it, the more impossible the task appeared. Matthewson waxed jubilant.

"Three to one!" he proclaimed. "I'll lay you another thousand at that figure, Thornton. What d'ye say?"

Thornton's doubt was strong in his face, but his fighting spirit was aroused—the fighting spirit that soars above odds, fails to recognize the impossible, and is deaf to all save the clamor for battle. He called Hans and Pete to him. Their sacks were slim, and with his own the three partners could rake together only two hundred dollars. In the ebb of their fortunes, this sum was their total capital; yet they laid it unhesitatingly against Matthewson's six hundred.

The team of ten dogs was unhitched, and Buck, with his own harness, was put into the sled. He had caught the contagion of the excitement, and he felt that in some way he must do a great thing for John Thornton. Murmurs of admiration at his splendid appearance went up. He was in perfect condition, without an ounce of superfluous flesh, and the one hundred and fifty pounds that he weighed were so many pounds of grit and virility. His furry coat shone with the sheen of silk. Down the neck and across the shoulders, his mane, in repose as it was, half bristled and seemed to lift with every movement, as though excess of vigor made each particular hair alive and active. The great breast and heavy fore legs were no more than in proportion with the rest of the body, where the muscles showed in tight rolls underneath the skin. Men felt these muscles and proclaimed them hard as iron, and the odds went down to two to one.

"Gad, sir! Gad, sir!" stuttered a member of the latest dynasty, a king of the Skookum Benches. "I offer you eight hundred for him, sir, before the test; eight hundred just as he stands."

Thornton shook his head and stepped to Buck's side.

"You must stand off from him," Matthewson protested. "Free play and plenty of room."

The crowd fell silent; only could be heard the voices of the gamblers vainly offering two to one. Everybody acknowledged Buck a magnificent animal, but twenty fifty-pound sacks of flour bulked too large in their eyes for them to loosen their pouch-strings.

Thornton knelt down by Buck's side. He took his head in his hands and rested cheek on cheek. He did not playfully shake him, as was his wont, or murmur soft love curses; but he whispered in his ear. "As you love me, Buck. As you love me," was what he whispered. Buck whined with suppressed eagerness.

The crowd was watching curiously. The affair was growing mysterious. It seemed like a conjuration. As Thornton got to his feet, Buck seized his mittened hand between his jaws, pressing in with his teeth and releasing slowly, half-reluctantly. It was the answer, in terms, not of speech, but of love. Thornton stepped well back.

"Now, Buck," he said.

Buck tightened the traces, then slacked them for a matter of several inches. It was the way he had learned.

"Gee!" Thornton's voice rang out, sharp in the tense silence.

Buck swung to the right, ending the movement in a plunge that took up the slack and with a sudden jerk arrested his one hundred and fifty pounds. The load quivered, and from under the runners arose a crisp crackling.

"Haw!" Thornton commanded.

Buck duplicated the manoeuver, this time to the left. The crackling turned into a snapping, the sled pivoting and the runners slipping and grating several inches to the side. The sled was broken out. Men were holding their breaths, intensely unconscious of the fact.

"Now, MUSH!"

Thornton's command cracked out like a pistol-shot. Buck threw himself forward, tightening the traces with a jarring lunge. His whole body was gathered compactly together in the tremendous effort, the muscles writhing and knotting like live things under the silky fur. His great chest was low to the ground, his head forward and down, while his feet were flying like mad, the claws scarring the hard-packed snow in parallel grooves. The sled swayed and trembled, half-started forward. One of his feet slipped, and one man groaned aloud. The sled lurched ahead in what appeared a rapid succession of jerks, though it never really came to a dead stop again . . . half an inch . . . an inch . . . two inches . . . The jerks perceptibly diminished; as the sled gained momentum, he caught them up, till it was moving steadily along.

Men gasped and began to breathe again, unaware that for a moment they had ceased to breathe. Thornton was running behind, encouraging Buck with short, cheery words. The distance had been measured off, and as he neared the pile of firewood which marked the end of the hundred yards, a cheer began to grow and grow, which burst into a roar as he passed the firewood and halted at command. Every man was tearing himself loose, even Matthewson. Hats and mittens were flying in the air. Men were shaking hands, it did not matter with whom, and bubbling over in a general incoherent babel.

But Thornton fell on his knees beside Buck. Head was against head, and he was shaking him back and forth. Those who hurried up heard him cursing Buck, and he cursed him long and fervently, and softly and lovingly.

"Gad, sir! Gad, sir!" sputtered the Skookum Bench king. "I'll give you a thousand for him, sir, a thousand, sir—twelve hundred, sir."

Thornton rose to his feet. His eyes were wet. The tears were streaming frankly down his cheeks. "Sir," he said to the Skookum Bench king, "no, sir. You can go to hell, sir. It's the best I can do for you, sir."

Buck seized Thornton's hand in his teeth. Thornton shook him back and forth. As though animated by a common impulse, the onlookers drew back to a respectful distance; nor were they again indiscreet enough to interrupt.

• • •

If you pick up a starving dog and make him prosperous,
he will not bite you; that is the principal difference
between a dog and a man.
—Mark Twain

stop kicking my dog around
(american folk song)

anonymous

Every time I come to town
The boys keep kicking my dog around.
Even if he is a hound
They've got to stop kicking my dog around!

part three

a breed apart

*From the dog's point of view, his master is an elongated
and abnormally cunning dog.*
—*Mabel Louise Robinson*

remarkable dog

mark twain

Mark Twain (1835–1910) was the pen name of Samuel Langhorne Clemens, who was born in Florida, Missouri. The name he used as an author was taken from a Mississippi riverboat term *mark twain*, which was called out when the shallow water was only two fathoms deep, placing the boat in danger. Sam Clemens was on his way to a career as a riverboat captain, a boyhood dream he had when living on the west bank of the Mississippi, in Missouri, when the Civil War erupted and motivated him to head west to Nevada and then California. It was there he began his long career as America's foremost writer and lecturer. Upon moving east, he became part of New York's prestigious literary circles. He was the author of two of the greatest American novels ever published, *The Adventures of Huckleberry Finn* and *The Adventures of Tom Sawyer*. He was an original American humorist and satirist, a master short story writer, novelist, and lecturer, and, as an international celebrity, the most famous man of his time. He died in Redding, Connecticut, on April 21, 1910. "Remarkable Dog" is from *Following the Equator* (1897).

. . . In the train, during a part of the return journey from Baroda, we had the company of a gentleman who had with him a remarkable looking dog. I had not seen one of its kind before, as far as I could remember. Though of course I might have seen one and not noticed it, for I am not acquainted with dogs, but only with cats. This dog's coat was smooth and shiny black, and I think it had tan trimmings around the edges of the dog, and perhaps underneath. It was a long low dog, with very short, strange legs—legs that curved inboard, something like parentheses turned the wrong way. Indeed, it was made on the plan of a bench for length and lowness. It seemed to be satisfied, but I thought the plan poor, and structurally weak, on account of the distance between the forward supports and those abaft. With age the dog's back was likely to sag; and it seemed to me that it would have been a stronger and more practicable dog if it had some more legs. It had not begun to sag yet, but the shape of the legs showed that the undue weight imposed upon them was beginning to tell. It had a long nose, and floppy ears that hung down, and a resigned expression of countenance. I did not like to ask what kind of dog it was, or how it became deformed, for it was plain that the gentleman was very fond of it, and naturally he could be sensitive about it. From delicacy I thought it best not to seem to notice it too much. No doubt a man with a dog like that feels just as a person does who has a child that is out of true. The gentleman was not merely fond of the dog, he was also proud of it—just the same, again as a mother feels about her child when it is an idiot. I could see that he was proud of it, not-withstanding it was such a long dog and looked so resigned and pious. It had been all over the world with him, and had been pilgriming like that for years and years. It had traveled 50,000 miles by sea and rail, and had ridden on front of him on his horse 8,000. It had a silver medal from the Geographical Society of Great Britain for its travels, and I saw it. It had won prizes in dog shows, both in India and in England—I saw them. He said that its pedigree was on record in the Kennel Club, and that it was a well-known dog. He said that a great many people in London could recognize it the moment they saw it. I did not say anything, but I did not think it anything strange. I should know that dog, again, myself, yet I am not careful about noticing dogs. He said that when he walked along in London, people often stopped and looked at the dog. Of course, I did not say anything, for I did not want to hurt his feelings, but I could have explained to him that if you take a great long low dog like that and waddle it along the street anywhere in the world and not charge anything, people will stop and look. He was gratified because the dog took prizes. But that was nothing; if I were built like that I could take prizes myself. I wished I knew what kind of dog it was, and what it was for, but I could not very well ask, for that would show that I did not know. Not that I want a dog like that, but only to know the secret of its birth.

I think he was going to hunt elephants with it, because I know, from remarks dropped by him, that he hunted large game in India and Africa, and likes it. But I think that if he tries to hunt elephants with it, he is going to be disappointed.

I do not believe that it is suited for elephants. It lacks energy, it lacks force of character, it lacks bitterness. These things all show in the meekness and resignation of its expression. It would not attack an elephant, I am sure of it. It might not run if it saw one coming, but it looked to me like a dog that would sit down and pray.

I wish he had told me what breed it was, if there are others, but I shall know the dog the next time, and then if I can bring myself to it I will put delicacy aside and ask. . . .

• • •

I wonder if other dogs think poodles are members
of a weird religious cult.
—Rita Rudner

gulliver the great

walter a. dyer

Walter A. Dyer (1878–1943) was the author of many successful books and short stories throughout his long career as a writer and editor. He was highly respected and greatly admired for the wide variety of subjects about which he wrote, from novels to short stories to magazine articles to books of nonfiction subjects such as antiques, American crafts, and furniture styles. He seemed to have always hit the mark for popularity. Several of his books have remained in print after all these decades, such as *The Lure of the Antique,* first published in 1910, which is still available as well as his 1915 novel, *Pierrot the Carabinier: Dog of Belgium.* Dyer began his long career as a staffer on the *Springfield Union* (Massachusetts) in 1900 and then continuing at *The Criterion* in New York from 1901 to 1905. The mainstay of his career was that of an editor for several magazines from 1907 until his death in 1943. He became the director of the Amherst College Press in 1933, his alma mater. "Gulliver, the Great" first appeared in his collection of short stories *Gulliver the Great and Other Dog Stories,* published in 1916. Judging by much of his fiction, he truly loved and admired dogs.

It was a mild evening in early spring, and the magnolias were in bloom. We motored around the park, turned up a side street, and finally came to a throbbing standstill before the Churchwarden Club.

There was nothing about its exterior to indicate that it was a club-house at all, but within there was an indefinable atmosphere of early Victorian comfort. There was something about it that suggested Mr. Pickwick. Old prints of horses and ships and battles hung upon the walls, and the oak was dark and old. There seemed to be no decorative scheme or keynote, and yet the atmosphere was utterly distinctive. It was my first visit to the Churchwarden Club, of which my quaint, old-fashioned Uncle Ford had long been a member, and I was charmed.

We dined in the rathskeller, the walls of which were completely covered with long churchwarden pipes, arranged in the most intricate and marvelous patterns; and after our mutton-chop and ale and plum pudding, we filled with the choicest of tobaccos the pipes which the old major-domo brought us.

Then came Jacob R. Enderby to smoke with us.

Tall and spare he was, with long, straight, black hair, large, aquiline nose, and piercing eyes. I disgraced myself by staring at him. I didn't know such a man existed in New York, and yet I couldn't decide whether his habitat should be Arizona or Cape Cod.

Enderby and Uncle Ford were deep in a discussion of the statesmanship of James G. Blaine, when a waiter summoned my uncle to the telephone.

I neglected to state that my uncle, in his prosaic hours, is a physician; and this was a call. I knew it the moment I saw the waiter approaching. I was disappointed and disgusted.

Uncle Ford saw this and laughed.

"Cheer up!" said he. "You needn't come with me to visit the sick. I'll be back in an hour, and meanwhile Mr. Enderby will take care of you; won't you, Jake?"

For answer Enderby arose, and refilling his pipe took me by the arm, while my uncle got into his overcoat. As he passed us on the way out he whispered in my ear:

"Talk about dogs."

I heard and nodded.

Enderby led me to the lounge or loafing-room, an oak-paneled apartment in the rear of the floor above, with huge leather chairs and a seat in the bay window. Save for a gray-haired old chap dozing over a copy of *Simplicissimus*, the room was deserted.

But no sooner had Enderby seated himself on the window-seat than there was a rush and a commotion, and a short, glad bark, and Nubbins, the steward's bull-terrier, bounded in and landed at Enderby's side with canine expressions of great joy.

I reached forward to pat him, but he paid absolutely no attention to me.

At last his wrigglings subsided, and he settled down with his head on Enderby's knee, the picture of content. Then I recalled my Uncle's parting injunction.

"Friend of yours?" I suggested.

Enderby smiled. "Yes," he said, "we're friends, I guess. And the funny part of it is that he doesn't pay any attention to any one else except his master. They all act that way with me, dogs do." And he pulled Nubbins's stubby ears.

But we hadn't lost sight of Manila Bay when I discovered that there was a dog aboard—and such a dog! I had never seen one that sent me into such a panic as this one, and he had free range of the ship. A Great Dane he was, named Gulliver, and he was the pride of the captain's rum-soaked heart.

"Natural attraction, I suppose," said I.

"Yes, it is," he answered, with the modest frankness of a big man.

"It's a thing hard to explain, though there's a sort of reason for it in my case."

I pushed toward him a little tobacco-laden teak-wood stand hopefully. He refilled and lighted.

"It's an extraordinary thing, even so," he said, puffing. "Every dog nowadays seems to look upon me as his long-lost master, but it wasn't always so. I hated dogs and they hated me."

Not wishing to say "Really" or "Indeed" to this big, outdoor man, I simply grunted my surprise.

"Yes, we were born enemies. More than that, I was afraid of dogs. A little fuzzy toy dog, ambling up to me in a room full of company, with his tail wagging, gave me the shudders. I couldn't touch the beast. And as for big dogs outdoors, I feared them like the plague. I would go blocks out of my way to avoid one.

"I don't remember being particularly cowardly about other things, but I just couldn't help this. It was in my blood, for some reason or other. It was the bane of my existence. I couldn't see what the brutes were put in the world for, or how any one could have anything to do with them.

"All the dogs reciprocated. They disliked me and distrusted me. The most docile old Brunos would growl and show their teeth when I came near."

"The change come suddenly?" I asked.

"Quite. It was in 1901. I accepted a commission from an importing and trading company to go to the Philippines to do a little quiet exploring, and spent four months in the sickly place. Then I got the fever, and when I recovered I couldn't get out of there too soon.

"I reached Manila just in time to see the mail steamer disappearing around the point, and I was mad. There would be another in six days, but I couldn't wait. I was just crazy to get back home.

"I made inquiries and learned of an old tramp steamer, named the *Old Squaw*, making ready to leave for Honolulu on the following day with a cargo of hemp and stuff, and a bunch of Moros for some show in the States, and I booked passage on that.

"She was the worst old tub you ever saw. I didn't learn much about her, but I verily believe her to have been a condemned excursion boat. She wouldn't have been allowed to run to Coney Island.

"She was battered and unpainted, and she wallowed horribly. I don't believe she could have reached Honolulu much before the regular boat, but I couldn't wait, and I took her.

"I made myself as comfortable as possible, bribed the cook to insure myself against starvation, and swung a hammock on the forward deck as far as possible from the worst of the vile smells.

"But we hadn't lost sight of Manila Bay when I discovered that there was a dog aboard—and such a dog! I had never seen one that sent me into such a panic as this one, and he had free range of the ship. A Great Dane he was, named Gulliver, and he was the pride of the captain's rum-soaked heart.

"With all my fear, I realized he was a magnificent animal, but I looked on him as a gigantic devil. Without exception, he was the biggest dog I ever saw, and as muscular as a lion. He lacked some points that show judges set store by, but he had the size and the build.

"I had seen Vohl's Vulcan and the Württemberg breed, but they were fox-terriers compared with Gulliver. His tail was as big around as my arm, and the cook lived in terror of his getting into the galley and wagging it; and he had a mouth that looked to me like the crater of Mauna Loa, and a voice that shook the planking when he spoke.

"I first caught sight of him appearing from behind a huge coil of cordage in the stern. He stretched and yawned, and I nearly died of fright.

"I caught up a belaying-ping, though little good that would have done me. I think he saw me do it, and doubtless he set me down for an enemy then and there.

"We were well out of the harbor, and there was no turning back, but I would have given my right hand to be off that boat. I fully expected him to eat me up, and I slept with that belaying-pin sticking into my ribs in the hammock, and with my revolver loaded and handy.

"Fortunately, Gulliver's dislike for me took the form of sublime contempt. He knew I was afraid of him, and he despised me for it. He was a great pet with the captain and crew, and even the Moros treated him with admiring respect when they werc allowed on deck. I couldn't understand it. I would as soon have made a pet of a hungry boa-constrictor.

"On the third day out the poor old boiler burst and the *Old Squaw* caught fire. She was dry and rotten inside and she burned like tinder. No attempt was made to extinguish the flames, which got into the hemp in the hold in short order.

"The smoke was stifling, and in a jiffy all hands were struggling with the boats. The Moros came tumbling up from below and added to the confusion with their terrified yells.

"The davits were old and rusty, and the men were soon fighting among themselves. One boat dropped stern foremost, filled, and sank immediately, and the *Old Squaw* herself was visibly settling.

"I saw there was no chance of getting away in the boats, and I recalled a life-raft on the deck forward near my hammock. It was a sort of catamaran—a double platform on a pair of hollow, watertight, cylindrical buoys. It wasn't twenty feet long and about half as broad, but it would have to do. I fancy it was a forgotten relic of the old excursion-boat days.

"There was no time to lose, for the *Old Squaw* was bound to sink presently. Besides, I was aft with the rest, and the flames were licking up the deck and running-gear in the waist of the boat.

"The galley, which was amidships near the engine-room, had received the full force of the explosion, and the cook lay moaning in the ice scuppers with a small water-cask thumping against his chest. I couldn't stop to help the man, but I did kick the cask away.

"It seemed to be nearly full, and it occurred to me that I should need it. I glanced quickly around, and luckily found a tin of biscuits that had also been blown out of the galley. I picked this up, and rolling the cask of water ahead of me as rapidly as I could, I made my way through the hot, stifling smoke to the bow of the boat.

"I kicked at the life-raft; it seemed to be sound, and I lashed the biscuits and water to it. I also threw on a coil of rope and a piece of sail-cloth. I saw nothing else about that could possibly be of any value to me. I abandoned my trunk for fear it would only prove troublesome.

"Then I hacked the raft loose with my knife and shoved it over the bulwark. Apparently no one had seen me, for there was no one else forward of the sheet of flame that now cut the boat in two.

"The raft was a mighty heavy affair, but I managed to raise one end to the rail. I don't believe I would ever have been able to heave it over under any circumstances, but I didn't have to.

"I felt a great upheaval, and the prow of the *Old Squaw* went up into the air. I grabbed the ropes that I had lashed the food on with and clung to the raft. The deck became almost perpendicular, and it was a miracle that the raft didn't slide down with me into the flames. Somehow it stuck where it was.

"Then the boat sank with a great roar and for about a thousand years, it seemed to me, I was under water. I didn't do anything, I couldn't think.

"I was only conscious of a tremendous weight of water and a feeling that I would burst open. Instinct alone made me cling to the raft.

"When it finally brought me to the surface I was as nearly dead as I care to be. I lay there on the thing in a half-conscious condition for an endless time. If my life had depended on my doing something, I would have been lost.

"Then gradually I came to, and began to spit out salt water and gasp for breath. I gathered my wits together and sat up. My hands were absolutely numb, and I had to loosen the grip of my fingers with the help of my toes. Odd sensation.

"Then I looked about me. My biscuits and water and rope were safe, but the sail-cloth had vanished. I remember that this annoyed me hugely at the time, though I don't know what earthly good it would have been.

"The sea was fairly calm, and I could see all about. Not a human being was visible, only a few floating bits of wreckage. Every man on board must have gone down with the ship and drowned, except myself.

"Then I caught sight of something that made my heart stand still. The huge head of Gulliver was coming rapidly toward me through the water!

"The dog was swimming strongly, and must have leaped from

the *Old Squaw* before she sank. My raft was the only thing afloat large enough to hold him, and he knew it.

"I drew my revolver, but it was soaking wet and useless. Then I sat down on the cracker tin and gritted my teeth and waited. I had been alarmed, I must admit, when the boiler blew up and the panic began, but that was nothing to the terror that seized me now.

"Here I was all alone on the top of the Pacific Ocean with a horrible demon making for me as fast as he could swim. My mind was benumbed, and I could think of nothing to do. I trembled and my teeth rattled. I prayed for a shark, but no shark came.

"Soon Gulliver reached the raft and placed one of his forepaws on it and then the other. The top of it stood six or eight inches above the water, and it took a great effort for the dog to raise himself. I wanted to kick him back, but I didn't dare to move.

"Gulliver struggled mightily. Again and again he reared his great shoulders above the sea, only to be cast back, scratching and kicking, at a lurch of the raft.

"Finally a wave favored him, and he caught the edge of the under platform with one of his hind feet. With a stupendous effort he heaved his huge bulk over the edge and lay sprawling at my feet, panting and trembling."

Enderby paused and gazed out of the window with a big sigh, as though the recital of his story had brought back some of the horror of his remarkable experience.

Nubbins looked up inquiringly, and then snuggled closer to his friend, while Enderby smoothed the white head.

"Well," he continued, "there we were. You can't possibly imagine how I felt unless you, too, have been afflicted with dog-fear. It was awful. And I hated the brute so. I could have torn him limb from limb if I had had the strength. But he was vastly more powerful than I. I could only fear him.

"By and by he got up and shook himself. I cowered on my cracker-tin, but he only looked at me contemptuously, went to the other end of the raft, and lay down to wait patiently for deliverance.

"We remained this way until nightfall. The sea was comparatively calm, and we seemed to be drifting but slowly. We were in the path of ships likely to be passing one way or the other, and I would have been hopeful of the outcome if it had not been for my feared and hated companion.

"I began to feel faint, and opened the cracker-tin. The biscuits were wet with salt water, but I ate a couple, and left the tin open to dry them. Gulliver looked around, and I shut the tin hastily. But the dog never moved. He was not disposed to ask any favors. By kicking the sides of the cask and prying with my knife, I managed to get the bung out and took a drink. Then I settled myself on the raft with my back against the cask, and longed for a smoke.

"The gentle motion of the raft produced a lulling effect on my exhausted nerves, and I began to nod, only to awake with a start, with fear gripping at my heart. I dared not sleep. I don't know what I thought Gulliver would do to me, for I did not understand dogs, but I felt that I must watch him constantly. In the starlight I could see that his eyes were open. Gulliver was watchful too.

Finally Gulliver, who had kept his distance all this time, arose and came toward me. My words died in my throat. What was he going to do?

"All night long I kept up a running fight with drowsiness. I dozed at intervals, but never for long at a time. It was a horrible night, and I cannot tell you how I longed for day and welcomed it when it came.

"I must have slept toward dawn, for I suddenly became conscious of broad daylight. I roused myself, stood up, and swung my arms and legs to stir up circulation, for the night had been chilly. Gulliver arose, too, and stood silently watching me until I ceased for fear. When he had settled down again I got my breakfast out of the cracker-tin. Gulliver was restless, and was evidently interested.

" 'He must be hungry,' I thought, and then a new fear caught me. I had only to wait until he became very hungry and then he would surely attack me. I concluded that it would be wiser to feed him, and I tossed him a biscuit.

"I expected to see him grab it ravenously, and wondered as soon as I had thrown it if the taste of food would only serve to make him more ferocious. But at first he would not touch it. He only lay there with his great head on his paws and glowered at me. Distrust was plainly visible in his face. I had never realized before that a dog's face could express the subtler emotions.

"His gaze fascinated me, and I could not take my eyes from his. The bulk of him was tremendous as he lay there, and I noticed the big, swelling muscles of his jaw. At last he arose, sniffed suspiciously at the biscuit, and looked up at me again.

" 'It's all right; eat it!' I cried.

"The sound of my own voice frightened me. I had not intended to speak to him. But in spite of my strained tone he seemed somewhat reassured.

"He took a little nibble, and then swallowed the biscuit after one or two crunches, and looked up expectantly. I threw him another and he ate that.

" 'That's all,' said I. 'We must be sparing of them.'

"I was amazed to discover how perfectly he understood. He lay down again and licked his chops.

"Late in the [morning] I saw a line of smoke on the horizon, and soon a steamer hove into view. I stood up and waved my coat frantically, but to no purpose. Gulliver stood up and looked from me to the steamer, apparently much interested.

" 'Too far off,' I said to Gulliver. 'I hope the next one will come nearer.'

"At midday I dined, and fed Gulliver. This time he took the two biscuits quite without reserve and whacked his great tail against the raft. It seemed to me that his attitude was less hostile, and I wondered at it.

"When I took my drink from the cask, Gulliver showed signs of interest.

" 'I suppose dogs get thirsty, too,' I said aloud.

"Gulliver rapped with his tail. I looked about for some sort of receptacle, and finally pulled off my shoe, filled it with water, and shoved it toward him with my foot. He drank gratefully.

"During the afternoon I sighted another ship, but it was too distant to notice me. However, the sea remained calm and I did not despair.

"After we had had supper, I settled back against my cask, resolved to keep awake, for still I did not trust Gulliver. The sun set suddenly and the stars came out, and I found myself strangely lonesome. It seemed as though I had been alone out there on the Pacific for weeks. The miles and miles of heaving waters, almost on a level with my eye, were beginning to get on my nerves. I longed for someone to talk to, and wished I had dragged the half-breed cook along with me for company. I sighed loudly, and Gulliver raised his head.

" 'Lonesome out here, isn't it?' I said, simply to hear the sound of my own voice.

"Then for the first time Gulliver spoke. He made a deep sound in his throat, but it wasn't a growl, and with all my ignorance of dog language I knew it.

"Then I began to talk. I talked about everything—the people back home and all that—Gulliver listened. I know more about dogs now, and I know that the best way to make friends with a dog is to talk to him. He can't talk back, but he can understand a heap more than you think he can.

"Finally Gulliver, who had kept his distance all this time, arose and came toward me. My words died in my throat. What was he going to do? To my immense relief he did nothing but sink down at my feet with a grunt and curl his huge body into a semicircle. He had dignity, Gulliver had. He wanted to be friendly, but he would not presume. However, I had lost interest in conversation, and sat watching him and wondering.

"In spite of my firm resolution, I fell asleep at length from sheer exhaustion, and never woke until daybreak. The sky was clouded and our raft was pitching. Gulliver was standing in the middle of the raft, looking at me in evident alarm. I glanced over my shoulder, and the blackness of the horizon told me that a storm was coming, and coming soon.

"I made fast our slender provender, tied the end of a line about my own waist for safety, and waited.

"In a short time the storm struck us in all its tropical fury. The raft pitched and tossed, now high up at one end, and now at the other, and sometimes almost engulfed in the waves.

"Gulliver was having a desperate time to keep aboard. His blunt claws slipped on the wet deck of the raft, and he fell and slid about dangerously. The thought flashed across my mind that the storm might prove to be a blessing in disguise, and that I might soon be rid of the brute.

"As I clung there to the lashings, I saw him slip down to the further end of the raft, his hind quarters actually over the edge. A wave swept over him, but still he clung, panting madly. Then the raft righted itself for a moment, and as he hung there he gave me a look I shall never forget—a look of fear, of pleading, of reproach, and yet of silent courage. And with all my stupidity I read that look. Somehow it told me that I was the master, after all, and he the dog. I could not resist it. Cautiously I raised myself and loosened the spare rope I had saved. As the raft tipped the other way Gulliver regained his footing and came sliding toward me.

"Quickly I passed the rope around his body, and as the raft dived again I hung on to the rope with one hand, retaining my own hold with the other. Gulliver's great weight nearly pulled my arm from its socket, but he helped mightily, and during the next moment of equilibrium I took another turn around his body and made the end of the rope fast.

"The storm passed as swiftly as it had come, and though it left us drenched and exhausted, we were both safe.

"That evening Gulliver crept close to me as I talked, and I let him. Loneliness will make a man do strange things.

"On the fifth day, when our provisions were nearly gone, and I had begun to feel the sinking dullness of despair, I sighted a steamer apparently coming directly toward us. Instantly I felt new life in my limbs and around my heart, and while the boat was yet miles away I began to shout and to wave my coat.

" 'I believe she's coming, old man!' I cried to Gulliver. 'I believe she's coming!'

"I soon wearied of this foolishness and sat down to wait. Gulliver came close and sat beside me, and for the first time I put my hand on him. He looked up at me and rapped furiously with his tail. I patted his head—a little gingerly, I must confess.

"It was a big, smooth head, and it felt solid and strong. I passed my hand down his neck, his back, his flanks. He seemed to quiver with joy. He leaned his huge body against me. Then he bowed his head and licked my shoe.

"A feeling of intense shame and unworthiness came over me, with the realization of how completely I had misunderstood him. Why should this great, powerful creature lick my shoe? It was incredible.

"Then, somehow, everything changed. Fear and distrust left me, and a feeling of comradeship and understanding took their place. We two had been through so much together. A dog was no longer a frightful beast to me; he was a dog! I cannot think of a nobler word. And Gulliver had licked my shoe! Doubtless it was only the fineness of his perception that had prevented him from licking my hand. I might have resented that. I put my arms suddenly around Gulliver's neck and hugged him, I loved that dog!

"Slowly, slowly, the steamer crawled along, but still kept to her course. When she was about a mile away, however, I saw that she would not pass as close to us I had hoped; so I began once more my waving and yelling. She came nearer, nearer, but still showed no sign of observing us.

"She was abreast of us, and passing. I was in a frenzy!

"She was so near that I could make out the figure of the captain on the bridge, and other figures on the deck below. It seemed as though they must see us, though I realized how low in the water we stood, and how pitifully weak and hoarse my voice was. I had been a fool to waste it. Then an idea struck me.

" 'Speak!' I cried to Gulliver, who stood watching beside me. 'Speak, old man!'

"Gulliver needed no second bidding. A roar like that of all the bulls of Bashan rolled out over the blue Pacific. Again and again Gulliver gave voice, deep, full, powerful. His great side heaved with the mighty effort, his red, cavernous mouth open, and his head raised.

" 'Good, old man!' I cried. 'Good!' And again that magnificent voice boomed forth.

"Then something happened on board the steamer. The figures came to the side. I waved my coat and danced. They saw us.

"I was pretty well done up when they took us aboard, and I slept for twenty-four hours straight. When I awoke there sat Gulliver by my bunk, and when I turned to look at him he lifted a great paw and put it on my arm."

Enderby ceased, and there was silence in the room save for the light snoring of Nubbins.

"You took him home with, I suppose?" I asked.

Enderby nodded.

"And you have him still?" I certainly wanted to have a look at that dog.

But he did not answer. I saw an expression of great sadness come into his eyes as he gazed out of the window, and I knew that Jacob Enderby had finished his story.

• • •

Our dogs, like our shoes, are comfortable. They might be a bit out of shape and a little worn around the edges, but they fit well.
—Chris Walkowicz

old dog tray

stephen collins foster

Stephen Collins Foster (1826–1864) is considered by many music historians to be America's quintessential songwriter. Foster's songs live in perpetuity as a lyrical expression of American popular culture, capturing the mood and the flavor of the country before, during, and after his time. His songs often exude melancholy, yearning for better times, sweet memories, and loving exuberance. Born in Lawrenceville, Pennsylvania, of American pioneer stock, his musical career began with various traveling minstrel shows. Many of his songs were written and performed for the E. P. Christy Minstrel troupe. His talent for capturing dialects in his songs, particularly African American dialects, has often created the misconception that his music is based on folk music. "Old Dog Tray" was one of Foster's most popular and best-selling songs. It expresses a reminiscence about better days when the dog, like all dogs, offered love, playfulness, and faithful companionship.

The morn of life is past,
And ev'ning comes at last;
It brings me a dream of a once happy day,
Of merry forms I've seen
Upon the village green,
Sporting with my old dog Tray.

Old dog Tray's ever faithful;
Grief cannot drive him away;
He's gentle, he is kind,
I'll never, never find
A better friend than old dog Tray.

The forms I called my own
Have vanish'd one by one,
The lov'd ones, the dear ones have all passed away;
Their happy smiles have flown,
Their gentle voices gone,
I've nothing left but old dog Tray.

Old dog Tray's ever faithful;
Grief cannot drive him away;
He's gentle, he is kind,
I'll never, never find
A better friend than old dog Tray.

When thoughts recall the past,
His eyes are on me cast,
I know that he feels what my breaking heart would say;
Although he cannot speak,
I'll vainly, vainly seek
A better friend than old dog Tray.

• • •

My father was a Saint Bernard, my mother was a collie,
but I am a Presbyterian.
—Mark Twain

the westminster kennel club

charles s. pelham-clinton

Charles S. Pelham-Clinton was a journalist of his time, contributing to several magazines in the later part of the nineteenth century. His article concerning the first decade of the Westminster Kennel Club and its celebrated dog shows appeared in the Vol. XII, June, 1888, issue of *Outing Magazine,* a periodical devoted to sporting activities and outdoor events and activities. It was first known as *Wheelman* in 1882 and had four title changes before ending publication in 1923.

"Sensation," call name Don, a lemon and white Pointer, has been the logo for the Westminster Kennel Club since 1877. His figure "on point" continues to grace the WKC show catalog every year.

The vast growth of public interest in outdoor sports, and the rapid increase of outdoor clubs, has, during the past decade, been a source of wonder to men of mature age. They marvel how in their young days they managed to do without the many amusements which nowadays are things "no fellow can do without."

The anglomaniac craze has undoubtedly been the main source of inspiration, for though the love of sport may be as deeply rooted in American as in English breasts, the sport itself, as a rule, comes over the ocean.

It is only during the last decade or two that the numerous hunt and shooting clubs have sprung up. The Westminster Kennel Club is one of the most notable of these. It was organized in December, 1877, and owes its origin in part to the dog-show held in Philadelphia in 1876, in connection with the Centennial Exhibition. This "show" excited a great deal of interest all over the country, and was one of the features of the exhibition. In the fall of that year and in the spring of 1877, various smaller bench shows were held, and each of them seemed so successful that several gentlemen who, previous to that date, had been engaged in the breeding of pointers, came to the conclusion that New York should not be behind in these matters, and determined to hold a bench show in New York.

A committee was appointed, consisting of Messrs. H. W. Webb, L. B. Wright, E. H. Dixon, C. DuB. Wagstaff, W. M. Tileston and Dr. Seward Webb, to conduct the undertaking.

These gentlemen lost but little time in fixing on the Madison Square Garden as the proper place to hold the show, and the late Charles Lincoln was engaged as superintendent. The estimation in which Mr. Lincoln was held is best shown by an extract from a short history published by the club for circulation among its members: "Mr. Lincoln's experience in England, where,

So successful an exhibit could not fail to make a permanent mark, and the promoters were encouraged to establish the club on a firm basis and make the show an annual affair.

at the age of nineteen years, he acted as secretary of the first Darlington Show, one of the earliest of any importance ever given in that country, and where he had been repeatedly engaged as a manager of exhibitions, both of dogs and horses, was of inestimable value to the committee." He was an excellent organizer, an indefatigable worker, of unimpeachable integrity, and his tact, judgment, and readiness in smoothing over difficulties and calming of the perturbed spirits of the ignorant or disappointed exhibitors (an office requiring all the estimable qualities for which Job was famous), had much to do with the success of that and the subsequent exhibitions of the club. There is little doubt that the club owes a vast deal to Mr. Lincoln, and without his aid would probably never have achieved its leading position among the bench shows of America.

The show took place on May 8, 1877, with 874 entries, and was such an unprecedented success that it was kept open four days instead of three, and the proceeds of the last day were handed over to Mr. Henry Bergh, to aid him in establishing a hospital for sick dogs.

So successful an exhibit could not fail to make a permanent mark, and the promoters were encouraged to establish the club on a firm basis and make the show an annual affair.

On December 9, 1877, it was resolved to incorporate the association. The roll of members at this time was as follows: Colonel LeGrand B. Cannon, General A. S. Webb, Dr. W. Seward Webb, Geo. De F. Grant, William F. Morgan, Edmund C. Stanton, C. DuBois Wagstaff, H. Walter Webb, Wm. M. Tileston, Frederick Barnard, Oliver Iselin, Lenox Belknap, J. Hopkins Smith, Louis B. Wright, F. O. De Luze, Robert C. Cornell, Huntingdon Denton, Dr. William G. Richards. The president elected was General Webb, with Dr. Seward Webb as secretary and treasurer and Mr. Wagstaff as vice-president. These three gentlemen, together with Messrs. Cannon, Tileston, Grant, Barnard, H. W. Webb and W. F. Morgan, forming the board of directors. The act of incorporation was signed on the 5th of January, 1878, and read that the particular business and the object of the society was "to study and improve the breed of dogs, to propagate and to protect game, and also to purchase, collect, own, sell, exhibit, breed and train dogs." Need we add that the breed of dog the club selected was the Pointer, for the improvement of which the Westminster Breeding Association, the parent of the present kennel club, had been formed?

Only sportsmen have any idea of the sagacity of this breed of dog. One instance of dog sense that will strike home is told by a Captain Brown. A gentleman requesting the loan of a pointer from a friend, was informed he was a perfect pointer, but could not stomach a bad shot. Unfortunately for the dog, the borrower was a poor shot, and missed bird after bird. Eventually the dog grew careless, but finally came to a good point, seemingly at a fern-bush. The sportsman advanced, and out sprang a fine black-cock. Both barrels missed him, and the dog's patience was so exhausted that he gave a howl, tucked his tail between his legs and put out for home. If more dogs of this kind existed half the powder manufacturers would shut up shop.

Some pointers do not care about emigration, as a story told by Mr. Edward Cook, of Tugsten, Northumberland, evinces. His brother went to America, taking with him a dog that was afterwards lost near Baltimore. Some months later Mr. and Mrs. Edward Cook were alarmed at hearing a dog attempting to break into their house. On admitting it, it was found to be the same dog that the brother had taken to America, and they never found how it returned, nor by what vessel.

Lieutenant Ship, in his memoirs, mentions the case of a soldier in India, who, having presented his dog to an acquaintance, by whom he was taken a distance of four hundred miles, was surprised to see him back a few days afterwards. These anecdotes show the pointers to be by no means deficient in other qualities than those which the sportsman requires.

The first kennels of the Westminster Kennel Club were at Passaic, New Jersey, near the residence of Mr. William Tileston. Here was first formed the nucleus of the present celebrated collection of pointers owned by the Kennel Club.

The first dog of great note owned was *Sensation*, who was purchased in England by Mr. George De Forest Grant, in 1876. His name originally was *Don*, and his record as good as could be desired. He was a large-sized lemon-and-white pointer, of about seventy pounds weight, and is generally admitted to have had the best head of any pointer in America, and probably in England, when there. He took part in the field trials of the Eastern Field Trials Club at Robins Island, and won the pointer cup, beating Mr. Godeffroy's well known *Croxteth*. During the first year after his importation he won no less than $1,200 in prizes, and the return from service fees was very large. He took prizes almost up to his death, which occurred in June of last year, and he has left a long list of good dogs, both in the field and on the bench, as his representatives. Together with him at Passaic were *Whiskey,* his daughters *Daisy* and *Flirt,* and many others equally good.

The show of 1878, the first given by the incorporated club, was a repetition of the success of that of the preceding year. This, together with the prestige acquired thereby and the great reputation that *Sensation* had by this time gained, both as a prize winner and sire, placed the club in the front rank of kennel associations. Applications for membership began to flow in, and the limit of twenty-five was very soon reached.

It was now considered a wise plan to procure a permanent and larger home, and, after innumerable places had been examined, Messrs. Cornell, Morgan and Wagstaff reported very favorably on the grounds now occupied by the club, at Babylon, L.I.; and a lease for two years was taken, with an option of purchase at $5,500 at the expiration of the lease.

The grounds contained about sixty-four acres, divided by roads into three sections, that on which the buildings stood being the largest, and containing about thirty acres. The land lies about a mile northwest of Babylon, and is admirably adapted for what is required of it. The soil is dry, and there is no trouble found in keeping the dogs in perfect health from that reason. The woods surrounding the club consist very largely of pine-trees, which are healthy in themselves, and certainly add a great deal to the beauty of the place, as, during the winter months, their verdure causes a pleasant change from the everlasting brown-gray that makes the country so monotonous in winter time. A fine pond lies south of the club-house, which supplies Babylon, as well as the club, with ice, and is a delightful adjunct to the scenery, the contrast between the blue of the water and deep tones of the pine-trees making a very pretty piece of perspective.

The buildings, when the club first entered into possession, were about a hundred years old, and seemed on their last legs; repairs, however, were made, a pigeon-ground laid out, and the barn turned into kennels, while the small house that was to be used as a club-house was made as comfortable as circumstances would permit.

At the time of moving *Sensation* was the stud dog and *Whiskey, Daisy I., Daisy II., Flirt, May* and *Gertie* were the best of the females.

The move proved extremely beneficial to the club in every way, and in 1882 the property was purchased, and two years afterwards, the list of members having quite outgrown the club-house, the old house was moved to a corner of the grounds, and a new building erected in its place. The designs were drawn by Mr. C. DuBois Wagstaff, who, with Messrs. L. K. Wilmerding and Elliott Smith, constituted the building committee. The building is a handsome and exceedingly comfortable structure, forty by sixty feet, and cost about $8,000.

The ground-floor, around which is a wide veranda, consists of a cozy hall, a billiard room, a gun-room and a handsome dining-room twenty feet by forty. As many as fifty have been seated at table. It is comfortably and neatly furnished in light wood, and has a huge fireplace, from which logs throw out an inspiring heat when the winter wind whistles across Long Island and the caloric gets very low. The sideboard is decorated with some handsome silver cups and jugs won by the different members in pigeon-matches against other clubs, while above the fireplace the mantel-board is still further adorned by pewter and silver cups won at different dog shows by members' dogs and presented to the club, and also by dogs belonging to the club.

On entering the dining-room, the first object to catch the eye are two magnificent heads, the one that of a moose and the other that of a huge elk, handsomely mounted, which would be hard to equal.

On each side of the fireplace are two extremely well executed oil paintings by J. M. Tracy, the one of *Tammany* and *Madstone*, and the other of *Croxteth* and old *Sensation*. Both paintings are very fine, and are said to be excellent likenesses of the dogs, particularly of old *Sensation*. The windows of the dining-room have an agreeable outlook, and there is certainly no lack of life in the background as one gets a good view of the kennels.

The hall has some excellent prints of dogs, some of which are very old and portray dogs as unlike those of the present day as can be imagined. The billiard room contains a single English table and has some handsome pictures on the walls, notably one of *Bang-Bang* and a fine picture of a St. Bernard. Beyond this is the gun-room and very cozy it is. Naturally the pictures are "doggy," but they are good ones, and the monotony is relieved by a caricature of Mr. G. De F. Grant, who is represented as having just blown a pigeon to innumerable fragments, while his face expresses unutterable satisfaction at the performance. Lockers surround the room which will hold from three to six guns, if required, and, as the room is kept warm, there is no danger of rust.

Upon the next floor are the bedrooms, ten in number, all neatly and comfortably furnished, and hung with shooting, coaching and hunting pictures. A charming view is had from the upper veranda, which overlooks the pigeon-shooting ground, and is a cool and pleasant place in summer.

The hum of the Long Island mosquito is to be heard at times in the summer, and is also to be felt, on occasions; but the grass is kept close around the house, and it is only when certain winds blow that the nuisance is at all troublesome.

The membership of the Westminster Kennel has of course immensely increased during the ten years of its existence. In 1878 there were only twenty-five members—to-day there are close on five times that number. . . .

If it had not been for the energy of such institutions as the Westminster Kennel Club dogs like these would never have been seen in this country, or, at all events, in very isolated cases: it is well, therefore, to give honor to whom honor is due. The press of New York appreciates the efforts of this and other clubs, and seconds such enterprise by lengthy reports of exhibitions, while the officers of the show in their turn do all they can to give correct and early information to the members of the press. . . .

four on the floor

mordecai siegal

When dog days are done
And the raptured tail is still,
I think about races won
And biscuits given in blackmail.
Barkless rooms reflect,
Swiveling eyes and chin on floor
Feelings of respect
And loving, missing all the more.

part four

poetry in motion

The dog has an enviable mind; it remembers the nice things
in life and quickly blots out the nasty.
—Barbara Woodhouse

elizabeth barrett browning and a spaniel named flush

mordecai siegal

Elizabeth Barrett Browning was born in Durham, England, in 1806 and died in Florence, Italy, in 1861. An adolescent Cocker Spaniel named Flush was given to the celebrated poet Elizabeth Barrett (before her marriage to Robert Browning) as a gift from her dear friend Mary Russell Mitford, a well-known writer of verse and prose. Mitford wanted her gift to be a positive source of pleasure and companionship for her good friend, hoping it would help her cope with her chronic, life-threatening illness. She made this very generous gesture during the darkest period of the poet's life. Elizabeth Barrett had no choice but to live as a reclusive invalid, confined to a quiet back room on the third floor of her father's house on affluent Wimpole Street in London. It was a gilded cage, to be sure. With her life hanging in the balance, her doctor confined her to her room to avoid physical and emotional stress. This was during the first third of the nineteenth century, almost a hundred years before the discovery of penicillin and other medical miracles we now take for granted. There was also no diagnosis available for her dangerous illness. She remained in her room, which she referred to as her "hermitage," or "prison," for more than five years, rarely leaving except when servants or one of her eleven brothers and sisters carried her to another part of the house or outdoors for an occasional excursion to get some fresh air.

Biographers have assumed her illness was tuberculosis, which swept in and out of her life like a deadly tide throughout all of her years. Almost instantly, Flush became the most important creature on earth to the frail writer, who never stopped composing and publishing throughout the time of her imposed seclusion. Near the end of that period, she published many notable works and developed into an important English poet. She was greatly admired, but only on rare occasions did she receive important writers of the time at home. It is safe to assume that the highly personal relationship between Elizabeth Barrett and Flush was enormously helpful, if not essential. They were two souls bound together first by circumstance and then by a strong emotional attachment based on mutual need. It seems to have been almost spiritual in nature.

For all the years of confinement, Flush, and only Flush, was constantly at Elizabeth's side, sharing her sofa, her meals, and her great affection while he learned to temper his behavior as a field dog with strong urges to run and scatter birds, as his name implied. He made the difficult adjustment as only a loving dog can. He was a typical-looking Cocker Spaniel of the red variety, with a full dark-colored coat. He was given to Miss Barrett within the first year of his young life to help ease her sadness at the death of a much-loved younger brother and to help abate her loneliness throughout the time of her seclusion. It was a generous sacrifice for her older friend, Miss Mitford, to give up her puppy, to which she had become quite attached, but she was a caring friend and admirer. It is quite likely that the dog's presence in Elizabeth Barrett's life was an important influence on the happiness and productivity of the poet during that difficult time. Few would dispute the therapeutic value of the depth and consistency of a dog's love and attention.

Literary scholars and critics have written that in her time, Elizabeth Barrett Browning was England's greatest woman poet. When William Wordsworth died, she was seriously considered for the position of poet laureate of England, but she lost out to Tennyson by a small margin. Beyond her poetry and her brilliant scholarship lies the most extraordinary story of this remarkable woman, which includes her lifelong illness, the importance of her dog, Flush, to her well-being, the romance and courtship of her affair with and marriage to Robert Browning, and her years afterward. So engrossing is her personal story, in addition to her literary output, that a number of books have been written about her, including several biographies; her letters have been published, as well as numerous collections of her poetry. Motion pictures were produced in Hollywood about her, most notably two versions of *The Barretts of Wimpole Street,* the first in 1934, starring Norma Shearer, and the second in 1957, with Jennifer Jones in the leading role. The films portrayed the romance of this literary giant and her equally gifted husband, Robert Browning. Important to her story is the fact that she was bedridden before her marriage for so long, stricken first with measles as a child and then with a chronic lung condition, which ultimately took her life when she was fifty-five.

Hers is a love story that has intrigued the most jaded of many generations. Her romance and marriage to poet and playwright Robert Browning is more compelling than a contemporary romance novel. Here, life makes fiction pale by comparison. Her prosperous but eccentric father had forbidden all twelve of his children to marry, Elizabeth having been the eldest. Three of the children married despite their father's wishes and were promptly disinherited and never allowed back in his house. No one has ever fully understood why he made this unreasonable demand. Throughout her childhood and adult life, Elizabeth's father loved her dearly and provided her with a superior education at home, the best medical attention available, and all the consideration and attention possible, including paying to have her first work published at the age of fourteen. What he demanded in return, as he did with all of his children, was obedience to his will.

In 1844, the last year of her seclusion, she published a collection of verse titled *Poems,* which received critical praise and secured her reputation as an important poet. As a result, she came to the attention of Robert Browning, whom she knew from his much-admired published work. Although six years younger than she, he wrote ardently to her in his first letter, dated January 10, 1845: "I love your verses with all my heart, dear Miss Barrett . . . and I love you too." So began a literary affair between these two great poets, who corresponded for five months before ever laying eyes on each other. These very letters fill two large published volumes. Many of the letters included extensive mention of Flush and Elizabeth's concern for him, as well as the dog's required acceptance of Browning, who was about to infringe on Flush's time with and attention from his mistress. The first meeting between Barrett and Browning, arranged by a mutual friend, was laden with the awkwardness and emotion of lovers who were not so young, she being thirty-nine and he thirty-three. Ultimately, however, this courtship led to their marriage sixteen months later. During that time, Browning visited Miss Barrett frequently, but only in the afternoons, avoiding contact with her father, who most certainly would have interfered had he been aware of the budding romance.

At the beginning of her relationship with Browning, her first obstacle was not her father, but, rather, her dog. During Browning's afternoon visits with Elizabeth, Flush began to sulk and presumably considered his mistress's new friend an interloper who was stealing her away from him. On two separate occasions, the jealous dog bit the tall suitor on the leg and was punished by a servant for his actions, receiving strong reprimands and being temporarily banished. In a short time, though, Flush came to accept Browning as a new, permanent part of his life, for the wise and sensitive man made great efforts to develop a rapport with him. It did not take long for him to gain the dog's acceptance, which was so important to his bride-to-be.

Defying the wishes of her father, they were secretly married in a nearby church, and a week later they left for Italy, where Elizabeth spent the balance of her life in great happiness. Flush, of course, went with them, settling in the sunny warmth of Florence. Leaving him behind was out of the question. The warm, gentle weather of Italy, the support of a loving husband and fellow artist, and the continued devotion of Flush all contributed to the prosperity of her health and happiness. The one sad note was that her father, with bitter rage, disowned her as well as expelling her from the family. It was a sad outcome for her, and all attempts at reconciliation failed. Father and daughter never saw each other again. From then on, she was known to the world as Elizabeth Barrett Browning.

The intense feelings that existed between Elizabeth and Flush constituted much more than a temporary relationship prior to Browning entering their lives. For Elizabeth, the bond provided a remedy for an ailing soul imprisoned by a failing body; and for Flush, her exalted love and need for him proved a fair trade for ancient hunting desires and impulses now supressed. It suggests that when you are very sick, you should first call your dog, and then your physician. What exists between dogs and humans are invisible cables made of entwined strands of feelings and needs, perhaps unworldly, perhaps divine.

to flush, my dog

elizabeth barrett browning

I

Loving friend, the gift of one
Who her own true faith has run
*   Through my lower nature,*
Be my benediction said
With hand upon thy head,
*   Gentle fellow-creature!*

II

Like a lady's ringlets brown,
Flow thy silken ears adown
          Either side demurely
Of thy silver-suited breast
Shining out from all the rest
          Of thy body purely.

III

Darkly brown thy body is,
Till the sunshine striking this
          Alchemize its dullness,
When the sleek curls manifold
Flash all over into gold
          With a burnished fullness.

IV

Underneath my stroking hand,
Startled eyes of hazel bland
          Kindling, growing larger,
Up thou leapest with a spring,
Full of prank and curveting,
          Leaping like a charger.

V

Leap! thy broad tail waves a light,
Leap! thy slender feet are bright,
          Canopied in fringes;
Leap! those tasselled ears of thine
Flicker strangely, fair and fine
          Down their golden inches.

VI

Yet, my pretty, sportive friend,
Little is't to such an end
  That I praise thy rareness;
Other dogs may be thy peers
Haply in these drooping ears
  And this glossy fairness.

VII

But of thee it shall be said,
This dog watched beside a bed
  Day and night unweary,
Watched within a curtained room
Where no sunbeam brake the gloom
  Round the sick and dreary.

VIII

Roses, gathered for a vase,
In that chamber died apace,
  Beam and breeze resigning;
This dog only, waited on,
Knowing that when light is gone
  Love remains for shining.

IX

Other dogs in thymy dew
Tracked the hares and followed through
  Sunny moor or meadow;
This dog only, crept and crept
Next a languid cheek that slept,
  Sharing in the shadow.

X

Other dogs of loyal cheer
Bounded at the whistle clear,
        Up the woodside hieing;
This dog only, watched in reach
Of a faintly uttered speech
        Or a louder sighing.

XI

And if one or two quick tears
Dropped upon his glossy ears
        Or a sigh came double,
Up he sprang in eager haste,
Fawning, fondling, breathing fast,
        In a tender trouble.

XII

And this dog was satisfied
If a pale thin hand would glide
        Down his dewlaps sloping—
Which he pushed his nose within,
After—platforming his chin
        On the palm left open.

XIII

This dog, if a friendly voice
Call him now to blither choice
        Than such a chamber-keeping,
"Come out!" praying from the door—
Presseth backward as before,
        Up against me leaping.

XIV

Therefore to this dog will I,
Tenderly not scornfully,
    Render praise and favor:
With my hand upon his head,
Is my benediction said
    Therefore and forever.

XV

And because he loves me so,
Better than his kind will do
    Often man or woman,
Give I back more love again
Than dogs often take of men,
    Leaning from my Human.

XVI

Blessings on thee, dog of mine,
Pretty collars make thee fine.
    Sugared milk make fat thee!
Pleasures wag on in thy tail,
Hands of gentle motion fail
    Nevermore, to pat thee!

XVII

Downy pillow take thy head,
Silken coverlid bestead,
    Sunshine help thy sleeping!
No fly's buzzing wake thee up,
No man break thy purple cup
    Set for drinking deep in.

XVIII

Whiskered cats arointed flee,
Sturdy stoppers keep from thee
  Cologne distillations;
Nuts lie in thy path for stones,
And thy feast-day macaroons
  Turn to daily rations!

XIX

Mock I thee, in wishing weal?—
Tears are in my eyes to feel
  Thou art made so straitly,
Blessing needs must straiten too—
Little canst thou joy or do,
  Thou who lovest greatly.

XX

Yet be blessèd to the height
Of all goods and all delight
  Pervious to thy nature;
Only loved beyond that line,
With a love that answers thine,
  Loving fellow—creature!

• • •

My little old dog: A heartbeat at my feet.
—Edith Wharton

flush or faunus

elizabeth barrett browning

You see this dog. It was but yesterday
I mused forgetful of his presence here
Till thought on thought drew downward tear on tear,
When from the pillow where wet-cheeked I lay,
A head as hairy as Faunus thrust its way
Right sudden against my face—two golden-clear
Great eyes astonished mine—a drooping ear
Did flap me on either cheek to dry the spray!
I started first as some Arcadian
Amazed by goatly god in twilight grove,
But as the bearded vision closelier ran
My tears off, I knew Flush, and rose above
Surprise and sadness—thanking the true PAN
Who, by low creatures, leads to heights of love.

flush: a biography

virginia woolf

When an author of the stature of Virginia Woolf, one of Britain's
most celebrated avant-garde writers, chose to devote her talent to

the biography of a dog, one must look beyond the obvious. True, she was a dog lover and even owned a much adored Cocker Spaniel of her own, but she was also an admirer of Elizabeth Barrett Browning, whom she regarded as an important poet and early advocate of women's issues. In the beautifully written biography of Flush, the author gives us an extraordinary view of the poet through the eyes of her dog. Although readers can enjoy the book for its surface content about a dog and his mistress, they will also appreciate what lies beneath the surface—a special view of Ms. Browning's life, the social conditions of Victorian England, and the prevailing attitudes of the time. It is a remarkable literary device and not as trivial as one would imagine. Many critics consider the biography of Flush to be Virginia Woolf's most pleasing work and more of a minor entertainment, rather than her usual serious, in-depth social commentary.

Virginia Woolf was born 1882 in London and died 1941 in Sussex, England. She was a distinguished British author who wrote innovative novels and important feminist essays. Woolf was also a critic for *The Times Literary Supplement* and one of the central figures of the Bloomsbury group, which was a literary circle of intellectual writers and editors who met socially in the Bloomsbury area of London. Initially, this group of friends met regularly for drinks, discussions, and witty repartee. Although they were serious thinkers and writers who shared similar antiestablishment attitudes, theirs was a tightly knit clique that exhibited snobbish mannerisms and expressed iconoclastic attitudes about art, religion, and sexual preferences and practices. The principal pursuit of this insulated group of writers and academics was maintaining its exclusivity while enjoying one another's company. A similar group developed in New York City and met regularly at a hotel there. These members of what became known as the Algonquin Round Table also enjoyed the snobbish pursuit of exclusivity and humor at the expense of others.

Flush: A Biography was published in 1933, after Virginia Woolf's greatest successes, and has remained in print ever since. It is especially admired by dog lovers everywhere.

from chapter two: the back bedroom

But the fine summer days were soon over; the autumn winds began to blow; and Miss Barrett settled down to a life of complete seclusion in her bedroom. Flush's life was also changed. His outdoor education was supplemented by that of the bedroom, and this, to a dog of Flush's temperament, was the most drastic that could have been invented. His only airings, and these were brief and perfunctory, were taken in the company of Wilson, Miss Barrett's maid. For the rest of the day he kept his station on the sofa at Miss Barrett's feet. All his natural instincts were thwarted and contradicted. When the autumn winds had blown last year in Berkshire he had run in wild scampering across the stubble; now at the sound of the ivy tapping on the pane Miss Barrett asked Wilson to see to the fastening of the window. When the leaves of the scarlet runners and nasturtiums in the window-box yellowed and fell she drew her Indian shawl more closely round her. When the October rain lashed the window Wilson lit the fire and heaped up the coals. Autumn deepened into winter and the first fogs jaundiced the air. Wilson and Flush could scarcely grope their way to the pillar-box or to the chemist. When they came back, nothing could be seen in the room but the pale busts glimmering wanly on the tops of the wardrobes; the peasants and the castle had vanished on the blind; blank yellow filled the pane. Flush felt that he and Miss Barrett lived alone together in a cushioned and fire-lit cave. The traffic droned on perpetually outside with muffled reverberations; now and again a voice went calling hoarsely, "Old chairs and baskets to mend," down the street: sometimes there was a jangle of organ music, coming nearer and louder; going further and fading away. But none of these sounds meant freedom, or action, or exercise. The wind and the rain, the wild days of autumn and the cold days of mid-winter, all alike meant nothing to Flush except warmth and still-ness; the lighting of lamps, the drawing of curtains and the poking of the fire.

At first the strain was too great to be borne. He could not help dancing round the room on a windy autumn day when the partridges must be scattering over the stubble. He thought he heard guns on the breeze. He could not help running to the door with his hackles raised when a dog barked outside. And yet when Miss Barrett called him back, when she laid her hand on his col-lar, he could not deny that another feeling, urgent, contradictory, disagreeable—he did not know what to call it or why he obeyed it—restrained him. He lay still at her feet. To resign, to control, to suppress the most violent instincts of his nature—that was the prime lesson of the bedroom school, and it was one of such por-tentous difficulty that many scholars have learnt Greek with less—many battles have been won that cost their generals not half such pain. But then, Miss Barrett was the teacher. Between them, Flush felt more and more strongly, as the weeks wore on, was a bond, an uncomfortable yet thrilling tightness; so that if his pleasure was her pain, then his pleasure was pleasure no longer but three parts pain. The truth of this was proved every day. Somebody opened the door and whistled him to come. Why should he not go out? He longed for air and exercise; his limbs were cramped with lying on the sofa. He had never grown alto-gether used to the smell of eau de cologne. But no—though the door stood open, he would not leave Miss Barrett. He hesitated halfway to the door and then went back to the sofa. "Flushie," wrote Miss Barrett, "is my friend—my companion—and loves me better than he loves the sunshine without." She could not go out. She was chained to the sofa. "A bird in a cage would have as good a story," she wrote, as she had. And Flush, to whom the whole world was free, chose to forfeit all the smells of Wimpole Street in order to lie by her side.

• • •

It is a terrible thing for an old lady to outlive her dogs.
—*Tennessee Williams,* Camino Real

to my dog

john galsworthy

My dear! When I leave you
I always drop a bit of me—
A holy glove or sainted shoe—
Your wistful corse I leave it to,
For all your soul has followed me—
How could I have the stony heart
So to abandon you!

My dear! When you leave me
You drop no glove, no sainted shoe;
And yet you know what humans be—
Mere blocks of dull monstrosity!
My spirit cannot follow you
When you're away, with all its heart
As you can follow me.

My dear! Since we must leave
(One sorry day) I you, you me;
I'll learn your wistful way to grieve;
Then through the ages we'll rerieve
Each other's scent and company;
And longing shall not pull my heart—
As now you pull my sleeve!

a midsummer night's dream, from act iv, scene 1

william shakespeare

HIPPOLYTA
I was with Hercules and Cadmus once,
When in a wood of Crete they bayed the bear
With hounds of Sparta. Never did I hear
Such gallant chiding; for, besides the groves,
The skies, the fountains, every region near
Seemed all one mutual cry. I never heard
So musical a discord, such sweet thunder.

THESEUS
My hounds are bred out of the Spartan kind,
So flewed, so sanded; and their heads are hung
With ears that sweep away the morning dew;
Crook-kneed, and dewlapped like Thessalian bulls;

Slow in pursuit, but matched in mouth like bells,
Each under each. A cry more tuneable
Was never holloed to, nor cheered with horn,
In Crete, in Sparta, nor in Thessaly.
Judge when you hear. But soft! What nymphs are these?

part five

the world according to dogs

Barking dogs don't bite, but they themselves don't know it.
—Sholom Aleichem

the bar sinister

richard harding davis

American author and journalist Richard Harding Davis (1864–1916) was born in Philadelphia, Pennsylvania. He began his career as a reporter, first for the *Philadelphia Press* and then for the *New York Evening Sun*. Eventually, his short stories and articles gained him an important reputation as a quality writer. In 1890, he was hired as managing editor of *Harper's Weekly*, a very prestigious job for the time, where he was given assignments to cover stories in many distant parts of the world. He soon became *Harper's* leading foreign correspondent and reported from the major trouble spots of the world, covering the Spanish-American War, the Greco-Turkish War, and the Boer War. During this period of his life, he wrote a number of books about his travels. In 1914, he became one of the highest-paid correspondents covering the first year of World War I. He returned to the United States in 1915, where he died one year later. *The Bar Sinister* is his best-remembered work. Unique for its time, it features a narration by its main character, Kid, who happens to be a dog of questionable lineage. The long life and popularity of *The Bar Sinister* is due to the fact that it is about an underdog living through hardships and overcoming many of society's prejudices. It was the *Rocky* story of its time, with Kid, the leading character, similar to Sylvester Stallone's immortal Rocky, a genuine champion.

. . . I don't fight because I like fighting. I fight because if I didn't the other dog would find my throat, and the Master would lose his stakes, and I would be very sorry for him, and ashamed. Dogs can pass me up and I can pass dogs, and I'd never pick a fight with none of them. When I see two dogs standing on their hind legs in the streets, clawing each other's ears, and snapping for each other's windpipes, or howling and swearing and rolling the mud, I feel sorry they should act so, and pretend not to notice. If he'd let me, I'd like to pass the time of day with every dog I meet. But there's something about me that no nice dog can abide. When I trot up to nice dogs, nodding and grinning, to make friends, they always tell me to be off. "Go to the devil!" they bark at me. "Get out!" And when I walk away they shout "Mongrel!" and "Gutter-dog!" and sometimes, after my back is turned, they rush me. I could kill most of them with three shakes, breaking the backbone of the little ones and squeezing the throat of the big ones, but what's the good? They *are* nice dogs; that's why I try to make up to them: and, though it's not for them to say it, I *am* a street-dog, and if I try to push into the company of my betters, I suppose it's their right to teach me my place.

"Every dog in Montreal knows," he says, "except you; and every Master knows. So I think it's time you knew."

Of course they don't know I'm the best fighting bull-terrier of my weight in Montreal. That's why it wouldn't be fair for me to take notice of what they shout. They don't know that if I once locked my jaws on them I'd carry away whatever I touched. The night I fought Kelley's White Rat, I wouldn't loosen up until the Master made a noose in my leash and strangled me; and, as for that Ottawa dog, if the handlers hadn't thrown red pepper down my nose I *never* would have let go of him. I don't think the handlers treated me quite right that time, but maybe they didn't know the Ottawa dog was dead. I did.

I learned my fighting from my mother when I was very young. We slept in a lumber-yard on the river-front, and by day hunted for food along the wharves. When we got it, the other tramp-dogs would try to take if off us, and then it was wonderful to see mother fly at them and drive them away. All I know of fighting I learned from mother, watching her picking the ash-heaps for me when I was too little to fight for myself. No one ever was so good to me as mother. When it snowed and the ice was in the St. Lawrence, she used to hunt alone, and bring me back new bones, and she'd sit and laugh to see me trying to swallow 'em whole. I was just a puppy then; my teeth was falling out. When I was able to fight we kept the whole river-range to ourselves. I had the genuine long "punishing" jaw, as mother said, and there wasn't a man or a dog that dared worry us. Those were happy days, those were; and we lived well, share and share alike, and when we wanted a bit of fun, we chased the fat old wharf-rats! My, how they would squeal!

Then the trouble came. It was no trouble to me. I was too young to care then. But mother took it so to heart that she grew ailing, wouldn't go abroad with me by day. It was the same old scandal that they're always bringing up against me. I was so young then that I didn't know. I couldn't see any difference between mother—and other mothers.

But one day a pack of curs we drove off snarled back some new names at her, and mother dropped her head and ran, just as though they had whipped us. After that she wouldn't go out with me except in the dark, and one day she went away and never came back, and, though I hunted for her in every court and alley and back street of Montreal, I never found her.

One night, a month after mother ran away, I asked Guardian, the old blind mastiff, whose Master is the night watchman on our slip, what it all meant. And he told me.

"Every dog in Montreal knows," he says, "except you; and every Master knows. So I think it's time you knew."

Then he tells me that my father, who had treated mother so bad, was a great and noble gentleman from London. "Your father had twenty-two registered ancestors, had your father," old Guardian says, "and in him was the best bull-terrier blood of England, the most ancientest, the most royal; the winning 'blue-ribbon' blood, that breeds champions. He had sleepy pink eyes and thin pink lips, and he was as white all over as his own white teeth, and under his white skin you could see his muscles, hard and smooth, like the links of a steel chain. When your father stood still, and tipped his nose in the air, it was just as though he was saying, 'Oh, yes, you common dogs and men, you may well stare. It must be a rare treat for you colonials to see real English royalty.' He certainly was pleased with hisself, was your father. He looked just as proud and haughty as one of them stone dogs in Victoria Park—them as is cut out of white marble. And you're like him," says the old mastiff—"by that, of course, meaning you're white, same as him. That's the only likeness. But, you see, trouble is, Kid—well, you see Kid, the trouble is—your mother—"

"That will do," I said, for then I understood without his telling, and I got up and walked away, holding my head and tail high in the air.

But I was, oh, so miserable, and I wanted to see mother that very minute, and tell her that I didn't care.

Mother is what I am, a street-dog; there's no royal blood in mother's veins, nor is she like that father of mine, nor—and that's the worst—she's not even like me. For while I, when I'm washed for a fight, am as white as clean snow, she—and this is our trouble—she, my mother, is a black-and-tan.

When mother hid herself from me, I was twelve months old and able to take care of myself, and as, after mother left, the wharves were never the same, I moved uptown and met the Master. Before he came, lots of other men-folks had tried to make up to me, and to whistle me home. But they either tried patting me or coaxing me with a piece of meat; so I didn't take to 'em. But one day Master pulled me out of a street-fight by the hind legs, and kicked me good.

"You want to fight, do you?" says he. "I'll give you all the *fighting* you want!" he says, and he kicks me again. So I knew he was

my Master, and I followed him home. Since that day I've pulled off
many fights for him, and they've brought dogs from all over the
province to have a go at me; but up to that night none, under thirty
pounds, had ever downed me.

But that night, so soon as they carried me into the ring, I saw
the dog was overweight, and that I was no match for him. It was
asking too much of a puppy. The Master should have known I
couldn't do it. Not that I mean to blame the Master, for when
sober, which he sometimes was—though not, as you might say, his
habit—he was most kind to me, and let me out to find food, if I
could get it, and only kicked me when I didn't pick him up at night
and lead him home.

But kicks will stiffen the muscles, and starving a dog so as to
get him ugly-tempered for a fight makes him nasty, but it's weak-
ening to his insides, and it causes the legs to wobble.

The ring was in a hall back of a public house. There was a red-
hot whitewashed stove in one corner, and the ring in the other. I
lay in the Master's lap, wrapped in my blanket, and, spite of the
stove, shivering awful; but I always shiver before a fight: I can't
help gettin' excited. While the men-folks were a-flashing their
money and taking their last drink at the bar, a little Irish groom in
gaiters came up to me and give me the back of his hand to smell,
and scratched me behind the ears.

"You poor little pup," says he; "you haven't no show," he says.
"That brute in the tap-room he'll eat your heart out."

"That's what *you* think," says the Master, snarling. "I'll lay you
a quid the Kid chews him up."

The groom he shook his head, but kept looking at me so sorry-
like that I begun to get a bit sad myself. He seemed like he couldn't
bear to leave off a-patting of me, and he says, speaking low just
like he would to a man-folk, "Well, good luck to you, little pup,"
which I thought so civil of him that I reached up and licked his
hand. I don't do that to many men. And the Master he knew I
didn't, and took on dreadful.

"What 'ave you got on the back of your hand?" says he, jumping up.

"Soap!" says the groom, quick as a rat. "That's more than you've got on yours. Do you want to smell of it?" and he sticks his fist under the Master's nose. But the pals pushed in between 'em.

"Tried to poison the Kid!" shouts the Master.

"Oh, one fight at a time," says the referee. "Get into the ring, Jerry. We're waiting." So we went into the ring.

I never could just remember what did happen in that ring. He give me no time to spring. He fell on me like a horse. I couldn't keep my feet against him, and though, as I saw, he could get his hold when he liked, he wanted to chew me over a bit first. I was wondering if they'd be able to pry him off me, when, in the third round, he took his hold; and I begun to drown, just as I did when I fell into the river off the Red C slip. He closed deeper and deeper on my throat, and everything went black and red and bursting; and then, when I were sure I were dead, the handlers pulled him off, and the Master gave me a kick that brought me to. But I couldn't move none, or even wink, both eyes being shut with lumps.

"He's a cur!" yells the Master, "a sneaking, cowardly cur! He lost the fight for me," says he, "because he's a—cowardly cur." And he kicks me again in the lower ribs, so that I go sliding across the sawdust. "There's gratitude fer yer," yells the Master. "I've fed that dog, and nussed that dog and housed him like a prince; and now he puts his tail between his legs and sells me out, he does. He's a coward! I've done with him, I am. I'd sell him for a pipeful of tobacco." He picked me up by the tail, and swung me for the men-folks to see. "Does any gentleman here want to buy a dog," he says, "to make into sausage-meat?" he says. "That's all he's good for."

But the Master calls out: "Yes, his father was Regent Royal; who's saying he wasn't? but the pup's a cowardly cur, that's what his pup is. And why? I'll tell you why: because his mother was a black-and-tan street-dog, that's why!"

Then I heard the little Irish groom say, "I'll give you ten bob for the dog."

And another voice says, "Ah, don't you do it; the dog's same as dead—mebbe he is dead."

"Ten shillings!" says the Master, and his voice sobers a bit; "make it two pounds and he's yours."

But the pals rushed in again.

"Don't you be a fool, Jerry," they say. "You'll be sorry for this when you're sober. The Kid's worth a fiver."

One of my eyes was not so swelled up as the other, and as I hung by my tail, I opened it, and saw one of the pals take the groom by the shoulder.

"You ought to give 'im five pounds for that dog, mate," he says; "that's no ordinary dog. That dog's got good blood in him, that dog has. Why, his father—that very dog's father—"

I thought he never would go on. He waited like he wanted to be sure the groom was listening.

"That very dog's father," says the pal, "is Regent Royal, son of Champion Regent Monarch, champion bull-terrier of England for four years."

I was sore, and torn, and chewed most awful, but what the pal said sounded so fine that I wanted to wag my tail, only couldn't, owing to my hanging from it.

But the Master calls out: "Yes, his father was Regent Royal; who's saying he wasn't? but the pup's a cowardly cur, that's what his pup is. And why? I'll tell you why: because his mother was a black-and-tan street-dog, that's why!"

I don't see how I got the strength, but, someway, I threw myself out of the Master's grip and fell at his feet, and turned over and fastened all my teeth in his ankle, just across the bone.

When I woke, after the pals had kicked me off him, I was in the smoking-car of a railroad-train, lying in the lap of the little groom, and he was rubbing my open wounds with a greasy yellow stuff, exquisite to the smell and most agreeable to lick off.

part II

"Well, what's your name—Nolan? Well, Nolan, these references are satisfactory," said the young gentleman my new Master called "Mr. Wyndham, sir." "I'll take you on as second man. You can begin to-day."

My new Master shuffled his feet and put his finger to his forehead. "Thank you, sir," says he. Then he choked like he had swallowed a fish-bone. "I have a little dawg, sir," says he.

"You can't keep him," says "Mr. Wyndham, sir," very short.

" 'E's only a puppy, sir," says my new Master; " 'e wouldn't go outside the stables, sir."

"I have a large kennel of very fine dogs; they're the best of their breed in America. I don't allow strange dogs on the premises."

The Master shakes his head, and motions me with his cap, and I crept out from behind the door. "I'm sorry, sir," says the Master. "Then I can't take the place. I can't get along without the dawg, sir."

"Mr. Wyndham, sir," looked at me that fierce that I guessed he was going to whip me, so I turned over on my back and begged with my legs and tail.

"You must keep away from the kennels," says he; "they're not for the likes of you. The kennels are for the quality. I wouldn't take a litter of them woolly dogs for one wag of your tail, Kid, but for all that they are your betters, same as the gentry up in the big house are my betters. I know my place and keep away from the gentry, and you keep away from the champions."

"Why, you beat him!" says "Mr. Wyndham, sir," very stern.

"No fear!" the Master says, getting very red. "The party I bought him off taught him that. He never learnt that from me!" He picked me up in his arms, and to show "Mr. Wyndham, sir," how well I loved the Master, I bit his chin and hands.

"Mr. Wyndham, sir," turned over the letters the Master had given him. "Well, these references certainly are very strong," he says. "I guess I'll let the dog stay. Only see you keep him away from the kennels—or you'll both go."

"Thank you, sir," says the Master, grinning like a cat when she's safe behind the area railing.

"He's not a bad bull-terrier," says "Mr. Wyndham, sir," feeling my head. "Not that I know much about the smooth-coated breeds. My dogs are St. Bernards." He stopped patting me and held up my nose. "What's the matter with his ears?" he says. "They're chewed to pieces. Is this a fighting dog?" he asks, quick and rough-like.

I could have laughed. If he hadn't been holding my nose, I certainly would have had a good grin at him. Me the best under thirty pounds in the Province of Quebec, and him asking if I was a fighting dog! I ran to the Master and hung down my head modest-like, waiting for him to tell my list of battles; but the Master he coughs in his cap most painful. "Fightin' dawg, sir!" he cries. "Lor' bless you, sir, the Kid don't know the word. " 'E's just a puppy, sir, same as you see; a pet dog, so to speak. 'E's a regular old lady's lap-dog, the Kid is."

"Well, you keep him away from my St. Bernards," says "Mr. Wyndham, sir," "or they might make a mouthful of him."

"Yes, sir; that they might," says the Master. But when we gets outside he slaps his knee and laughs inside hisself, and winks at me most sociable.

The Master's new home was in the country, in a province they called Long Island. There was a high stone wall about his home with big iron gates to it, same as Godfrey's brewery; and there was a house with five red roofs; and the stables, where I lived, was cleaner than the aërated bakery-shop. And then there was the kennels; but they was like nothing else in this world that ever I see. For the first days I couldn't sleep of nights for fear some one would catch me lying in such a cleaned-up place, and would chase me out of it; and when I did fall to sleep I'd dream I was back in the old Master's attic, shivering under the rusty stove, which never had no coals in it, with the Master flat on his back on the

cold floor, with his clothes on. And I'd wake up scared and whim-
pering, and find myself on the new Master's cot with his hand on
the quilt beside me; and I'd see the glow of the big stove, and hear
the high-quality horses below-stairs stamping in the straw-lined
boxes, and I'd snoop the sweet smell of hay and harness-soap and
go to sleep again.

The stables was my jail, so the Master said, but I don't ask no
better home than that jail.

"Now, Kid," says he, sitting on the top of a bucket upside down,
"you've got to understand this. When I whistle it means you're not
to go out of this 'ere yard. These stables is your jail. If you leave 'em
I'll have to leave 'em too, and over the seas, in the County Mayo, an
old mother wil 'ave to leave her bit of a cottage. For two pounds
I must be sending her every month, or she'll have naught to eat, nor
no thatch over 'er head. I can't lose my place, Kid, so see you don't
lose it for me. You must keep away from the kennels," says he;
"they're not for the likes of you. The kennels are for the quality. I
wouldn't take a litter of them woolly dogs for one wag of your tail,
Kid, but for all that they are your betters, same as the gentry up in
the big house are my betters. I know my place and keep away from
the gentry, and you keep away from the champions."

So I never goes out of the stables. All day I just lay in the sun on
the stone flags, licking my jaws, and watching the grooms wash
down the carriages, and the only care I had was to see they didn't
get gay and turn the hose on me. There wasn't even a single rat to
plague me. Such stables I never did see.

"Nolan," says the head groom, "some day that dog of yours
will give you the slip. You can't keep a street-dog tied up all his life.
It's against his natur'." The head groom is a nice old gentleman,
but he doesn't know everything. Just as though I'd been a street-
dog because I liked it! As if I'd rather poke for my vittles in ash-
heaps than have 'em handed me in a wash-basin, and would
sooner bite and fight than be polite and sociable. If I'd had mother
there I couldn't have asked for nothing more. But I'd think of her

snooping in the gutters, or freezing of nights under the bridges, or, what's worst of all, running through the hot streets with her tongue down, so wild and crazy for a drink that the people would shout "mad dog" at her and stone her. Water's so good that I don't blame the men-folks for locking it up inside their houses; but when the hot days come, I think they might remember that those are the dog-days, and leave a little water outside in a trough, like they do for the horses. Then we wouldn't go mad, and the policemen wouldn't shoot us. I had so much of everything I wanted that it made me think a lot of the days when I hadn't nothing, and if I could have given what I had to mother, as she used to share with me, I'd have been the happiest dog in the land. Not that I wasn't happy then, and most grateful to the Master, too, and if I'd only minded him, the trouble wouldn't have come again.

But one day the coachman says that the little lady they called Miss Dorothy had come back from school, and that same morning she runs over to the stables to pat her ponies, and she sees me.

"Oh, what a nice little, white little dog!" said she. "Whose little dog are you?" says she.

"That's my dog, miss," says the Master. "'Is name is Kid." And I ran up to her most polite, and licks her fingers, for I never see so pretty and kind a lady.

"You must come with me and call on my new puppies," says she, picking me up in her arms, and starting off with me.

"Oh, but please, miss," cries Nolan, "Mr. Wyndham give orders that the Kid's not to go to the kennels."

"That'll be all right," says the

I could not help thinking that if Woodstock Wizard III tried to follow a fire-engine he would die of apoplexy, and seeing he'd lost his teeth, it was lucky he had no taste for fighting; but, after his being so condescending, I didn't say nothing.

"Anyway," says he, "every smooth-coated dog is better than any hairy old camel like those St. Bernards, and if ever you're hungry down at the stables, young man, come up to the house and I'll give you a bone."

little lady; "they're my kennels too. And the puppies will like to play with him."

You wouldn't believe me if I was to tell you of the style of them quality-dogs. If I hadn't seen it myself I wouldn't have believed it neither. The Viceroy of Canada don't live no better. There was forty of them, but each one had his own house and a yard—most exclusive and a cot and a drinking-basin all to hisself. They had servants standing round waiting to feed 'em when they was hungry, and valets to wash 'em; and they had their hair combed and brushed like the grooms must when they out on the box. Even the puppies had overcoats with their names on 'em in blue letters, and the name of each of those they called champions was painted up fine over his front door just like it was a public house or a veterinary's. They were the biggest St. Bernards I ever did see. I could have walked under them if they'd have let me. But they were very proud and haughty dogs, and looked only once at me, and then sniffed in the air. The little lady's own dog was an old gentleman bull-dog. He'd come along with us, and when he notices how taken aback I was with all I see, 'e turned quite kind and affable and showed me about.

"Jimmy Jocks," Miss Dorothy called him, but, owing to his weight, he walked most dignified and slow, waddling like a duck, as you might say, and looked much too proud and handsome for a silly name.

"That's the runway, and that's the trophy-house," says he to me, "and that over there is the hospital, where you have to go if you get distemper, and the vet gives you beastly medicine."

"And which of these is your 'ouse, sir?" asks I, wishing to be respectful. But he looked that hurt and haughty. "I don't live in the kennels," says he, most contemptuous. "I am a house-dog. I sleep in Miss Dorothy's room. And at lunch I'm let in with the family, if the visitors don't mind. They 'most always do, but they're too polite to say so. Besides," says he, smiling most condescending, "visitors are

always afraid of me. It's because I'm so ugly," says he. "I suppose,"
says he, screwing up his wrinkles and speaking very slowly and
impressive, "I suppose I'm the ugliest bull-dog in America"; and as
he seemed to be so pleased to think hisself so, I said, "Yes, sir; you
certainly are the ugliest ever I see," at which he nodded his head
most approving.

"But I couldn't hurt 'em, as you say," he goes on, though I
hadn't said nothing like that, being too polite. "I'm too old," he
says; "I haven't any teeth. The last time one of those grizzly
bears," said he, glaring at the big St. Bernards, "took a hold of me,
he nearly was my death," says he. I thought his eyes would pop out
of his head, he seemed so wrought up about it. "He rolled me
around in the dirt, he did," says Jimmy Jocks, "an I couldn't get
up. It was low," says Jimmy Jocks, making a face like he had a bad
taste in his mouth. "Low, that's what I call it—bad form, you understand, young man, not done in my set—and—and low." He
growled 'way down in his stomach, and puffed hisself out, panting
and blowing like he had been on a run.

"I'm not a street fighter," he says, scowling at a St. Bernard
marked "Champion." "And when my rheumatism is not troubling
me," he says, "I endeavor to be civil to all dogs, so long as they are
gentlemen."

"Yes, sir," said I, for even to me he had been most affable.

At this we had come to a little house off by itself, and Jimmy
Jocks invites me in. "This is their trophy-room," he says, "where
they keep their prizes. Mine," he says, rather grand like, "are on
the sideboard." Not knowing what a sideboard might be, I said,
"Indeed, sir, that must be very gratifying." But he only wrinkled
up his chops as much as to say, "It is my right."

The trophy-room was as wonderful as any public house I ever
see. On the walls was pictures of nothing but beautiful St. Bernard
dogs, and rows and rows of blue and red and yellow ribbons; and
when I asked Jimmy Jocks why they was so many more of blue

than of the others, he laughs and says, "Because these kennels always win." And there was many shining cups on the shelves, which Jimmy Jocks told me were prizes won by the champions.

"Now, sir, might I ask you, sir," says I, "wot is a champion?"

At that he panted and breathed so hard I thought he would bust hisself. "My dear young friend!" says he, "wherever have you been educated? A champion is a—a champion," he says. "He must win nine blue ribbons in the 'open' class. You follow me—that is—against all comers. Then he has the title before his name, and they put his photograph in the sporting papers. You know, of course, that *I* am a champion," says he. "I am Champion Woodstock Wizard III, and the two other Woodstock Wizards, my father and uncle, were both champions."

"But I thought your name was Jimmy Jocks," I said.

He laughs right out at that.

"That's my kennel name, not my registered name," he says. "Why, certainly, you know that every dog has two names. Now, for instance, what's your registered name and number?" says he.

"I've got only one name," I says. "Just Kid."

Woodstock Wizard puffs at that and wrinkles up his forehead and pops out his eyes.

"Who are your people?" says he. "Where is your home?"

"At the stable, sir," I said. "My Master is the second groom."

At that Woodstock Wizard III looks at me for quite a bit without winking, and stares all around the room over my head.

"Oh, well," says he at last, "you're a very civil young dog," says he, "and I blame no one for what he can't help," which I thought most fair and liberal. "And I have known many bull-terriers that were champions," says he, "thought as a rule they mostly run with fire-engines and to fighting. For me, I wouldn't care to run through the streets after a hose-cart, nor to fight," says he; "but each to his taste."

I could not help thinking that if Woodstock Wizard III tried to follow a fire-engine he would die of apoplexy, and seeing he'd lost

his teeth, it was lucky he had no taste for fighting; but, after his being so condescending, I didn't say nothing.

"Anyway," says he, "every smooth-coated dog is better than
any hairy old camel like those St. Bernards, and if ever you're hungry down at the stables, young man, come up to the house and I'll
give you a bone. I can't eat them myself, but I bury them around
the garden from force of habit and in case a friend should drop in.
"Ah, I see my mistress coming," he says, "and I bid you good day. I
regret," he says, "that our different social position prevents our
meeting frequent, for you're a worthy young dog with a proper respect for your betters, and in this country there's precious few of
them have that." Then he waddles off, leaving me alone and very
sad, for he was the first dog in many days that had spoke to me.
But since he showed, seeing that I was a stable-dog, he didn't want
my company, I waited for him to get well away. It was not a cheerful place to wait, the trophy-house. The pictures of the champions
seemed to scowl at me, and ask what right such as I had even to
admire them, and the blue and gold ribbons and the silver cups
made me very miserable. I had never won no blue ribbons or silver
cups, only stakes for the old Master to spend in the publics; and I
hadn't won them for being a beautiful high-quality dog, but just
for fighting—which, of course, as Woodstock Wizard III says, is low.
So I started for the stables, with my head down and my tail between my legs, feeling sorry I had ever left the Master. But I had
more reason to be sorry before I got back to him.

The trophy-house was quite a bit from the kennels, and as I left
it I see Miss Dorothy and Woodstock Wizard III walking back toward them, and, also, that a big St. Bernard, his name was Champion Red Elfberg, had broke his chain and was running their way.
When he reaches old Jimmy Jocks he lets out a roar like a grain-
steamer in a fog, and he makes three leaps for him. Old Jimmy
Jocks was about a fourth his size; but he plants his feet and curves
his back, and his hair goes up around his neck like a collar. But he
never had no show at no time, for the grizzly bear, as Jimmy Jocks

had called him, lights on old Jimmy's back and tries to break it, and old Jimmy Jocks snaps his gums and claws the grass, panting and groaning awful. But he can't do nothing, and the grizzly bear just rolls him under him, biting and tearing cruel. The odds was all that Woodstock Wizard III was going to be killed; I had fought enough to see that: but not knowing the rules of the game among champions, I didn't like to interfere between two gentlemen who might be settling a private affair, and, as it were, taking it as presuming of me. So I stood by, though I was shaking terrible, and holding myself in like I was on a leash. But that Woodstock Wizard III, who was underneath, sees me through the dust, and calls very faint, "Help, you!" he says. "Take him in the hind leg," he says. "He's murdering me," he says. And then the little Miss Dorothy, who was crying, and calling to the kennel-men, catches at the Red Elfberg's hind legs to pull him off, and the brute, keeping his front pats well in Jimmy's stomach, turns his big head and snaps at her. So that was all I asked for, thank you. I went up under him. It was really nothing. He stood so high that I had only to take off about three feet from him and come in from the side, and my long "punishing jaw," as mother was always talking about, locked on his woolly throat, and my back teeth met. I couldn't shake him, but I shook myself, and every time I shook myself there was thirty pounds of weight tore at his windpipes. I couldn't see nothing for his long hair, but I heard Jimmy Jocks puffing and blowing on one side, and munching the brute's leg with his old gums. Jimmy was an old sport that day, was Jimmy, or Woodstock Wizard III, as I should say. When the Red Elfberg was out and down I had to run, or those kennel-men would have had my life. They chased me right into the stables; and from under the hay I watched the head groom take down a carriage-whip and order them to the right about. Luckily Master and the young grooms were out, or that day there'd have been fighting for everybody.

Well, it nearly did for me and the Master. "Mr. Wyndham, sir," comes raging to the stables. I'd half killed his best prize-winner, he says, and had oughter be shot, and he gives the Master his notice. But Miss Dorothy she follows him, and says it was his Red Elfberg what began the fight, and that I'd saved Jimmy's life, and that old Jimmy Jocks was worth more to her than all the St. Bernards in the Swiss mountains—wherever they may be. And that I was her champion, anyway. Then she cried over me most beautiful, and over Jimmy Jocks, too, who was that tied up in bandages he couldn't even waddle. So when he heard that side of it, "Mr. Wyndham, sir," told us that if Nolan put me on a chain we could stay. So it came out all right for everybody but me. I was glad the Master kept his place, but I'd never worn a chain before, and it disheartened me. But that was the least of it. For the quality-dogs couldn't forgive my whipping their champion, and they came to the fence between the kennels and the stables, and laughed through the bars, barking most cruel words at me. I couldn't understand how they found it out, but they knew. After the fight Jimmy Jocks was most condescending to me, and he said the grooms had boasted to the kennel-men that I was a son of Regent Royal, and that when the kennel-men asked who was my mother they had had to tell them that too. Perhaps that was the way of it, but, however, the scandal got out, and every one of the quality-dogs knew that I was a street-dog and the son of a black-and-tan.

About a month after my fight, the word was passed through the kennels that the New York Show was coming, and such goings on as followed I never did see. If each of them had been matched to fight for a thousand pounds and the gate, they couldn't have trained more conscientious. But perhaps that's just the envy. The kennel-men rubbed 'em and scrubbed 'em, and trims their hair and curls and combs it, and some dogs they fatted and some they starved. No one talked of nothing but the Show, and the chances "our kennels" had against the other kennels, and if this one of our champions would win over that one, and whether them as hoped to be champions had better show in the "open" or the "limit" class, and whether this dog would beat his own dad, or whether his little puppy sister couldn't beat the two of 'em. Even the grooms had their money up, and day or night you heard nothing but praises of "our" dogs, until I being so far out of it, couldn't have felt meaner if I had been running the streets with a can to my tail. I knew shows were not for such as me, and so all day I lay stretched at the end of my chain, pretending I was asleep, and only too glad that they had something so important to think of that they could leave me alone.

But one day, before the Show opened, Miss Dorothy came to the stables with "Mr. Wyndham, sir," and seeing me chained up and so miserable, she takes me in her arms.

"You poor little tyke!" says she. "It's cruel to tie him up so; he's eating his heart out, Nolan," she says. "I don't know nothing about bull-terriers," says she,

" 'Dam unknown," says "Mr. Wyndham, sir," and writes it down. Then he takes the paper and reads out loud: " 'Sire unknown, dam unknown, breeder unknown, date of birth unknown.' You'd better call him the 'Great Unknown,' " says he. "Who's paying his entrance fee?"

"I am," says Miss Dorothy.

"but I think Kid's got good points," says she, "and you ought to show him. Jimmy Jocks has three legs on the Rensselaer Cup now, and I'm going to show him this time, so that he can get the fourth; and, if you wish, I'll enter your dog too. How would you like that, Kid?" says she. "How would you like to see the most beautiful dogs in the world? Maybe you'd meet a pal or two," says she. "It would cheer you up, wouldn't it, Kid?" says she. But I was so upset I could only wag my tail most violent. "He says it would!" says she, though, being that excited, I hadn't said nothing.

So "Mr. Wyndham, sir," laughs, and takes out a piece of blue paper and sits down at the head groom's table.

"What's the name of the father of your dog, Nolan?" says he.

And Nolan says: "The man I got him off told me he was a son of Champion Regent Royal, sir. But it don't seem likely, does it?" says Nolan.

"It does not!" says "Mr. Wyndham, sir," short-like.

"Aren't you sure, Nolan?" says Miss Dorothy.

"No, miss," says the Master.

"Sire unknown," says "Mr. Wyndham, sir," and writes it down.

"Date of birth?" asks "Mr. Wyndham, sir."

"I—I—unknown, sir," says Nolan. And "Mr. Wyndham, sir," writes it down.

"Breeder?" says "Mr. Wyndham, sir."

"Unknown," says Nolan, getting very red around the jaws, and I drops my head and tail. And "Mr. Wyndham, sir," writes that down.

"Mother's name?" says "Mr. Wyndham, sir."

"She was a—unknown," says the Master. And I licks his hand.

"Dam unknown," says "Mr. Wyndham, sir," and writes it down. Then he takes the paper and reads out loud: " 'Sire unknown, dam unknown, breeder unknown, date of birth unknown.' You'd better call him the 'Great Unknown,' " says he. "Who's paying his entrance fee?"

"I am," says Miss Dorothy.

Two weeks after we all got on a train for New York, Jimmy Jocks and me following Nolan in the smoking-car, and twenty-two of the St. Bernards in boxes and crates and on chains and leashes. Such a barking and howling I never did hear; and when they sees me going, too, they laughs fit to kill.

"Wot is this—a circus?" says the railroad man.

But I had no heart in it. I hated to go. I knew I was no "show" dog, even though Miss Dorothy and the Master did their best to keep me from shaming them. For before we set out Miss Dorothy brings a man from town who scrubbed and rubbed me, and sandpapered my tail, which hurt most awful, and shaved my ears with the Master's razor, so you could 'most see clear through 'em, and sprinkles me over with pipe-clay, till I shines like a Tommy's cross-belts.

"Upon my word!" says Jimmy Jocks when he first sees me. "Wot a swell you are! You're the image of your grand-dad when he made his début at the Crystal Palace. He took four firsts and three specials." But I knew he was only trying to throw heart into me. They might scrub, and they might rub, and they might pipe-clay, but they couldn't pipe-clay the insides of me, and they was black-and-tan.

> . . . and when I dozed I dreamed horrible. All the dogs in the hall seemed coming at me for daring to intrude, with their jaws red and open, and their eyes blazing like the lights in the roof. "You're a street-dog! Get out, you street-dog!" they yells.

Then we came to a garden, which it was not, but the biggest hall in the world. Inside there was lines of benches a few miles long, and on them sat every dog in America. If all the dog-snatchers in Montreal had worked night and day for a year, they couldn't have caught so many dogs. And they was all shouting and barking and howling so vicious that my heart stopped beating. For at first I thought they was all enraged at my presuming to intrude. But after I got in my place they kept at it just the same, barking at every dog as he come in: daring him to fight, and ordering him out, and asking him what breed of dog he thought he was, anyway. Jimmy Jocks was chained just behind me, and he said he never see so fine a show. "That's a hot class you're in, my lad," he says, looking over into my street, where there were thirty bull-terriers. They was all as white as cream, and each so beautiful that if I could have broke my chain I would have run all the way home and hid myself under the horse-trough.

All night long they talked and sang, and passed greetings with old pals, and the homesick puppies howled dismal. Them that couldn't sleep wouldn't let no others sleep, and all the electric lights burned in the roof, and in my eyes. I could hear Jimmy Jocks snoring peaceful, but I could only doze by jerks, and when I dozed

I dreamed horrible. All the dogs in the hall seemed coming at me for daring to intrude, with their jaws red and open, and their eyes blazing like the lights in the roof. "You're a street-dog! Get out, you street-dog!" they yells. And as they drives me out, the pipe-clay drops off me, and they laugh and shriek; and when I looks down I see that I have turned into a black-and-tan.

They was most awful dreams, and next morning, when Miss Dorothy comes and gives me water in a pan, I begs and begs her to take me home; but she can't understand. "How well Kid is!" she says. And when I jumps into the Master's arms and pulls to break my chain, he says, "If he knew all as he had against him, miss, he wouldn't be so gay." And from a book they reads out the names of the beautiful high-bred terriers which I have got to meet. And I can't make 'em understand that I only want to run away and hide myself where no one will see me.

Then suddenly men comes hurrying down our street and begins to brush the beautiful bull-terriers; and the Master rubs me with a towel so excited that his hands trembles awful, and Miss Dorothy tweaks my ears between her gloves, so that the blood runs to 'em, and they turn pink and stand up straight and sharp.

The judging-ring, which is where the judge holds out, was so like a fighting-pit that when I come in it, and find six other dogs there, I springs into position, so that when they lets us go I can defend myself. But the Master smoothes down my hair and whispers, "Hold 'ard, Kid, hold 'ard. This ain't a fight," says he. "Look your prettiest," he whispers. "Please, Kid, look your prettiest"; and he pulls my leash so tight that I can't touch my pats to the sawdust, and my nose goes up in the air. There were millions of people a-watching

If the judge had ordered me right out it wouldn't have disgraced us so, but it was keeping me there while he was judging the high-bred dogs that hurt so hard. With all those people staring, too. And his doing it so quick, without no doubt nor questions. You can't fool the judges. They see inside you.

us from the railings, and three of our kennel-men, too, making fun of the Master and me, and Miss Dorothy with her chin just reaching to the rail, and her eyes so big that I thought she was a-going to cry. It was awful to think that when the judge stood up and exposed me, all those people, and Miss Dorothy, would be there to see me driven from the Show.

The judge he was a fierce-looking man with specs on his nose, and a red beard. When I first come in he didn't see me, owing to my being too quick for him and dodging behind the Master. But when the Master drags me round and I pulls at the sawdust to keep back, the judge looks at us careless-like, and then stops and glares through his specs, and I knew it was all up with me.

"Are there any more?" asks the judge to the gentleman at the gate, but never taking his specs from me.

The man at the gate looks in his book. "Seven in the novice class," says he. "They're all here. You can go ahead," and he shuts the gate.

The judge he doesn't hesitate a moment. He just waves his hand toward the corner of the ring. "Take him away," he says to the Master, "over there, and keep him away"; and he turns and looks most solemn at the six beautiful bull-terriers. I don't know how I crawled to that corner. I wanted to scratch under the sawdust and dig myself a grave. The kennel-men they slapped the rail with their hands and laughed at the Master like they would fall over. They pointed at me in the corner, and their sides just shaked. But little Miss Dorothy she presses her lips tight against the rail, and I see tears rolling from her eyes. The Master he hangs his head like he had been whipped. I felt most sorry for him than all. He was so red, and he was letting on not to see the kennel-men, and blinking his eyes. If the judge had ordered me right out it wouldn't have disgraced us so, but it was keeping me there while he was judging the high-bred dogs that hurt so hard. With all those people staring, too. And his doing it so quick, without no doubt nor questions. You can't fool the judges. They see inside you.

But he couldn't make up his mind about them high-bred dogs. He scowls at 'em, and he glares at 'em, first with his head on the one side and then on the other. And he feels of 'em, and orders 'em to run about. And Nolan leans against the rails, with his head hung down, and pats me. And Miss Dorothy comes over beside him, but don't say nothing, only wipes here eyes with her finger. A man on the other side of the rail he says to the Master, "The judge don't like your dog?"

"No," says the Master.

"Have you ever shown him before?" says the man.

"No," says the Master, "and I'll never show him again. He's my dog," says the Master, "and he suits me! And I don't care what no judges think." And when he says them kind words, I licks his hand most grateful.

The judge had two of the six dogs on a little platform in the middle of the ring, and he had chased the four other dogs into the corners, where they was licking their chops, and letting on they didn't care, same as Nolan was.

The two dogs on the platform was so beautiful that the judge hisself couldn't tell which was the best of 'em, even when he stoops down and holds their heads together. But at last he gives a sigh, and brushes the sawdust of his knees, and goes to the table in the ring, where there was a man keeping score, and heaps and heaps of blue and gold and red and yellow ribbons. And the judge picks up a bunch of 'em and walks to the two gentlemen who was holding the beautiful dogs, and he says to each, "What's his number?" and he hands each gentleman a ribbon. And then he turned sharp and comes straight at the Master.

"What's his number?" says the judge. And Master was so scared that he couldn't make no answer.

But Miss Dorothy claps her hands and cries out like she was laughing. "Three twenty-six," and the judge writes it down and shoves Master the blue ribbon.

I bit the Master, and I jumps and bit Miss Dorothy, and I waggled so hard that the Master couldn't hold me. When I get to the gate Miss Dorothy snatches me up and kisses me between the ears, right before millions of people, and they both hold me so tight that I didn't know which of them was carrying of me. But one thing I knew, for I listened hard, as it was the judge hisself as said it.

"Did you see that puppy I gave first to?" says the judge to the gentleman at the gate.

"I did. He was a bit out of his class," says the gate gentleman.

"He certainly was!" says the judge, and they both laughed.

But I didn't care. They couldn't hurt me then, not with Nolan holding the blue ribbon and Miss Dorothy hugging my ears, and the kennel-men sneaking away, each looking like he'd been caught with his nose under the lid of the slop-can.

We sat down together, and we all three just talked as fast as we could. They was so pleased that I couldn't help feeling proud myself, and I barked and leaped about so gay that all the bull-terriers in our street stretched on their chains and howled at me.

"Just look at him!" says one of those I had beat. "What's he giving hisself airs about?"

"Because he's got one blue ribbon!" says another of 'em. "Why, when I was a puppy I used to eat 'em, and if that judge could ever learn to know a toy from a mastiff, I'd have had this one."

But Jimmy Jocks he leaned over from his bench and says, "Well done, Kid. Didn't I tell you so?" What he 'ad told me was that I might get a "commended," but I didn't remind him.

"Didn't I tell you," says Jimmy Jocks, "that I saw your grandfather make his début at the Crystal—"

"Yes, sir, you did, sir," says I, for I have no love for the men of my family.

A gentleman with a showing-leash around his neck comes up just then and looks at me very critical. "Nice dog you've got, Miss Wyndham," says he; "would you care to sell him?"

"He's not my dog," says Miss Dorothy, holding me tight. "I wish he were."

"He's not for sale, sir," says the Master, and I was *that* glad.

"So, he's yours, is he?" says the gentleman, looking hard at Nolan. "Well, I'll give you a hundred dollars for him," says he, careless-like.

"Thank you, sir; he's not for sale," says Nolan, but his eyes get very big. The gentleman he walked away; but I watches him, and he talks to a man in a golf-cap, and by and by the man comes along our street, looking at all the dogs, and stops in front of me.

"This your dog?" says he to Nolan. "Pity he's so leggy," says he. "If he had a good tail, and a longer stop, and his ears were set higher, he'd be a good dog. As he is, I'll give you fifty dollars for him."

"Oh, you know him," says the gentleman. "He is the champion of champions, Regent Royal."

The Master's face went red.

"And this is Regent Royal's son," cries he, and he pulls me quick into the ring, and plants me on the platform next to my father.

But, before the Master could speak, Miss Dorothy laughs and says: "You're Mr. Polk's kennel-man, I believe. Well, you tell Mr. Polk from me that the dog's not for sale now any more than he was five minutes ago, and that when he is, he'll have to bid against me for him."

The man looks foolish at that, but he turns to Nolan quicklike. "I'll give you three hundred for him," he says.

"Oh, indeed!" whispers Miss Dorothy, like she was talking to herself. "That's it, is it?" And she turns and looks at me just as though she had never seen me before. Nolan he was a-gaping, too, with his mouth open. But he holds me tight.

"He's not for sale," he growls, like he was frightened; and the man looks black and walks away.

"Why, Nolan!" cries Miss Dorothy, "Mr. Polk knows more about bull-terriers than any amateur in America. What can he mean? Why, Kid is no more than a puppy!"

"And he ain't no thoroughbred, neither!" cries the Master.

"He's 'Unknown,' ain't he? Kid can't help it, of course, but his mother, miss—"

I dropped my head. I couldn't bear he should tell how I had stolen my blue ribbon.

But the Master never told, for at that a gentleman runs up, calling "Three twenty-six, three twenty-six!" And Miss Dorothy says, "Here he is; what is it?"

Nolan tries to get me off the chain on to a showing-leash, but he shakes so, he only chokes me. "What is it, miss?" he says. "What is it?"

"The Winners' class," says Miss Dorothy. "The judge wants him with the winners of the other classes—to decide which is the best. It's only a form," says she. "He has the champions against him now."

"Yes," says the gentleman, as he hurries us to the ring. "I'm afraid it's only a form for your dog, but the judge wants all the winners, puppy class even."

We had got to the gate, and the gentleman there was writing down my number.

"Who won the open?" asks Miss Dorothy.

"Oh, who would?" laughs the gentleman. "The old champion, of course. He's won for three years now. There he is. Isn't he wonderful?" says he; and he points to a dog that's standing proud and haughty on the platform in the middle of the ring.

I never seen so beautiful a dog—so fine and clean and noble, so white like he had rolled hisself in flour, holding his nose up and his eyes shut, same as though no one was worth looking at. Aside of him we other dogs, even though wc had a blue ribbon apiece, seemed like lumps of mud. He was a royal gentleman, a king, he was. His master didn't have to hold his head with no leash. He held it hisself, standing as still as an iron dog on a lawn, like he knew all the people was looking at him. And so they was, and no one around the ring pointed at no other dog but him.

"Oh, what a picture!" cried Miss Dorothy. "He's like a marble figure by a great artist—one who loved dogs. Who is he?" says she, looking in her book. "I don't keep up with terriers."

"Oh, you know him," says the gentleman. "He is the champion of champions, Regent Royal."

The Master's face went red.

"And this is Regent Royal's son," cries he, and he pulls me quick into the ring, and plants me on the platform next to my father.

I trembled so that I near fell. My legs twisted like a leash. But my father he never looked at me. He only smiled the same sleepy smile, and he still kept his eyes half shut, like as no one, no, not even his own son, was worth his lookin' at.

The judge he didn't let me stay beside my father, but, one by one, he placed the other dogs next to him and measured and felt and pulled at them. And each one he put down, but he never put my father down. And then he comes over and picks up me and sets me back on the platform, shoulder to shoulder with the Champion Regent Royal, and goes down on his knees, and looks into our eyes.

The gentleman with my father he laughs, and says to the judge, "Thinking of keeping us here all day, John?" But the judge he doesn't hear him, and goes behind us and runs his hand down my side, and holds back my ears, and takes my jaws between his fingers. The crowd around the ring is very deep now, and nobody says nothing. The gentleman at the score-table, he is leaning forward, with his elbows on his knees and his eyes very wide, and the gentleman at the gate is whispering quick to Miss Dorothy, who has turned white. I stood as stiff as stone. I didn't even breathe. But out of the corner of my eye I could see my father licking his pink chops, and yawning just a little, like he was bored.

The judge he had stopped looking fierce and was looking solemn. Something inside him seemed a-troubling him awful. The more he stares at us now, the more solemn he gets, and when he touches us he does it gentle, like he was patting us. For a long time he kneels in the sawdust, looking at my father and at me, and no one around the ring says nothing to nobody.

Then the judge takes a breath and touches me sudden. "It's his," he says. But he lays his hand just as quick on my father. "I'm sorry," says he.

The gentleman holding my father cries:

"Do you mean to tell me—"

And the judge he answers, "I mean the other is the better dog." He takes my father's head between his hands and looks down at him most sorrowful. "The king is dead," says he. "Long live the king! Good-bye, Regent," he says.

The crowd around the railings clapped their hands, and some laughed scornful, and every one talks fast, and I start for the gate, so dizzy that I can't see my way. But my father pushes in front of me, waking very daintily, and smiling sleepy, same as he had just been waked, with his head high and his eyes shut, looking at nobody.

So that is how I "came by my inheritance," as Miss Dorothy calls it; and just for that, though I couldn't feel where I was any different, the crowd follows me to my bench, and pats me, and coos at me, like I was a baby in a baby-carriage. And the handlers have to hold 'em back so that the gentlemen from the papers can make pictures of me, and Nolan walks me up and down so proud, and the men shake their heads and say, "He certainly is the true type, he is!" And the pretty ladies ask Miss Dorothy, who sits beside me letting me lick her gloves to show the crowd what friends we is, "Aren't you afraid he'll bite you?" And Jimmy Jocks calls to me, "Didn't I tell you so? I always knew you were one of us. Blood will out, Kid; blood will out. I saw your grandfather," says he, "make his début at the Crystal Palace. But he was never the dog you are!"

After that, if I could have asked for it, there was nothing I couldn't get. You might have thought I was a snow-dog, and they was afeared I'd melt. If I wet my pats, Nolan gave me a hot bath and chained me to the stove; if I couldn't eat my food, being stuffed full by the cook—for I am a house-dog now, and let in to lunch, whether there is visitors or not—Nolan would run to bring the vet. It was all tommy rot, as Jimmy says, but meant most kind. I couldn't scratch myself comfortable, without Nolan giving me nasty drinks, and rubbing me outside till it burnt awful; and I wasn't let to eat bones for fear of spoiling my "beautiful" mouth, what mother used to call my "punishing jaw"; and my food was cooked special on a gas-stove; and Miss Dorothy gives me an overcoat, cut very stylish like the champions', to wear when we goes out carriage-driving.

After the next Show, where I takes three blue ribbons, four silver cups, two medals, and brings home forty-five dollars for Nolan, they gives me a "registered" name, same as Jimmy's. Miss Dorothy wanted to call me "Regent Heir Apparent"; but I was *that* glad when Nolan says, "No; Kid don't owe nothing to his father, only to you and hisself. So, if you please, miss, we'll call him Wyndham Kid." And so they did, and you can see it on my overcoat in blue letters, painted top of my kennel. It was all too hard to understand. For days I just sat and wondered if I was really me, and how it all come about, and why everybody was so kind. But oh, it was so good they was, for if they hadn't been I'd never have got the thing I most wished after. But, because they was kind, and not liking to deny me nothing, they gave it me, and it was more to me than anything in the world.

It came about one day when we was out driving. We was in the cart they calls the dog-cart because it's the one Miss Dorothy keeps to take Jimmy and me for an airing. Nolan was up behind, and me, in my new overcoat, was sitting beside Miss Dorothy. I was admiring the view, and thinking how good it was to have a horse pull you about so that you needn't get yourself splashed and have to be washed, when I hears a dog calling loud for help, and I pricks up my ears and looks over the horse's head. And I sees something that makes me tremble down to my toes. In the road before us three big dogs was chasing a little old lady-dog. She had a string to her tail, where some boys had tied a can, and she was dirty with mud and ashes, and torn most awful. She was too far done up to get away, and too old to help herself, but she was making a fight for her life, snapping her old gums savage, and dying game. All this I see in a wink, and then the three dogs pinned her down, and I can't stand it no longer, and clears the wheel and lands in the road on my head. It was my stylish overcoat done that, and I cursed it proper, but I gets my pats again quick, and makes a rush for the fighting. Behind me I hear Miss Dorothy cry: "They'll kill that old dog. Wait, take my whip. Beat them off her! The Kid can take care of himself"; and I hear Nolan fall into the road, and the horse come to a stop. The old lady-dog was down, and the three was eating her vicious; but as I come up, scattering the pebbles, she hears, and thinking it's one more of them, she lifts her head, and my heart breaks open like some one had sunk his teeth in it. For, under the ashes and the dirt and the blood, I can see who it is, and I know that my mother has come back to me.

I gives a yell that throws them three dogs off their legs.

"Mother!" I cries. "I'm the Kid," I cries. "I'm coming to you. Mother, I'm coming!"

And I shoots over her at the throat of the big dog, and the other two they sinks their teeth into that sylish overcoat and tears it off me, and that sets me free, and I lets them have it. I never had so fine a fight as that! What with mother being there to see, and not having been let to mix up in no fights since I become a prize-winner, it just naturally did me good, and it wasn't three shakes before I had 'em yelping. Quick as a wink, mother she jumps in to help me, and I just laughed to see her. It was so like old times. And Nolan he made me laugh, too. He was like a hen on a bank, shaking the butt of his whip, but not daring to cut in for fear of hitting me.

"Stop it, Kid," he says, "stop it. Do you want to be all torn up?" says he. "Think of the Boston show," says he. "Think of Chicago. Think of Danbury. Don't you never want to be a champion?" How was I to think of all them places when I had three dogs to cut up at the same time? But in a minute two of 'em begs for mercy, and mother and me lets 'em run away. The big one he ain't able to run away. Then mother and me we dances and jumps, and barks and laughs, and bites each other and rolls each other in the road. There never was two dogs so happy as we. And Nolan he whistles and calls and begs me to come to him; but I just laugh and play larks with mother.

"Now, you come with me," says I, "to my new home, and never try to run away again." And I shows her our house with the five red roofs, set on the top of the hill. But mother trembles awful, and says: "They'd never let me in such a place. Does the Viceroy live there, Kid?" says she. And I laugh at her. "No; I do," I says. "And if they won't let you live there, too, you and me will go back to the streets together, for we must never be parted no more." So we trots up the hill side by side, with Nolan trying to catch me, and Miss Dorothy laughing at him from the cart.

"The Kid's made friends with the poor old dog," says she. "Maybe he knew her long ago when he ran the streets himself. Put her in here beside me, and see if he doesn't follow."

So when I hears that I tells mother to go with Nolan and sit in the cart; but she says no—that she'd soil the pretty lady's frock; but I tells her to do as I say, and so Nolan lifts her, trembling still, into the cart, and I runs alongside, barking joyful.

When we drives into the stables I takes mother to my kennel, and tells her to go inside it and make herself at home. "Oh, but he won't let me!" says she.

"Who won't let you?" says I, keeping my eye on Nolan, and growling a bit nasty, just to show I was meaning to have my way.

"Why, Wyndham Kid," says she, looking up at the name on my kennel.

"But I'm Wyndham Kid!" says I.

"You!" cries mother. "You! Is my little Kid the great Wyndham Kid the dogs all talk about?" And at that, she being very old, and sick, and nervous, as mothers are, just drops down in the straw and weeps bitter.

Well, there ain't much more than that to tell. Miss Dorothy she settled it.

"If the Kid wants the poor thing in the stables," says she, "let her stay.

"You see," says she, "she's a black-and-tan, and his mother was a black-and-tan, and maybe that's what makes Kid feel so friendly toward her," says she.

"Indeed, for me," says Nolan, "she can have the best there is. I'd never drive out no dog that asks for a crust nor a shelter," he says. "But what will Mr. Wyndham do?"

"He'll do what I say," says Miss Dorothy, "and if I say she's to stay, she will stay, and I say—she's to stay!"

And so mother and Nolan and me found a home. Mother was scared at first—not being used to kind people; but she was so gentle and loving that the grooms got fonder of her than of me, and tried to make me jealous by patting of her and giving her the pick of the vittles. But that was the wrong way to hurt my feelings. That's all, I think. Mother is so happy here that I tell her we ought to call it the Happy Hunting Grounds, because no one hunts you, and there is nothing to hunt; it just all comes to you. And so we live in peace, mother sleeping all day in the sun, or behind the stove in the head groom's office, being fed twice a day regular by Nolan, and all the day by the other grooms most irregular. And as for me, I go hurrying around the country to the bench-shows, winning money and cups for Nolan, and taking the blue ribbons away from father.

• • •

If nature hadn't created dogs, some clever, needful person would
have, because dogs make it possible to survive some
of the harsher aspects of life.
—Mordecai Siegal

angel on a leash

music and lyrics by murray weinstock

An original song to honor the work of the Westminster Kennel Club's therapy dog program, *Angel on a Leash*, benefiting the young patients at Morgan Stanley Children's Hospital of NewYork-Presbyterian. This program has proven to enhance the healing process for the hospital's pediatric patients. Therapy dogs bring unconditional love from an animal to the bedside, which greatly contributes to the emotional and physical healing process.

I've got a story
And I know I'm not alone.
My body's in trouble—
In my life that's all I've known.

But there's a furry friend that I'm happy to see
When he comes to my door,
He loves me unconditionally,
With four paws on the floor.

My Angel on a Leash
Leading to my heart.
Hope will light the way
Give me strength to live another day. . . .

Angel on a Leash,
His soul is in his play,

He gives his love away
Gentle hero of the day.

three's company

steve dale

Steve Dale was born in Chicago, Illinois. He is the author of Tribune Media Services syndicated column, "My Pet World," a contributing editor at *USA Weekend,* and special correspondent for *Cat Fancy* magazine. He is the host of "Pet Central," heard on WGN Radio, Chicago, and two syndicated radio programs, "Steve Dale's Pet World" and "The Pet Minute." He's the editor in chief of *Pawprints,* a publication for veterinary clinics. He's the recipient of many awards, including the American Veterinary Medical Association Humane Award, the American Kennel Club Distinguished Service Award, and the General Feature Newspaper Writer of the Year award from *Editor & Publisher.* The Dog Writers' and the Cat Writers' associations have bestowed upon Steve numerous honors for Best Newspaper Column, Best Online Feature, Best Radio Show, and Best Radio Presentation. The following article is adapted from one of his "My Pet World" columns.

Kerchunk, klop, klop, kerplunk . . . Then we heard an awful sounding loud clang and the elevator comes to an abrupt halt.

You know how passengers are in an elevator. At first no one said a word. But when the elevator hit the skids, you could tell they were alarmed. They all had what I call "a Barney Fife face"—their eyes spoke sheer terror. They looked at me for action. I took the initiative and sounded the alarm button. Like a dinner bell magnified by a thousand, it rang loudly enough to be heard down the block. But no one from our five-story vintage condo building on Chicago's near North Side replied.

Finally, one of the passengers spoke up, or, I should say, broke up. She melted and began to whimper. Attempting to console her, I touched her shoulder and said, "It's okay, no need to worry."

Again, I pushed that red alarm button. At that point, another passenger began to walk in circles.

"Lucy, sit," I said. Chaser was already positioned in a sit, and the third passenger, Boots Montgomery, began to bark when she heard our neighbor Blake. "Hello, is someone in the elevator?"

Over Boots's barking, I explained the problem. Blake called the elevator company and then reported that the rescue crew would take a few hours to get to the building because they were on the other side of town and it was rush hour.

No worries. I was counting my blessings—after all, we were going up in the elevator, if you know what I mean. Well, I mean the dogs had just done their business.

I took off my coat, sat on the floor, and held Lucy in my lap. Poor Lucy was shaking with fright. Lucy is cute as a button and she knows it. She revels at showing off her parlor tricks—like playing dead or jumping through a hula hoop. She's even performed little routines countless times as a therapy dog. But at this moment, Lucy, who is a nineteen-pound North American shepherd (miniature Australian shepherd), was shakier than Jell-O. I held her as she whimpered.

Could it be that Lucy knew something was wrong? Certainly, this wasn't our regular routine.

Lucy wasn't the only frightened pooch. Boots Montgomery, as she likes to be called, is our neighbor's dog. Her entire twenty-two-pound Tibetan terrier frame squirms with delight at the mere mention of her complete and proper name. Boots's outlook on life is to bark and then ask questions later. Boots didn't want to act afraid, but at that moment, if she could have gotten any closer to me, she would have been under my shirt.

Forget about the half-full or half-empty glass of water test to determine an optimist. If you think our elevator is quaint, you're an optimist. Most people—the pessimists and the realists, too— call it "cramped" or "claustrophobic." Indeed, this elevator is only about half the size of most, even smaller than the elevators in French or Italian pensions.

Our elevator is so antiquated that I swear it's operated by a rodent going around and around in a cylinder that pulls ropes, just like an elevator in *The Flintstones*.

I was so busy consoling Lucy and Boots Montgomery, I barely noticed how unruffled Chaser, our then four-and-a-half-year-old, thirty-five-pound Brittany was. Chaser sat staring at me with her amber-colored eyes. I realized that she had been looking at me for the entire time we had been trapped. She never took her eyes off me. Now, finally, Chaser had my full attention. Sometimes, I get the feeling that Chaser isn't just looking at me; she's looking into my soul.

I hugged Chaser and thought about her first days in our home. She was about nine months old at the time; we had little knowledge of her checkered past.

It seemed all Chaser did for her first few months in our home was to urinate and cry. When I did my business on one side of the bathroom door, she'd do the same thing on the other side of the door. She just couldn't stand being behind a closed door.

Chaser was terrified of loud noises, even not so loud ones. She was afraid of other dogs, other people, and all forms of public transportation, from buses to commuter trains. Living on a bus route and near the Chicago elevated trains, if it were up to Chaser, we would have moved—maybe to Mars.

When we went out for a walk, the expression on Chaser's face could have been a poster for animal abuse. It was so bad that on two occasions, hardened Chicago cops—apparently assuming

Chaser had been stolen—stopped and asked if she was *really* our dog. That's just how pitiful she looked.

Chaser liked my wife, Robin, fine. But she was attached to me like a shadow, following my every move. And when I moved somewhere she couldn't, everything inside her came out, even when she was crated.

In desperation, when we left the house, Robin displayed an impostor kit. She had enlarged a giant life-size photo of me and draped an old T-shirt over it. She would put this dummy out, along with a tape recorder playing my voice. She figured that if Chaser could see, smell, and hear me whenever we left the house, she might be fooled.

She wasn't.

Chaser was certainly humbling. At that time, I periodically wrote pet stories, and even then was supposed to know a little something. She taught me that I knew nothing.

After visiting several experts for advice, attending puppy classes for confidence boosting, and getting out in the world for many months, Chaser began her Pygmalion transformation, finally succeeding in converting into My Fair Canine when she earned her American Kennel Club Canine Good Citizen certificate. And all along the way, Chaser was the best teacher I ever had. It's as if Chaser entered my life for a reason.

Little Lucy's whimpers were now few and far between, and Boots Montgomery was actually lying down, but then she'd get up again. And then she'd lie down, and then get up. But Chaser was strangely at ease.

Then it happened. Chaser, who was sitting only about six or seven inches away, got up and placed herself nearly on me. She continued staring the entire time; our noses were almost close enough to touch. The next moment seemed to last for several minutes. But I'm sure that it was only a split second. It was a moment that I'll never forget. It was the kind of thing that I thought happened only to Timmy and Lassie, or maybe when a pet psychic was around.

For that second, I felt Chaser's soul in a way that I never had before with any animal. I can't translate what Chaser told me. It was more like a feeling, a warm feeling of unadulterated love. I was moved to tears, though I didn't quite know why.

I had been offered the syndicated newspaper column (with Tribune Media Services) only a day earlier. I didn't know whether or not I should take the gig.

I realized that it wasn't likely that I would ever again enjoy an intense relationship like the one I'd developed with Chaser. Yet, it would have been so easy for me to give up on her. Just in the time you've read this, at least one person in America has given up on a dog and maybe two cats. Most often, the reason for relinquishing an animal is that it exhibits what we call "bad behavior," but that's not always the right way to put it—as Chaser taught me.

Chaser also taught me that dogs and cats can change, just as people can. At that moment in the elevator, I thought, If I can write about pets, I'll affect a change, helping others to understand this.

Chaser licked away a tear, and then she smiled, opening her mouth and pulling back her lips, as many dogs are able to do. Then in a sort of restrained way, she said, "Woof." I can't claim to translate that "Woof." Then Chaser did what Chaser does best: She nodded off.

By now, I was more relaxed. Perhaps Lucy and Boots picked up on my comfort level, or perhaps Chaser's. They, too, appeared more at ease. The three of us sprawled in a heap, crammed together in the tight confines of the boxy elevator for another twenty minutes or so before the repair crew arrived. In a way, I wish we would have been stuck inside the elevator longer.

I like my career. I'm grateful to have been able to help countless people and their pets. It never would have happened without

Chaser, and maybe without getting stuck in that elevator in 1993. Chaser is now fifteen. She still stares at me—at least that's what people say she's doing. I know better. I know she's reading my soul.

Some of my best leading men have been dogs and horses.
—Elizabeth Taylor

• • •

Heaven goes by favor. If it went by merit, you would
stay out and your dog would go in.
—Mark Twain

when i get to heaven

questions from an anxious dog

anonymous

Dear God: When I get to heaven, do I have to roll over and play dead to get through the gates?

Dear God: I can understand verbal instructions, hand signals, whistles, horns, clickers, beepers, scent IDs, electromagnetic fields, and flight paths for Frisbees. What else do I need to know to get to heaven?

Dear God: Will I be allowed on your couch, or will it be the same old story?

Dear God: If a dog barks in heaven and no human hears him, is he still a bad dog?

Dear God: Is it true that in heaven, dining room tables have on-ramps?

Dear God: More meatballs, less spaghetti, please.

Dear God: Are there dogs on other planets? I have been howling at the moon and the stars all my life, but all I ever hear back is the dog next door.

Dear God: Will our mailman be in heaven, too? If he is, will I have to apologize?

Dear God: Will I be allowed in restaurants when I get to heaven, or will I be kept out because of the government again?

Dear God: My family always blesses their food but never mine. So, I wag my tail extra hard when they fill my bowl. Have you noticed?

Dear God: The cat in the house pees on the Oriental rug all the time and they blame me. How would they know? They can't smell the difference. Can you help me out here, please?

Dear God: If we come back as humans, is that a good thing or a bad thing?

Dear God: I hate to complain, but do you know that a lot of us live in shelters, waiting for a home? I'd sure like it if you could get the others into a home as nice as mine. Or will they have to wait until they get to heaven?

• • •

No animal should ever jump up on the dining-room furniture
unless absolutely certain that he can hold his
own in the conversation.
—Fran Lebowitz

old blue
(american folk song)

anonymous

I had a dog and his name was Blue,
And I betcha five dollars he's a good dog too.
Saying, "Come on, Blue, you good dog, you."

Shouldered my axe and I tooted my horn,
Gonna get me a possum in the new-ground corn.
"Go on, Blue, I'm comin' too."

Chased that possum up a 'simmon tree;
Blue looked at the possum, possum looked at me,
Saying, "Go on, Blue, you can have some too."

Baked that possum good and brown,
Laid them sweet potatoes 'round and 'round,
Saying, "Come on, Blue, you can have some too."

"Blue, what makes your eyes so red?"
"I've run them possums till I'm almost dead."
"Go on, Blue, I'm comin' too."

Old Blue died, and he died so hard
That he dug little holes in my backyard
Saying, "Go on, Blue, I'm comin' too."

I dug his grave with a silver spade,
And I let him down with a golden chain,
Saying, "Go on, Blue, I'm comin' too."

When I get to Heaven, first thing I'll do,
Grab my horn, and I'll blow for old Blue.
Saying, "Come on, Blue, finally got here too."

part six

love unleashed

The greatness of a nation and its moral progress can be judged by the way its animals are treated.
—Mahatma Gandhi

garm—a hostage

rudyard kipling

Rudyard Kipling (1865–1936) was born in Bombay, India. In his time, he was known as "the people's laureate" and "poet of the Empire," and was celebrated for his books, stories, and poems throughout the world, but especially within the vast British Empire. Kipling was the first Englishman to win the Nobel Prize for Literature, in 1907. At the age of six, he was sent to live with a foster family in Hampshire, England, while his parents remained in India. He returned to India at the age of sixteen and immediately began his long and distinguished career, first as a journalist and then as a master short story writer, then a novelist and a poet. His first published collection of short stories, *The Phantom Rickshaw and other Tales,* brought him instant fame in 1888, followed in 1893 by the highly successful poetry collection *Barrack-Room Ballads.* His three most important novels were produced as successful motion pictures. The first of these was *Captains Courageous,* produced in 1937, for which Spencer Tracy won an Academy Award. *Kim* was another highly successful Kipling film; Errol Flynn starred in the 1950 version and Peter O'Toole in the 1984 remake. Another successful film based on Kipling's work was *Jungle Book,* produced in 1942, which made an international star of the Indian actor Sabu. It has since been remade twice. His poem "Gunga Din" was the basis for a classic action film (1939) starring Cary Grant and it frequently runs on television. Kipling's most successful works were created during the height of the British Empire and reflected its practices and attitudes toward other races and peoples. Many of the expressions

Kipling used are no longer acceptable in today's world. His much-admired poem "If" has remained in print since it first appeared at the beginning of the twentieth century and continues to be a source of motivation and inspiration to all who read it. As you will learn by reading "Garm—a Hostage," taken from Kipling's *Actions and Reactions,* he was a great lover of dogs and wrote about them frequently with humor and sometimes with profound sadness, as expressed in his poem "The Power of the Dog." When he died in London, his ashes were interred in the Poet's Corner in Westminster Abby, an honor reserved for England's most distinguished subjects.

One night, a very long time ago, I drove to an Indian military encampment called Mian Mir to see amateur theatricals. At the back of the Infantry barracks a soldier, his cap over one eye, rushed in front of the horses and shouted that he was a dangerous highway robber. As a matter of fact, he was a friend of mine, so I told him to go home before any one caught him; but he fell under the pole, and I heard voices of a military guard in search of some one.

The driver and I coaxed him into the carriage, drove home swiftly, undressed him and put him to bed, where he waked next morning with a sore headache, very much ashamed. When his uniform was cleaned and dried, and he had been shaved and washed and made neat, I drove him back to barracks with his arm in a fine white sling, and reported that I had accidentally run over him. I did not tell this story to my friend's sergeant, who was a hostile and unbelieving person, but to his lieutenant, who did not know us quite so well.

Three days later my friend came to call, and at his heels slobbered and fawned one of the finest bull-terriers—of the old-fashioned breed, two parts bull and one terrier—that I had ever set eyes on. He was pure white, with a fawn-colored saddle just behind his neck, and a fawn diamond at the root of his thin whippy tail. I had admired him distantly for more than a year; and Vixen, my own fox-terrier, knew him too, but did not approve.

" 'E's for you," said my friend; but he did not look as though he liked parting with him.

"Nonsense! That dog's worth more than most men, Stanley," I said.

" 'E's that and more. 'Tention!"

The dog rose on his hind legs, and stood upright for a full minute.

"Eyes right!"

He sat on his haunches and turned his head sharp to the right. At a sign he rose and barked thrice. Then he shook hands with his right paw and bounded lightly to my shoulder. Here he made himself into a necktie, limp and lifeless, hanging down on either side of my neck. I was told to pick him up and throw him in the air. He fell with a howl, and held up one leg.

. . . but a dog with whom one lives alone for at least six months in the year; a free thing, tied to you so strictly by love that without you he will not stir or exercise; a patient, temperate, humorous, wise soul, who knows your moods before you know them yourself, is not a dog under any ruling.

"Part o' the trick," said his owner. "You're going to die now. Dig yourself your little grave an' shut your little eye."

Still limping, the dog hobbled to the garden-edge, dug a hole and lay down in it. When told that he was cured, he jumped out, wagging his tail, and whining for applause. He was put through half-a-dozen other tricks, such as showing how he would hold a man safe (I was that man, and he sat down before me, his teeth bared, ready to spring), and how he would stop eating at the word of command. I had no more than finished praising him when my friend made a gesture that stopped the dog as though he had been shot, took a piece of blue-ruled canteen-paper from his helmet, handed it to me and ran away, while the dog looked after him and howled. I read:

SIR—I give you the dog because of what you got me out of. He is the best I know, for I made him myself, and he is as good as a

man. Please do not give him too much to eat, and please do not
give him back to me, for I'm not going to take him, if you will
keep him. So please do not try to give him back any more. I have
kept his name back, so you can call him anything and he will answer. But please do not give him back. He can kill a man as easy
as anything, but please do not give him too much meat. He knows
more than a man.

Vixen sympathetically joined her shrill little yap to the bull-
terrier's despairing cry, and I was annoyed, for I knew that a man
who cares for dogs is one thing, but a man who loves one dog is
quite another. Dogs are at the best no more than verminous va-
grants, self-scratchers, foul feeders, and unclean by the law of
Moses and Mohammed; but a dog with whom one lives alone for
at least six months in the year; a free thing, tied to you so strictly
by love that without you he will not stir or exercise; a patient, temperate, humorous, wise soul, who knows your moods before you
know them yourself, is not a dog under any ruling.

I had Vixen, who was all my dog to me; and I felt what my
friend must have felt, at tearing out his heart in this style and leaving it in my garden.

However, the dog understood clearly enough that I was his
master, and did not follow the soldier. As soon as he drew breath I
made much of him, and Vixen, yelling with jealousy, flew at him.
Had she been of his own sex, he might have cheered himself with
a fight, but he only looked worriedly when she nipped his deep
iron sides, laid his heavy head on my knee, and howled anew. I
meant to dine at the Club that night; but as darkness drew in, and
the dog snuffed through the empty house like a child trying to recover from a fit of sobbing, I felt that I could not leave him to suf-
fer his first evening alone. So we fed at home, Vixen on one side,
and the stranger-dog on the other; she watching his every mouthful, and saying explicitly what she thought of his table manners,
which were much better than hers.

· · ·

There was one corner of a village near by, which we generally passed with caution, because all the yellow pariah-dogs of the place gathered about it. They were half-wild, starving beasts, and though utter cowards, yet where nine or ten of them get together they will mob and kill and eat an English dog. I kept a whip with a long lash for them. That morning they attacked Vixen, who, perhaps of design, had moved from beyond my horse's shadow.

The bull was ploughing along in the dust, fifty yards behind, rolling in his run, and smiling as bull-terriers will. I heard Vixen squeal; half a dozen of the curs closed in on her; a white streak came up behind me; a cloud of dust rose near Vixen, and, when it cleared, I saw one tall pariah with his back broken, and the bull wrenching another to earth. Vixen retreated to the protection of my whip, and the bull paddled back smiling more than ever, covered with the blood of his enemies. That decided me to call him "Garm of the Bloody Breast," who was a great person in his time, or "Garm" for short; so, leaning forward, I told him what his temporary name would be. He looked up while I repeated it, and then raced away. I shouted "Garm!" He stopped, raced back, and came up to ask my will.

Then I saw that my soldier friend was right, and that that dog knew and was worth more than a man. At the end of the ride I gave an order which Vixen knew and hated: "Go away and get washed!" I said. Garm understood some part of it, and Vixen interpreted the rest, and the two trotted off together soberly. When I went to the back veranda Vixen had been washed snowy-white, and was very proud of herself, but the dog-boy would not touch Garm on any account unless I stood by. So I waited while he was being scrubbed, and Garm, with the soap creaming on the top of his broad head, looked at me to make sure that this was what I expected him to endure. He knew perfectly that the dog-boy was only obeying orders.

Sometimes a company of soldiers would move along on their way to the Fort, and Garm rolled forth to inspect them; or an officer in

uniform entered into the office, and it was pitiful to see poor
Garm's welcome to the cloth—not the man. He would leap at
him, and sniff and bark joyously, then run to the door and back
again. One afternoon I heard him bay with a full throat—a thing I
had never heard before—and he disappeared. When I drove into
my garden at the end of the day a soldier in white uniform scram-
bled over the wall at the far end, and the Garm that met me was a
joyous dog. This happened twice or thrice a week for a month.

I pretended not to notice, but Garm knew and Vixen knew. He
would glide homewards from the office about four o'clock, as
though he were only going to look at the scenery, and this he did
so quietly that but for Vixen I should not have noticed him. The
jealous little dog under the table would give a sniff and a snort,
just loud enough to call my attention to the flight. Garm might go
out forty times in the day and Vixen would never stir, but when he
slunk off to see his true master in my garden she told me in her
own tongue. That was the one sign she made to prove that Garm
did not altogether belong to the family. They were the best of
friends at all times, but, Vixen explained that I was never to forget
Garm did not love me as she loved me.

I never expected it. The dog was not my dog—could never be
my dog—and I knew he was as miserable as his master who
tramped eight miles a day to see him. So it seemed to me that the
sooner the two were reunited the better for all. One afternoon I
sent Vixen home alone in the dog-cart (Garm had gone before),
and rode over to cantonments to find another friend of mine, who
was an Irish soldier and a great friend of the dog's master.

I explained the whole case, and wound up with:

"And now Stanley's in my garden crying over his dog. Why
doesn't he take him back? They're both unhappy."

"Unhappy! There's no sense in the little man any more. But 'tis
his fit."

"What *is* his fit? He travels fifty miles a week to see the brute, and he pretends not to notice me when he sees me on the road; and I'm as unhappy as he is. Make him take the dog back."

"It's his penance he's set himself. I told him by way of a joke, after you'd run over him so convenient that night, when he was drunk—I said if he was a Catholic he'd do penance. Off he went wid that fit in his little head an' a dose of fever, an nothin' would suit but givin' you the dog as a hostage."

"Hostage for what? I don't want hostages from Stanley."

"For his good behaviour. He's keepin' straight now, the way it's no pleasure to associate wid him."

"Has he taken the pledge?"

"If 'twas only that I need not care. Ye can take the pledge for three months on an' off. He sez he'll never see the dog again, an' so mark you, he'll keep straight for evermore. Ye know his fits? Well, this is wan of them. How's the dog takin' it?"

"Like a man. He's the best dog in India. Can't you make Stanley take him back?"

"I can do no more than I have done. But ye know his fits. He's just doin' his penance. What will he do when he goes to the Hills? The doctor's put him on the list."

It is the custom in India to send a certain number of invalids from each regiment up to stations in the Himalayas for the hot weather; and though the men ought to enjoy the cool and the comfort, they miss the society of the barracks down below, and do their best to come back or to avoid going. I felt that this move would bring matters to a head, so I left Terrence hopefully, though he called after me:

"He won't take the dog, sorr. You can lay your month's pay on that. Ye know his fits."

I never pretended to understand Private Ortheris; and so I did the next best thing—I left him alone.

That summer the invalids of the regiment to which my friend belonged were ordered off to the Hills early, because the doctors

thought marching in the cool of the day would do them good.
Their route lay south to a place called Umballa, a hundred and
twenty miles or more. Then they would turn east and march up
into the hills to Kasauli or Dugshai or Subathoo. I dined with the
officers the night before they left—they were marching at five in
the morning. It was midnight when I drove into my garden, and
surprised a white figure flying over the wall.

"That man," said my butler, "has been here since nine, making
talk to that dog. He is quite mad." I did not tell him to go away because he has been here many times before, and because the dog-
boy told me that if I told him to go away, that great dog would
immediately slay me. He did not wish to speak to the Protector of
the Poor, and he did not ask for anything to eat or drink."

"Kadir Buksh," said I, "that was well done, for the dog would
surely have killed thee. But I do not think the white soldier will
come any more."

Garm slept ill that night and whimpered in his dreams. Once
he sprang up with a clear, ringing bark, and I heard him wag his
tail till it waked him and the bark died out in a howl. He had
dreamed he was with his master again, and I nearly cried. It was
all Stanley's silly fault.

The first halt which the detachment of invalids made was some
miles from their barracks, on the Amritsar road, and ten miles distant from my house. By a mere chance one of the officers drove
back for another good dinner at the Club (cooking on the line of
march is always bad), and there we met. He was a particular friend
of mine, and I knew that he knew how to love a dog properly. His
pet was a big fat retriever who was going up to the Hills for his
health, and, though it was still April, the round, brown brute puffed
and panted in the Club veranda as though he would burst.

"It's amazing," said the officer, "what excuses these invalids of
mine make to get back to barracks. There's a man in my company
now asked me for leave to go back to cantonments to pay a debt he'd
forgotten. I was so taken by the idea I let him go, and he jingled off

in an *ekka* as pleased as Punch. Ten miles to pay a debt! Wonder what it was really?"

"If you'll drive me home I think I can show you," I said.

So he went over to my house in his dog-cart with the retriever; and on the way I told him the story of Garm.

"I was wondering where that brute had gone to. He's the best dog in the regiment," said my friend. "I offered the little fellow twenty rupees for him a month ago. But he's a hostage, you say, for Stanley's good conduct. Stanley's one of the best men I have when he chooses."

"That's the reason why," I said. "A second-rate man wouldn't have taken things to heart as he has done."

We drove in quietly at the far end of the garden, and crept round the house. There was a place close to the wall all grown about with tamarisk trees, where I knew Garm kept his bones. Even Vixen was not allowed to sit near it. In the full Indian moonlight I could see a white uniform bending over the dog.

"Good-bye, old man," we could not help hearing Stanley's voice. "For 'Eving's sake don't get bit and go mad by any measly pi-dog. But you can look after yourself, old man. You don't get drunk an' run about 'ittin' your friends. You takes your bones an' you eats your biscuit, an' kills your enemy like a gentleman. I'm goin' away—don't 'owl—I'm goin' off to Kasauli, where I won't see you no more."

I could hear him holding Garm's nose as the dog threw it up to the stars.

"You'll stay here an' be'ave, an'—an' I'll go away an' try to be'ave, an' I don't know 'ow to leave you. I don't think—"

"I think this is damn silly," said the officer, patting his foolish

"Beast?" said the officer. "I value that dog considerably more than I value any man I know. It's all very fine for you to talk—your dog's here."

So she was—under my feet—and, had she been missing, food and wages would have stopped in my house till her return. But some people grow fond of dogs not worth a cut of the whip.

fubsy old retriever. He called to the private who leaped to his feet, marched forward, and saluted.

"You here?" said the officer, turning away his head.

"Yes, sir, but I'm just goin' back."

"I shall be leaving here at eleven in my cart. You come with me. I can't have sick men running about all over the place. Report yourself at eleven, *here*."

We did not say much when we went indoors, but the officer muttered and pulled his retriever's ears.

He was a disgraceful, overfed doormat of a dog; and when he waddled off to my cookhouse to be fed, I had a brilliant idea.

At eleven o'clock that officer's dog was nowhere to be found, and you never heard such a fuss as his owner made. He called and shouted and grew angry, and hunted through my garden for half an hour.

Then I said:

"He's sure to turn up in the morning. Send a man in by rail, and I'll find the beast and return him."

"Beast?" said the officer. "I value that dog considerably more than I value any man I know. It's all very fine for you to talk—your dog's here."

So she was—under my feet—and, had she been missing, food and wages would have stopped in my house till her return. But some people grow fond of dogs not worth a cut of the whip. My friend had to drive away at last with Stanley in the back seat; and then the dog-boy said to me:

"What kind of animal is Bullen Sahib's dog? Look at him!"

I went to the boy's hut, and the fat old reprobate was lying on a mat carefully chained up. He must have heard his master calling for twenty minutes, but had not even attempted to join him.

"He has no face," said the dog-boy scornfully. "He is a *punniar-kooter* [a spaniel]. He never tried to get that cloth off his jaws when his master called. Now Vixen-baba would have jumped through the window, and that Great Dog would have slain me

with his muzzled mouth. It is true that there are many kinds of
dogs."

Next evening who should turn up but Stanley. The officer had
sent him back fourteen miles by rail with a note begging me to return the retriever if I had found him, and, if I had not, to offer
huge rewards. The last train to camp left at half-past ten, and
Stanley stayed till ten talking to Garm. I argued and entreated, and
even threatened to shoot the bull-terrier, but the little man was as
firm as a rock, though I gave him a good dinner and talked to him
most severely. Garm knew as well as I that this was the last time he
could hope to see his man, and followed Stanley like a shadow.
The retriever said nothing, but licked his lips after his meal and
waddled off without so much as saying "Thank you" to the disgusted dog-boy.

Once, and only once, did I see Garm at all contented with his sur-
roundings. He had gone for an unauthorised walk with Vixen
early one Sunday morning, and a very young and foolish artilleryman (his battery had just moved to that part of the world) tried to
steal both. Vixen, of course, knew better than to take food from
soldiers, and, besides, she had just finished her breakfast. So she
trotted back with a large piece of the mutton that they issue to our
troops, laid it down on my veranda, and looked up to see what I
thought. I asked her where Garm was, and she ran in front of the
house to show me the way.

About a mile up the road we came across our artilleryman sitting very stiffly on the edge of a culvert with a greasy handkerchief
on his knees. Garm was in front of him, looking rather pleased.
When the man moved leg or hand, Garm bared his teeth in silence.
A broken string hung from his collar, and the other half of it lay,
all warm, in the artilleryman's still hand. He explained to me,
keeping his eyes straight in front of him, that he had met this dog
(he called him awful names) walking alone, and was going to take
him to the Fort to be killed for a masterless pariah.

I said that Garm did not seem to me much of a pariah, but that he had better take him to the Fort if he thought best. He said he did not care to do so. I told him to go to the Fort alone. He said he did not want to go at that hour, but would follow my advice as soon as I had called off the dog. I instructed Garm to take him to the Fort, and Garm marched him solemnly up to the gate, one mile and a half under a hot sun, and I told the quarter-guard what had happened; but the young artilleryman was more angry than was at all necessary when they began to laugh. Several regiments, he was told, had tried to steal Garm in their time.

That month the hot weather shut down in earnest, and the dogs slept in the bathroom on the cool wet bricks where the bath is placed. Every morning, as soon as the man filled the bath, the two jumped in, and every morning the man filled the bath a second time. I said to him that he might as well fill a small tub specially for the dogs. "Nay," said he smiling, "it is not their custom. They would not understand. Besides, the big bath gives them more space."

The punkah-coolies who pull the punkahs day and night came to know Garm intimately. He noticed that when the swaying fan stopped I would call out to the coolie and bid him pull with a long stroke. If the man still slept I would wake him up. He discovered, too, that it was a good thing to lie in the wave of air under the punkah. Maybe Stanley had taught him all about this in barracks. At any rate, when the punkah stopped, Garm would first growl and cock his eye at the rope, and if that did not wake the man—it nearly always did—he would tiptoe forth and talk in the sleeper's ear. Vixen was a clever little dog, but she could never connect the punkah and the coolie; so Garm gave me grateful hours of cool sleep. But he was utterly wretched—as miserable as a human being; and in his misery he clung so closely to me that other men noticed it, and were envious. If I moved from one room to another Garm followed; if my pen stopped scratching, Garm's head was thrust into my hand; if I turned, half awake, on the pillow, Garm was up and at my side, for he knew that I was his only link with his master, and day and night, and night and day, his eyes asked one question—"When is this going to end?"

Living with the dog as I did, I never noticed that he was more than ordinarily upset by the hot weather, till one day at the Club a man said: "That dog of yours will die in a week or two. He's a shadow." Then I dosed Garm with iron and quinine, which he hated; and I felt very anxious. He lost his appetite, and Vixen was allowed to eat his dinner under his eyes. Even that did not make him swallow, and we held a consultation on him, of the best man-doctor in the place; a lady-doctor, who cured the sick wives of kings; and the Deputy Inspector-General of the veterinary service of all India. They pronounced upon his symptoms, and I told them his story, and Garm lay on a sofa licking my hand.

"He's dying of a broken heart," said the lady-doctor suddenly.

" 'Pon my word," said the Deputy Inspector-General, "I believe Mrs. Macrae is perfectly right—as usual."

The best man-doctor in the place wrote a prescription, and the veterinary Deputy Inspector-General went over it afterwards to be sure that the drugs were in the proper dog-proportions; and that was the first time in his life that our doctor ever allowed his prescriptions to be edited. It was a strong tonic, and it put the dear boy on his feet for a week or two; then he lost flesh again. I asked a man I knew to take him up to the Hills with him when he went, and the man came to the door with his kit packed on the top of the carriage. Garm took in the situation at one red glance. The hair rose along his back; he sat down in front of me and delivered the most awful growl I have ever heard in the jaws of a dog. I shouted to my friend to get away at once, and as soon as the carriage was out of the garden Garm laid his head on my knee and whined. So I knew his answer, and devoted myself to getting Stanley's address in the Hills.

My turn to go to the cool came late in August. We were allowed thirty days' holiday in a year, if no one fell sick, and we took it as we could be spared. My chief and Bob the Librarian had their holiday first, and when they were gone I made a calendar, as I always did, and hung it up at the head of my cot, tearing off one day at a time till they returned. Vixen had gone up to the Hills with me five times before; and she appreciated the cold and the damp and the beautiful wood fires there as much as I did.

"Garm," I said, "we are going back to Stanley at Kasauli. Kasauli—Stanley; Stanley Kasauli." And I repeated it twenty times. It was not Kasauli really, but another place. Still I remembered what Stanley had said in my garden on the last night, and I dared not change the name. Then Garm began to tremble; then he barked; and then he leaped up at me, frisking and wagging his tail.

"Not now," I said, holding up my hand. "When I say 'Go,' we'll go, Garm." I pulled out the little blanket coat and spiked collar that Vixen always wore up in the Hills to protect her against sudden chills and thieving leopards, and I let the two smell them and talk it over. What they said of course I do not know; but it made a new dog of Garm. His eyes were bright; and he barked joyfully when I spoke to him. He ate his food, and he killed his rats for the next three weeks, and when he began to whine I had only to say "Stanley—Kasauli; Kasauli—Stanley," to wake him up. I wish I had thought of it before.

My chief came back, all brown with living in the open air, and very angry at finding it so hot in the plains. That same afternoon we three and Kadir Buksh began to pack for our month's holiday, Vixen rolling in and out of the bullock-trunk twenty times a minute, and Garm grinning all over and thumping on the floor with his tail. Vixen knew the routine of travelling as well as she knew my office-work. She went to the station, singing songs, on the front seat of the carriage, while Garm sat with me. She hurried into the railway carriage, saw Kadir Buksh make up my bed for the night, got her drink of water, and curled up with her black-patch eye on the tumult of the platform. Garm followed her (the crowd gave him a lane all to himself) and sat down on the pillows with his eyes blazing, and his tail a haze behind him.

We came to Umballa in the hot misty dawn, four or five men, who had been working hard for eleven months, shouting for our diks—the two-horse travelling carriages that were to take us up to Kalka at the foot of the Hills. It was all new to Garm. He did not understand carriages where you lay at full length on your bedding, but Vixen knew and hopped into her place at once; Garm following. The Kalka Road, before the railway was built, was about forty-seven miles long, and the horses were changed every eight miles. Most of them jibbed, and kicked, and plunged, but they had to go, and they went rather better than usual for Garm's deep bay in their rear.

When we climbed to the top we spied that very Stanley, who had given me all this trouble, sitting on a rock with his face in his hands, and his overcoat hanging loose about him. I never saw anything so lonely and dejected in my life as this one little man, crumpled up and thinking, on the great gray hillside.

Here Garm left me.

There was a river to be forded, and four bullocks pulled the carriage, and Vixen stuck her head out of the sliding-door and nearly fell into the water while she gave directions. Garm was silent and curious, and rather needed reassuring about Stanley and Kasauli. So we rolled, barking and yelping, into Kalka for lunch, and Garm ate enough for two.

After Kalka the road wound among the hills, and we took a curricle with half-broken ponies, which were changed every six miles. No one dreamed of a railroad to Simla in those days, for it was seven thousand feet up in the air. The road was more than fifty miles long, and the regulation pace was just as fast as the ponies could go. Here, again, Vixen led Garm from one carriage to the other; jumped into the back seat, and shouted. A cool breath from the snows met us about five miles out of Kalka, and she whined for her coat, wisely fearing a chill on the liver. I had had one made for Garm too, and, as we climbed to the fresh breezes, I put it on, and Garm chewed it uncomprehendingly, but I think he was grateful.

"Hi-yi-yi-yi!" sang Vixen as we shot round the curves; "Toot-toot-toot!" went the driver's bugle at the dangerous places, and "Yow! Yow! Yow! Yow!" bayed Garm. Kadir Buksh sat on the front seat and smiled. Even he was glad to get away from the heat of the Plains that stewed in the haze behind us. Now and then we would meet a man we knew going down to his work again, and he would say: "What's it like below?" and I would shout: "Hotter than cinders. What's it like up above?" and he would shout back: "Just perfect!" and away we would go.

Suddenly Kadir Buksh said, over his shoulder: "Here is Solon"; and Garm snored where he lay with his head on my knee. Solon is an unpleasant little cantonment, but it has the advantage of being cool and healthy. It is all bare and windy, and one generally stops at a rest-house nearby for something to eat. I got out and took both dogs with me, while Kadir Buksh made tea. A soldier told us we should find Stanley "out there," nodding his head towards a bare, bleak hill.

When we climbed to the top we spied that very Stanley, who had given me all this trouble, sitting on a rock with his face in his hands, and his overcoat hanging loose about him. I never saw anything so lonely and dejected in my life as this one little man, crumpled up and thinking, on the great gray hillside.

Here Garm left me.

He departed without a word, and, so far as I could see, without moving his legs. He flew through the air bodily, and I heard the whack of him as he flung himself at Stanley, knocking the little man clean over. They rolled on the ground together, shouting, and yelping, and hugging. I could not see which was dog and which was man, till Stanley got up and whimpered.

He told me that he had been suffering from fever at intervals, and was very weak. He looked all he said, but even while I watched, both man and dog plumped out to their natural sizes, precisely as dried apples swell in water. Garm was on his shoulder, and his breast and feet all at the same time, so that Stanley spoke all through a cloud of Garm—gulping, sobbing, slavering Garm. He did not say anything that I could understand, except that he had fancied he was going to die, but that now he was quite well, and that he was not going to give up Garm any more to anybody under the rank of Beelzebub.

Then he said he felt hungry, and thirsty, and happy.

We went down to tea at the rest-house, where Stanley stuffed himself with sardines and raspberry jam, and beer, and cold mutton and pickles, when Garm wasn't climbing over him; and then Vixen and I went on.

Garm saw how it was at once. He said good-bye to me three times, giving me both paws one after another, and leaping on to my shoulder. He further escorted us, singing Hosannas at the top of his voice, a mile down the road. Then he raced back to his own master.

Vixen never opened her mouth, but when the cold twilight came, and we could see the lights of Simla across the hills, she snuffled with her nose at the breast of my ulster. I unbuttoned it, and tucked her inside. Then she gave a contented little sniff, and fell fast asleep, her head on my breast, till we bundled out at Simla, two of the four happiest people in all the world that night.

• • •

Trained or not, he'll always be his own dog to a degree.
—Carol Lea Benjamin

the power of the dog

rudyard kipling

There is sorrow enough in the natural way
From men and women to fill our day;
But when we are certain of sorrow in store,
Why do we always arrange for more?
Brothers and sisters, I bid you beware
Of giving your heart to a dog to tear.

Buy a pup and your money will buy
Love unflinching that cannot lie—
Perfect passion and worship fed
By a kick in the ribs or a pat on the head.
Nevertheless it is hardly fair
To risk your heart for a dog to tear.

When the fourteen years which Nature permits
Are closing in asthma, or tumour, or fits,
And the vet's unspoken prescription runs
To lethal chambers or loaded guns,
Then you will find—it's your own affair—
But . . . you've given your heart for a dog to tear.

When the body that lived at your single will
When the whimper of welcome is stilled (how still!);
When the spirit that answered your every mood
Is gone—wherever it goes—for good,
You will discover how much you care,
And will give your heart for the dog to tear!

We've sorrow enough in the natural way,
When it comes to burying Christian clay.
Our loves are not given, but only lent,
At compound interest of cent per cent.
Though it is not always the case, I believe,
That the longer we've kept 'em, the more do we grieve:
For, when debts are payable, right or wrong,
A short-time loan is as bad as a long—
So why in Heaven (before we are there!)
Should we give our hearts to a dog to tear?

Some days you're the dog, some days you're the hydrant.
—Anonymous

• • •

If a dog will not come to you after having looked you in the face,
you should go home and examine your conscience.
—Woodrow Wilson

the checkers affair: a cocker spaniel, a speech, and the political survival of richard m. nixon

mordecai siegal

In September 1952, Senator Richard M. Nixon was the Republican vice presidential candidate and Dwight D. Eisenhower's running mate, but after the first week of the campaign, he found his candidacy about to come to an abrupt end, along with his political future. The incident began with the front page of the *New York Post* charging that Nixon had a secret fund of eighteen thousand dollars that was set aside for personal use.*

High-powered Republicans applied intense pressure for him to step down and give up his candidacy for the vice presidency. An aggressive national press made this their primary story for days on end, fueling the allegations. Adding to the pressure was silence from General Eisenhower, a beloved hero of World War II, who refused to say whether or not he would keep Nixon on the ticket. In effect, he did not defend him.

Up to this point, Nixon's rise in politics had been meteoric; in just six years, he had come from obscurity to become a U.S. senator and a candidate for vice president. The public challenge to his honesty and integrity was overwhelming. Based on advice from his own campaign advisers, Nixon raised money and purchased airtime on television and radio in a desperate attempt to convince

---

*Earl Mazo's *Richard Nixon: A Political Potrait* was consulted when this piece was written.

the Republican party and the American people that the charges were false. Hence, he broadcast the "Checkers Speech" on television and radio, one of the most bizarre episodes in the history of American politics.

On Tuesday night, September 23, 1952, Richard M. Nixon sat before the cameras in NBC's El Capitan Theater in Hollywood and fought for his political life. The advertising agency for the Republican party, Batten, Barton, Durstine & Osborn, had originally wanted the speech to follow *I Love Lucy* for the huge ready-made audience that it would provide, but that slot would not have given Nixon enough time to prepare. Their second choice was that he should follow *The Milton Berle Show*. If the speech did not make a positive impression on the leaders of the Republican party, such as Thomas E. Dewey, governor of New York and a former presidential candidate, they would have removed him from the ticket, bringing about a possible failed campaign for Eisenhower, who was favored to win the election. The situation could have handed an easy victory to the Democratic candidate, Adlai Stevenson. It was a potential disaster for the Republican campaign.

Nixon paid for a national hookup of 64 NBC television stations, 194 CBS radio stations, and practically the entire 560-station Mutual Broadcasting System radio network for $75,000. No one, however, knew what he was going say. Nixon had made only handwritten notes, which he'd jotted down on a yellow legal pad and had kept to himself. It seemed as if the entire country was waiting in anticipation of what he would say; certainly, General Eisenhower and the entire Republican party were sternly attentive and upset with the thirty-nine-year-old candidate. They were ready to pounce on him publicly. Here was pure political drama being played out for the first time on national television.

Nixon worked on the speech for almost twenty-four hours before the broadcast, and no matter how hard important Republicans and members of the press tried to pressure him to reveal what he was going to say, he remained tight-lipped. Eisenhower was set up in a room above the stage of an auditorium in Cleveland, just before he was to have a rally that night. He watched the speech on television, along with his wife, Mamie, and a number of campaign advisers. He was still undecided about Nixon staying on the ticket. The tension was reported to be unbearable while he and the nation held its breath. At that point, it was entirely up to Richard Nixon to work a miracle, and very few thought he would.

Offering no explanation, the harried candidate had refused to discuss the speech with the program director or to rehearse that day. A stand-in who resembled Nixon allowed the technicians to preset the lights, sound levels, and camera angles. Ted Rogers, Nixon's television adviser, instructed the program director to keep the camera on Nixon no matter what he did, but to focus on Mrs. Nixon when the senator talked about her. They had rehearsed all day Tuesday, but without Nixon.

Thirty minutes before leaving his hotel for the studio, Nixon accepted a call from Governor Dewey, the head of the Republican party, who coldly informed him that most of the campaign leaders felt he should resign from the ticket, implying that Eisenhower agreed. It was a crushing emotional blow, and Nixon sat alone in his room in the Ambassador Hotel, trying to decide what to do, his mood gravitating toward despair. His campaign manager and adviser, Murray Chotiner, a Beverly Hills lawyer, convinced him to make the broadcast anyway and rallied the candidate with a show of fierce loyalty. They left the hotel and drove to the NBC studio. The dice was rolling.

> And you know, the kids, like all kids, love the dog, and I just want to say this, right now, that regardless of what they say about it, we are going to keep it.

A photo of Nixon introduced the beginning of the broadcast, the lights came on, and the camera showed a young, almost callow-looking senator in a plain single-breasted suit sitting at a desk in front of bland draperies. With his hands clasped together, almost as if in prayer, he began:

"My Fellow Americans, I come before you tonight as a candidate for the Vice-Presidency and as a man whose honesty and integrity has been questioned. . . .

. . . the best and only answer to a smear or to an honest misunderstanding of the facts is to tell the truth. . . .

I am sure that you have read the charges, and you have heard it, that I, Senator Nixon, took $18,000 from a group of my supporters.

. . . I say that it was morally wrong—if any of that $18,000 went to Senator Nixon, for my personal use. I say that it was morally wrong if it was secretly given, and secretly handled.

And I say that it was morally wrong if any of the contributors got special favors for the contributions that they made.

After a vigorous denial that the fund was used for any purpose other than campaign expenses and that it was ever a secret, Nixon went on to explain why he needed additional campaign funds.

. . . First of all, the Senator gets $15,000 a year in salary. He gets enough money to pay for one trip a year, a round trip, that is, for himself, and his family between his home and Washington, D.C., and then he gets an allowance to handle the people that work in his office to handle his mail.

And the allowance for my State of California, is enough to hire 13 people. . . .

He continued, speaking next of an independent audit and an official letter that stated he had not obtained any financial gain from the collection and disbursement of the fund, that he had not violated any federal or state law, and that it was clearly designated for office expenses.

. . . I am going at this time to give to this television and radio audience a complete financial history, everything I have earned,

everything I have spent, and everything I own, and I want you to
know the facts.

Nixon went on to reveal his humble beginnings, his life since
that time, and his very modest financial status, mentioning the gro-
cery store run by his family, in which he had worked, how he had
put himself through college and law school, met and married his
wife, Pat, served during World War II as a naval officer, and begun
his political career in 1946, running for Congress. He then gave
what appeared to be a very complete list of his earnings, his debts,
and his holdings, which amounted to the house he occupied in
Washington, on which he had a twenty-thousand-dollar mortgage,
plus a house in Whittier, California, on which he still owed three
thousand dollars and in which his parents now lived. He revealed
that he had a meager life insurance policy, a 1950 car, the family's
furniture, a small bank loan, and no stocks or bonds whatsoever.

Well, that's about it. That's what we have. And that's what we
owe. It isn't very much. But Pat and I have the satisfaction that
every dime that we have got is honestly ours.
    I should say this, that Pat doesn't have a mink coat. But she
does have a respectable Republican cloth coat, and I always tell
her she would look good in anything.

And then he added what turned out to be the part of the
speech that made it immortal, as if it were an afterthought or an
aside.

One other thing I probably should tell you, because if I don't
they'll probably be saying this about me, too. We did get something, a gift, after the election.
    A man down in Texas heard Pat on the radio mention the fact
that our two youngsters would like to have a dog, and believe it or
not, the day before we left on this campaign trip we got a message

from Union Station in Baltimore, saying they had a package for us. We went down to get it. You know what it was?

It was a little Cocker Spaniel dog, in a crate that he had sent all the way from Texas, black and white, spotted, and our little girl Tricia, the six year old, named it Checkers.

And you know, the kids, like all kids, love the dog, and I just want to say this, right now, that regardless of what they say about it, we are going to keep it.

And now, finally, I know that you wonder whether or not I am going to stay on the Republican ticket or resign. Let me say this: I don't believe that I ought to quit, because I am not a quitter. . . .

But the decision, my friends, is not mine. I would do nothing that would harm the possibilities of Dwight Eisenhower to become President of the United States. And for that reason I am submitting to the Republican National Committee tonight through this television broadcast the decision which it is theirs to make. Let them decide whether my position on the ticket will help or hurt. And I am going to ask you to help them decide. Wire and write the Republican National Committee whether you think I should stay or whether I should get off. And whatever their decision is, I will abide by it.

But let me say this last word: Regardless of what happens, I am going to continue this fight. I am going to campaign up and down America until we drive the crooks and the Communists and those that defend them out of Washington. . . .

The instant response across the country was wildly enthusiastic. There was great excitement at the hotel. Telephone calls began pouring in from Republicans everywhere. Darryl F. Zanuck, the Hollywood producer, said it was the most tremendous performance he'd ever seen.

The speech continued at considerable length after the portion concerning Checkers. Nixon mentioned much about smears and misunderstandings, made reference to the Alger Hiss case, and asserted his belief in the fight against Communists in the American government. The balance of the broadcast meandered away from the "secret fund," with gratuitous barbs aimed at Adlai Stevenson. But he had sunk his emotional harpoon deftly into the sentimental heart of the American public, especially with reference to his wife's Republican cloth coat and the fact that he was keeping Checkers for his two young daughters, no matter what. The reference to the dog brought tears to the eyes of many viewers, including Mrs. Eisenhower and others watching in Cleveland.

On reflection, Nixon later said that the inspiration for the Checkers portion of the speech came from a speech delivered by President Roosevelt in 1944. In it, Roosevelt referred comically to his Scottie, Fala, and made a laughingstock of the Republican party. It was not in Nixon to go for a laugh. Instead, he went for the pathos of a man who wanted to please his children.

Who could resist the touching image of a young Cocker Spaniel and two needy little girls? It was a master stroke, one that made this among the most notable speeches of the twentieth century, if only for its impact and intended results. Nixon had beaten the impossible odds. The Eisenhower-Nixon ticket went on to win the White House by a landslide, twice.

There was so much more involving Nixon to follow in the next twenty-two years, including the threat of impeachment over the Watergate break-in and cover-up. Ironically, that, too, involved a secret fund, this time resulting in Nixon being the first and only president to resign from office. It's all history now, owing in part to the conjuring up of a pretty Cocker Spaniel by a politician who tugged at America's heartstrings with an emotional leash. He understood completely the feelings most Americans have for dogs and the children who love them. Not before or since has one little dog so completely influenced American history. Checkers is a dog to remember.

another speech, another dog

mordecai siegal

Another presidential dog worth noting is Fala, Franklin Delano Roosevelt's Scottish Terrier. Although the rambunctious Scottie never influenced the nation's history as did Checkers, he was a beloved companion for the 32nd President of the United States and during his lifetime was the most famous dog in the country. If the dog had any influence on the affairs of state, it was indirectly as a source of happiness and pleasure for the wheelchair-bound FDR, who, at that time, was waging a deadly war with Germany, Italy, and Japan. Based on all accounts Fala was deeply loved by the president and was a joyful distraction for the wartime commander-in-chief.

Fala was born April 7, 1940, in Westport, Connecticut, into the family of Augustus Kellogg, a friend of Margaret "Daisy" Suckley, the president's cousin. The puppy was presented to FDR by the Kellogg family as a thoughtful gift. The president promptly changed his name from Big Boy to Fala after an obscure Scottish ancestor known only as "Murray the Outlaw of Falahill." It was typical of the Roosevelt sense of humor.

In one short year, the young dog had become a major publicity asset for the president as a means of obtaining upbeat publicity during the dark days of World War II. The public rarely saw the president outside of the White House without his beloved Scottie. The two were inseparable. In his lifetime, Fala's photograph appeared in every newspaper and nearly every magazine throughout the United States once he took up residence with his presidential companion.

In early August 1941, FDR secretly slipped out of the country to meet for the first time with England's Prime Minister, Winston Churchill, to create an alliance for the coming war, which came to be known as the Atlantic Charter. The leaders met aboard the heavy cruiser, U.S.S. *Augusta,* in Argentia Bay, Newfoundland. A footnote to this meeting is that Fala also attended the momentous "Atlantic Conference" because the head of state never left home without him.

During Roosevelt's 1944 campaign for an unprecedented fourth term the president's opponents accused him of spending millions of taxpayer dollars to send a destroyer back to the Aleutian Islands, where it was rumored Fala had been accidentally left behind during an official visit. Never missing an opportunity to skewer his Republican opposition with humorous ridicule, he answered the charges in a tongue-in-cheek speech heard nationwide. Here, in part, is that speech, from an address to the Teamsters Union on September 23, 1944:

the fala speech

. . . These Republican leaders have not been content with attacks on me, or my wife, or on my sons. No, not content with that, they now include my little dog, Fala. Well, of course, I don't resent attacks, and my family doesn't resent attacks, but Fala does resent them. You know, Fala is Scotch, and . . . being a Scottie, as soon as he learned that the Republican fiction-writers in Congress and out had concocted a story that I had left him behind on the Aleutian Islands and had sent a destroyer back to find him—at a cost to the taxpayers of two or three, or eight or twenty million dollars— his Scotch soul was furious. He has not been the same dog since. I am accustomed to hearing malicious falsehoods about myself— such as that old, worm-eaten chestnut that I have represented myself as indispensable. But I think I have a right to resent, to object to libelous statements about my dog. . . .

Although Fala did not change American history, as did Checkers, the Fala speech did have some impact on the election that year. Richard Nixon, by his own admission, was inspired by the Fala speech when he included Checkers in his historic television plea in 1952.

We can only conclude from these two celebrated speeches that most Americans, including presidents, have deep feelings about dogs and are capable of having their heartstrings tugged to a great degree by national politicians. Since that time, the American public has never seen a president without a dog in the White House.

• • •

You want a friend in Washington? Get a dog.
—Harry S Truman

dog names of the great and not so great

mordecai siegel

King Arthur's favorite dog	Cavall
Elizabeth Barrett Browning	Flush
Charles Lamb	Dash
Sir Edwin Landseer	Brutus
Sir Isaac Newton	Diamond
Richard II	Mathe
Sir Walter Scott	Maida
Ulysses	Argos
The Thin Man	Asta

Gunnar Kasson	Balto
St. Bernard Hospice	Barry
Gertrude Stein	Basket
Frank Inn (trainer)	Higgins, the dog who played Benji
Sailor Jack of Cracker Jack fame	Bingo
Adolf Hitler	Blondi
Franklin Delano Roosevelt	Fala
Alexander Pope	Bounce
Morris Frank	Buddy
Roy Rogers	Bullet
John Steinbeck	Charley
Tricia Nixon	Checkers
Willie and Tad Lincoln	Fido
Emily Brontë	Keeper
John Gray	Greyfriars Bobby
Lyndon Johnson	Him and Her
Richard Nixon	King Timahoe
Albert Payson Terhune	Lad
The Actual Lassie	Pal
RCA dog "His Master's Voice"	Nipper
Lee Duncan	Rin Tin Tin
Meriwether Lewis	Scannon
Charlie Chaplin's costar	Scraps
Westminster Kennel Club	Sensation
Charles Schulz's real dog	Spike
Konrad Lorenz	Tito

part seven

god is coming, look busy

Kindness to all living things is the true religion.
—Buddha

the soul of caliban

emma-lindsay squier

Emma-Lindsay Squier (1892–1941) was born in Marion, Indiana. She was a precocious child and began a weekly newsletter in Terre Haute in her preteen years. She moved with her family during her childhood to Salem, Oregon, and then to Glendale, California. As a young adult, she was a reporter for the *Los Angeles Times* and eventually wrote a society column under her own byline. She became assistant editor of a monthly periodical published in Pasadena called *California Life*. She then moved on to become a successful author, writing adventure and animal books for young adults. Her published short stories appeared in her first collection, *The Wild Heart,* and brought her national recognition. Although she died at the age of forty-eight of tuberculosis in Saranac Lake, New York, she left behind many books and short stories. Among her books is *The Wild Heart* (1922), *On Autumn Trails* (1922), *Children of the Twilight* (1926), *The Bride of the Sacred Well* (1928), and *Gringa* (1934), in addition to dozens of short stories for such magazines as *Collier's, Ladies' Home Journal, McCall's,* and *The American Girl.* "Glorious Buccaneer," a short story, was produced as a Hollywood film retitled *The Dancing Pirate* (1936), along with another of her stories, "The Wild Heart." "The Soul of Caliban" is a short story that first appeared in the December 1924 issue of *Everybody's Magazine.* Since then it has been included in many anthologies of classic dog stories.

From French Louie I had this story, which you will accept as true or scout as impossible, according to your liking and knowledge of dogs. For myself, I think it is true, for he was not blessed—or cursed—with imagination.

French Louie is a curious mixture of savagery and simplicity. For many years he lived by trapping in the northern woods. And yet, despite his cruel occupation, he has always loved animals. Many a fox cub he has reared to adulthood when it came to grief in his traps. Many a tear has he shed—I can well believe it—when a dragged and bloody trap told the mute story of an animal's desperate gnawing of a foot or a leg as the price of freedom. One day when he heard a visitor to the menagerie remark that it was a pity that animals had no souls, he flew into a rage, fairly booted the visitor out of the place, and was still sputtering French and English when I dropped in upon him.

"No souls, they say!" he snorted, spreading his hands and puckering his lips in contemptuous mimicry. "Faugh! They give me the gran' pain! The only animal they ever have, I bet you, he is a canary bird that say 'Pretty Poll' all day long!"

"That's a parrot," I said mildly. But he only snorted.

"No soul, they say! Listen, I tell you somet'ing I bet you nobody believe, by Gar! Or they say, 'Oh, dat dog he obey hees instinct.' Bien, all I say ees, who know what ees instinct and what ees soul? And I bet you many a man he ain't got the soul that that dog got instinct—no, by Gar!"

A dog of strange, tumultuous jealousies, and incomprehensible tenderness. So rough was he, when herding the sheep, that Leon Suprenon was always shouting: "Caliban, you devil! Stop biting that sheep . . . !"

It was in the sheep country of Alberta that Louie knew the dog, Caliban. Leon Suprenon was his owner, and Louie used to visit the sheep man at his ranch, far removed from civilization.

"Leon he was one fine educated man, by Gar," he told me. "Books—with pictures—he had many of them in hees 'ouse. Dat dog, Caliban, he name' heem from a pleh by Shakespeare—you have heard of heem?"

"Yes," I said, unsmiling.

"You know a pleh with a dog name' Caliban in eet?"

"Not a dog," I answered, "but a poor imprisoned monster, ugly, deformed, and very wicked, yet somehow very pitiful." French Louie nodded vigorously.

"*C'est la meme chose,*" he assured me. "Dat dog, Caliban—oh, *mon Dieu,* he was ogly! Hees lip she always lifted up like zis—in a snar—all the time dat lip. And hees eyes—leetle, mean-looking eyes, wid a frown between dem always, and teeth dat would snap together—*clop*! No tramps ever came near the place of Leon Suprenon. Dey know dat dog, Caliban; he was not a beast to be trifle' with."

"What kind of a dog was he?" I asked of Louie the Frenchman.

He shrugged his shoulders, spread out his hands and shook his head. No kind, and every kind, was what I gathered from his description a big, shaggy dog, as large as a sheep dog, and much more stockily built. His hair had no silky smoothness to it. Rather it was like the rough, matted fur of a wolf—and Louie maintained that that Caliban had wolf blood in him. There was a strain of bull-dog, too, that made his legs short and bowed a bit. His under jaw came out pugnaciously—always with that lifted lip which was no fault of his, but which gave his face a perpetually savage expression.

Ugly he must have been; yet useful, too. As a guard against tramps and the lawless characters who are to be found in any part of the country where civilization is at a distance, he was invalu-able. As a sheep dog, too, he had not his equal in Alberta. Perhaps it is too much to say that he could count the sheep his master owned. But it is true that he would watch them, passing into the big corrals, his sharp, shaggy ears pointed, his small, close-set eyes never wavering in their intense regard, his whole body taut with concentration. And if any lingered or did not come, Caliban would need no word of command to stir him to action. Like an arrow he would dart out, snapping at the lagging heels, turning in a scatter-brained ewe, or dashing off across the fields to find a sheep which he knew had strayed or had fallen into the river.

A dog of strange, tumultuous jealousies, and incomprehensible tenderness. So rough was he, when herding the sheep, that Leon Suprenon was always shouting: "Caliban, you devil! Stop biting that sheep or I'll beat your ugly brains out!"

Caliban would stop short, regard his master with a long, disdainful stare, and then look back at the sheep, as if to say: "Those silly things! What difference does it make whether I bite their heels or not?"

And yet—that was the dog that, after seeing the sheep into the corral one winter afternoon when a blizzard was threatening to blow down from the north, did not come into the house to dream and twitch under the kitchen stove as was his custom. When darkness fell Leon noticed the dog's absence at first with unconcern, and then with growing uneasiness. The rising wind flung itself viciously upon doors and windows, the white snow whirled up against the panes with sharp, sibilant flurries. Leon went to the door and called. The blizzard drove his voice back in his throat; the wind hurled him against the portals, and drove an icy blast of snow into the hall.

Leon Suprenon was not the man to be daunted by a storm. He remembered that after the gates were shut, Caliban had stood steadily gazing away toward the dim fields, where the menacing curtain of oncoming wind and snow was blotting out the contours of stream and distant forest.

So he took a lantern and fought his way out into the terrible night, out toward the sheep corrals, and then out toward the invisible fields beyond the stream. A mile he went—perhaps more—fighting his way against the fury of the storm. It was out by the cluster of pine trees that marks the east line of the ranch that he met Caliban, coming home.

The dim light of the lantern threw a weak golden circle against the driving white mistiness of the snow. And into the nebulous ring of light came Caliban, grim, staggering, a grotesque monster looming out of the white darkness, his mouth strangely misshapen by something he was carrying—a lamb, newly born. Beside him, struggling weakly yet valiantly against the driving snow, came the mother sheep, which had given birth to her baby in the midst of the dreadful blizzard. Caliban was coming slowly, adapting his pace to hers, stopping when she would stop, yet with unmistakable signs that he expected her to struggle forward with him. And the lamb—the weak, bleating little thing that swung from his teeth as lightly as if it had been a puff of thistledown.

Now the dog Caliban never begged for caresses. He was not the sort of dog to leap and bark and wag his tail when the master came home. Between him and Leon Suprenon there was an understanding—a man's understanding of mutual respect and restraint. A word of commendation sufficed him, or sometimes a pat on the head. But never, as long as Leon had owned the dog, could he recall a time when Caliban had ever sought to ingratiate himself by being friendly and playful, as the other dogs would do.

Nevertheless, Caliban had his jealousies, fierce, deep and primitive. He killed a dog that Leon petted casually; he took it by the throat and crushed it with his great teeth, then flung the quivering body down and stared at it with those baleful, close-set eyes. There was blood on the perpetual snarl of his lifted lip.

Then fearlessly he awaited his punishment. Leon beat him cruelly. But Caliban never flinched or whimpered, just stood there hunching himself up and shutting his eyes, licking his lips a bit as the blows hurt him more and more. When it was over, he shook himself, stretched, then pricked up his ears and looked Leon in the face, as if to say: "Well, that's over. Now have you any orders?" If he had whimpered once—but he did not. Leon swore furiously, and had the dead dog buried in the meadow. He did not caress the other dogs after that. They were valuable to him—but Caliban was priceless. And Leon knew that the only way of breaking his stubborn spirit would be to kill him.

Caliban had one abiding hatred: cats. Whereas the other dogs chased them joyously, or ignored them as inferior creatures, Caliban loathed them, chased them savagely, killed them mercilessly. He had a short, brutal way of doing it; if he caught a luckless cat—and he would run like a yearling buck, that dog Caliban—he would give it one shake, like the crack of a whip, and then toss the cat into the air. It usually died with a broken neck and a broken back. And by the law of the survival of the fittest, the cats that escaped from Caliban's savage sallies were wise in their generation and kept out of his way.

But there was one small cat, not yet out of kittenhood, that had either come recently to the ranch, or else by an accident had not crossed Caliban's path—a gentle little cat, all gray, with a white paw which she was always licking as if proud of it.

One day she sat sunning herself on the porch before the house. Caliban came by that way, and saw her.

With the savage, deep-throated growl that all the other cats had learned to fear as the most deadly thing of life, he leaped at her, caught her, flung her up into the air.

Perhaps it was supreme ignorance of danger that saved her from death. For the gentle little cat had not tried to run from the oncoming whirlwind of teeth and gleaming eyes. She lay where Caliban had flung her, dazed, inert, staring at the terrible dog, with round, uncomprehending eyes. He saw that he had not killed her. He came nearer, ready to shake her with the peculiarly deadly twist that he knew so well. Still she did not move. She could not. She only mewed, a very small, pitiful mew, and her stunned body twitched a little.

Caliban hesitated, sniffed at her, turned away. After all, he seemed to tell himself, you could not kill a weak, helpless thing like that—a thing that could not run.

Leon Suprenon came out and found the little cat. He took her up very gently, and she tried to purr as he stroked her quivering, hurt body.

"Caliban," Leon said sternly, "that was not a sportsmanlike thing to do. I am ashamed of you!"

And to his great surprise, Caliban, the insolent, the ever-snarling, put his tail between his legs and slunk down the porch steps. He too was ashamed.

But Caliban, that ugly, misshapen dog with the perpetual snarl on his lifted lip, could make amends. And to the best of his ability he did. The gentle little cat did not die, but never did she fully recover the use of her limbs. She had a slow, halting way of walking, and running was an impossibility. She would have been an easy prey for the joyous, roistering dogs that chased cats, not from enmity, but because it was the proper thing to do. But Caliban stood between her and eager, sniffing dogs like a savage, sinister warrior. Too well did the other ranch dogs know the menace of those close-set eyes, the ugly, undershot jaw, and the snarl that showed the glitter of deadly, clamping teeth. They learned—through experience—that the little gray cat was not to be molested.

Not only did Caliban become the little gray cat's protector; he became her friend. She would sit on the fence and watch for the sheep dogs to come up to the house after the day's work was done. When the other dogs filed past her, she paid no attention, realizing perfectly that they dared not harm her. And when Caliban came, close at the heels of Leon Suprenon, she would yawn and stretch, purr loudly, and drop squarely and lightly on the big dog's back. He would

Caliban had accepted the girl, Amelie, stoically, without apparent resentment. It was as if he knew that sooner or later his master would bring home a woman to share the lonely ranch house. But the baby—that was a different thing. He had not bargained on the small intruder who became at once the lord and tyrant of the household. When Leon took up the tiny baby in his arms, Caliban growled, and his eyes became a baleful red.

carry her gravely into the kitchen, lie down while she got slowly off his back, and would lie under the stove, with the little cat purring and rubbing about his face. It was not in him to show affection. But he permitted her carefully to wash his face and ears, tug at burrs that matted his heavy coat, and to sleep between his forefeet.

Once another cat, emboldened by the gray cat's immunity from danger, went to sleep between Caliban's great paws. When he awoke and found the intruder peacefully purring against his chest, he gave one terrific growl, sprang to his feet, seized the strange cat and shook it. Savagely he flung it across the room. It was dead before ever it struck the floor.

Now it was at this time that Leon Suprenon married Amelie Morin, from Dubuiqui, and brought her to the ranch that was bounded by dark forests and deep, turbulent rivers. She chafed a little under the isolation of the place, and shivered when at night the wolves howled far back on the distant slopes. But she loved Leon Suprenon, and in time became reconciled to the loneliness of the ranch—still more reconciled when a baby was born to her, and was strong and healthy and beautiful.

Caliban had accepted the girl, Amelie, stoically, without apparent resentment. It was as if he knew that sooner or later his master would bring home a woman to share the lonely ranch house. But the baby—that was a different thing. He had not bargained on the small intruder who became at once the lord and tyrant of the household. When Leon took up the tiny baby in his arms, Caliban growled, and his eyes became a baleful red.

When Leon put the baby in its crib, and spoke to it foolishly, fondly, as all fathers do, Caliban came and stood beside him, looking down at the red-faced crinkly-eyed baby; and again the dog growled, deep in his throat.

One day when Leon caressed the child, Caliban sprang, trying to tear the infant out of his arms. Leon kicked the dog furiously aside, and beat him with a leather whip. "Caliban, you devil!" he panted between the blows. "If you ever touch that baby, I'll kill you!"

And, as if the dog understood, he hunched himself and shut his eyes, licking his lips as the heavy lash fell again and again. Then he shook himself, stared at his master with somber, unwavering eyes, and went out of the house without once looking back.

For a whole week he did not return. One of the ranchmen reported that he had seen Caliban in the forest, that the dog had mated with a female wolf.

Leon Suprenon said that it was not true, and that Caliban would come back. But Amelie cried out:

"No, no! That dog, he is a monster! Never again would I feel that my baby was safe!"

"You misjudge him," Leon said soothingly. "He is a little jealous of the baby, it is true, but he will overcome that in time. An ugly-looking dog, I grant you, but he is very gentle, nevertheless."

"*Gentle*—that beast!" The girl shut her eyes and shuttered. Caliban did come back. He appeared at the kitchen door one day when Leon was out looking after the sheep—sullen, defiant, his glittering, close-set eyes seeming to question whether or not he would be welcomed. The perpetual snarl on his lifted lip and the misshapen ugliness of his powerful body made him even more repellent to the girl Amelie, who snatched up her baby from where he was playing on the floor, ran with him to the bedroom, and closed and bolted the door. But a royal welcome he received from the little gray cat, that dragged herself toward him with purring sounds of joy. She mewed delightedly, rubbed against his bowed legs, and tried to lick his face. Caliban, for the first and last time, bent his ugly head, and licked the little gray cat, briefly and furtively.

The dog had learned his lesson as to the status of the baby. And whether or not his heart was seared with that savage, primitive jealousy which he had shown at first so plainly, no hint of it now appeared. At first he ignored the child, even when it crawled toward him as he lay under the kitchen stove. Later he would watch the round-faced baby with rigid, attentive eyes—eyes in which there were blue-green wolf gleams behind the honest brown. Sometimes he would sniff at the child questioningly, as if trying to ascertain for himself what charm such a helpless crawling little animal could possibly have for the man who was his master and his idol.

Little by little Amelie's distrust lessened, and she was willing that the baby should lie in his crib on the sunny porch, when Caliban was stretched out on the steps with the little gray cat sleeping between his paws.

Then one day, after a morning of housework within doors, she came out to take the baby—and he was gone. The crib was empty, the little blankets were rumpled into confusion. The dog Caliban still lay sleeping upon the porch, and the little gray cat purred drowsily against his furry chest.

"Caliban," said Leon Suprenon sternly, "you have spoiled my belief in you. I will never be able to trust you again."

Amelie screamed, and the men came running up from the sheep pens and barns, snatching up sticks of wood, or fumbling with guns. Leon came running with a face the color of chalk; and Amelie clung to him, screaming, sobbing, wild with hysterical fear. She was certain that some wild animal had snatched her baby out of his crib and devoured him.

"Nonsense!" said Leon Suprenon positively. "No wild animal could have come near the house with Caliban on guard." After an hour of frantic searching, they found the child. Back of the ranch house where the garbage was dumped and burned, there they found the baby, playing happily with an old tin can, dirty and bedraggled, yet quite unhurt and unharmed.

In the first moment of acute relief, no one thought to question how the child had come so far. But afterward—

Leon stood in deep thought, staring down at Caliban, who returned his look steadily, unflinchingly, as was his wont. For the first time a doubt of the dog's integrity came into his mind. He knew Caliban's great strength, knew that the dog could have carried the baby as easily as he had carried the newborn lamb. And the garbage pile—there was a grim humor in that which pointed to Caliban's line of reasoning. Undesirable things were thrown out there; things put upon the garbage pile were never brought back into the house; therefore, if the baby were put out there, with the rest of the rubbish . . .

"Caliban, you devil!" said Leon Suprenon between clenched teeth. Yet he could not beat the dog. The evidence was only circumstantial.

Had the thing happened to any one else's child, he would have laughed heartily at the story. But to him it was not so funny. Anything might have happened to the child. The dog might have dropped it; or stray wolves might have come down out of the woods. The baby might have cut its hands terribly on broken glass or rusty tin cans.

"Caliban," said Leon Suprenon sternly, "you have spoiled my belief in you. I will never be able to trust you again."

The great ugly dog stared at him with those glittering, close-set eyes, then turned away abruptly and lay down. It was as if he accepted the defeat of his plans, the humiliation, the loss of his master's trust, with stoical resignation. It was almost as if he had shrugged his shoulders.

Now there came the winter time—a lean, terrible winter, when the wolves howled about the ranch, sometimes becoming so bold as to come close to the barns, and corrals, and the house.

The spring was late, and even when the snow began to melt, and the first warm breezes to come up from the south, still the howling of the wolf pack was heard on distant hills, and still tracks were found in the crusted snow about the barn and the sheep corrals.

One day in the spring an urgent message came to Amelie Suprenon, begging her to come to a neighboring ranch where a woman lay in child-birth.

She could only go on horseback—and the need for her help was imminent. She saddled her horse herself, for the men were out on the ranges. Then she hesitated as to leaving or taking the baby.

But Leon had said he would return at noon, and the sun was then almost at the zenith. She scribbled a note for him, put the baby in the bedroom in the little pen which Leon had made for it, and shut the door.

Then she mounted her horse and rode hard and fast to the woman who was in need of her.

Leon Suprenon did not get the note. A hint of spring sickness had come upon some of the sheep, and he worked all through the morning and late into the afternoon with sheep dip and sprays. When he was about to return to the ranch house, one of the men told him that he had seen Amelie riding by, at noon, in the direction of the Pourers' ranch. Leon frowned at it. He did not like to have Amelie ride alone, especially on the forest roads. He flung himself upon his horse, shouted to his men to go on with their work, and took a short cut across the fields to ride home with Amelie.

He met her just as she came out of the door, tired, but smiling. "Such a sweet little baby boy!" she called to Leon as he rode nearer. Then her face suddenly clouded.

"The baby—our baby—" she said uncertainly. "You did not leave him alone?"

Leon stared back at her, his forehead wrinkled.

"The baby?" he repeated. "Why, surely, Amelie, he is with you?" For an instant she did not reply. A slow fear was dawning in her heart that stretched her eyes wide and made them hard and glassy.

"No—no," she almost whispered. "I left a note—I thought you would come at noon. The baby then—he is there alone—perhaps with—*Caliban*—" Her voice died away, as if she were afraid of the name she had spoken.

Leon tried to laugh, to make light of her fears. But his lips were a bit stiff, and he breathed as he helped her into the saddle.

"Come, come, Amelie, you worry too much. The little one will be quite well—you shall see—only very hungry perhaps and exercising his small lungs terrifically. As for Caliban—"

Amelie slashed at her horse's flank with the whip. Her face was dead-white.

"Where was that dog—that terrible beast, when you came away?" she gasped as they galloped down the snowy road.

"I don't know," Leon jerked out grimly, as if thinking aloud. "I can't remember seeing him—yes, yes, he stood looking away toward the ranch house; I remember now that he barked once—then trotted away. I thought he was rounding up a sheep. I did not call him back. One of the men laughed and said that he was going to meet the Lady—"

"*Wolf!*" the girl finished hoarsely. "O *grand Dieu*, guard my baby! He is in danger, I tell you, Leon; I feel it, I know it! That beast—that horrible beast who mates with bloodthirsty wolves— you would not believe it, Leon, but I tell you it is true—true! Oh, my baby, my little baby!"

She lashed her horse with frenzied, hysterical hands, and the startled animal reared and plunged forward. Fast, faster, the slender hoofs pounded through the snowy slush of the road, and Leon's horse followed, breathing hard and straining at the bit.

They did not speak again, the husband and wife, but rode, rode as if for the saving of a life.

It was Amelie who dismounted first, when at the end of that wild ride her horse came to a stop, panting and trembling. She dashed the unlocked door wide open, and an instant later a wild scream sent the blood ebbing from Leon's face and made his hands numb clods of flesh as they fumbled for the gun in his belt.

The scene he saw as he stumbled through the hallway turned him sick with a deadly nausea of horror and despair.

Amelie lay fainting in the open doorway of the bedroom. Beyond, an empty cradle, an open window, with muddy tracks on the window sill, told a dreadful story. But the thing that made him cry out, savagely, hoarsely, was the dog—Caliban. The snarling, misshapen beast stood in the doorway, staring at him with red, malevolent eyes—*and there was blood on the heavy jowls and the thick-matted hair of the chest.*

"You—you devil!" Leon screamed like a madman—and fired.

The dog still stood there, just an instant. The small, close-set eyes blinked slightly, the ugly head jerked back once—and he fell in a silent, twitching heap.

"Oh, God! Oh, God!" Leon was sobbing, hardly knowing what he said or did. And then—he heard a baby crying.

Stunned, incredulous, almost believing himself in a tortured dream, the man went slowly forward. The baby lay behind the door, lay where it had been dragged to safety. It was crying with fright and was beating the air vaguely with its pink little hands. And over behind the dresser, in a pool of blood—lay a dead wolf.

"There is a grave on the ranch of Leon Suprenon," said French Louie solemnly, in the language of his people, "where the dog, Caliban, lies buried. And above it is a tombstone of marble—yes, the whitest of marble—with this inscription:

" 'Here lies Caliban, a dog. He died as he lived, misjudged, maligned, yet unafraid. In life he never failed in duty, and in death he was faithful to his trust.' '

"And dat is why," said Louie, the Frenchman, lapsing into the argot of his daily life, "dat I get so mad inside of me when people say animals dey have no souls. Did not the dog, Caliban, have a soul? Oh, *mon Dieu!* I know dis: when he died that day, and hees spirit went out of hees big, ugly body and rose up to the skies, the good Saint who guards the gates up dere he look out and say: 'Why, Caliban, ees dat you? Come in, *mon brave.* I did not know you. How beautiful you have grown!"

• • •

The greatest love is a mother's; then a dog's; then a sweetheart's.
—Polish proverb

the barking dog

zen master hsu yun

Master Hsu Yun (Empty Cloud) was the most famous Chinese Chan (Zen) master of the nineteenth and twentieth centuries. He was born circa 1839 in Guangzhou province, China, and died at Zhen Ru Monastery on October 13,1959. By all available accounts, he lived to be 120 years old. The Zen Buddhist Order of Hsu Yun is a virtual order, which one can easily access on the Internet at www .hsuyun.org. "The Barking Dog" is representative of the quietly powerful poetry of Hsu Yun.

We went up across the ridge for the fun of it.
Didn't need to pack any more wine.
On the precipice, flowers opened, smiling.
By the river, willows grew bright.
In the drizzling rain the village smoke congealed,
        concealed.

The wind was slight and the grass was cool.
There in the woods' underbrush, startled,
We suddenly heard a dog bark.
It wanted us to know the Master was aware.

for ashley whippet: a testimonial

mordecai siegal

By now you have probably read something about the passing of the great disc-catching dog that was known and admired by millions of fans, dog owners or not.

For the record, Ashley Whippet was born on June 4, 1971, in Oxford, Ohio. He died March 11, 1985, in Sierra Madre, California, in the arms of his owner, trainer, and best friend, Alex Stein, after a brief illness.

Sooner or later, all of us who love dogs must cope with the fact that they live only one-sixth as long as the average person. The result is the coming and going of many dogs in our lives. Pet owners enjoy fewer dogs than those more actively involved. So why is the passing of one thirteen-year-old Whippet receiving more attention than any other dog? Easy. He was very special. Truly, he was.

In the tradition of Ch. Braeburn's Close Encounter or Ch. My Own Brucie, adored crowd-pleasers, Ashley Whippet was a great dog. The public admired and adored him, as they did Brucie and Close Encounter.

To my knowledge, he never won a single conformation show and was probably not show material at all. But blue ribbons and silver trophies are not necessarily what make a great dog. Ashley's devoted fans could never boast of a single Best of Breed, much less a Best in Show, win. But if thrilling crowds of people by the millions is any mark of a special dog, then that little Whippet was something else.

His fame began in the summer of 1974, when his daring owner,

Alex Stein, smuggled him onto the field at Dodger Stadium during a tense pennant game between the Dodgers and the Cincinnati Reds. The two of them commenced to give a demonstration of "fetch" the likes of which had never been seen before. Alex sent a plastic Frisbee sailing high into the air and Ashley did his thing. He made spectacular leaps high into the air, catching the Frisbee in his mouth each time. The millions of fans in the stands and at home in front of their TV screens were amazed, amused, and absolutely thrilled with the unscheduled display. No one had ever seen a dog do that before. The show went on for eight brazen minutes as the crowd roared with delight. Alex Stein and Ashley Whippet went into the archives of baseball history. No one person, much less a dog, had in the past been able to steal a baseball crowd's attention away from a crucial game.

Sitting in the stands that day was Irv Lander, a Los Angeles public-relations consultant, who took dog and owner in tow and steered them into the successful career that ensued. I guess you should know that the team of Whippet and Stein went to jail for three days for their brazen stunt. Stein said of the incident, "I got thrown in the clink and Ashley was lost for three agonizing days."

When they were reunited, twenty-eight-pound Ashley went on to break all records, covering 106.5 yards at thirty-five miles per hour and winning the Catch & Fetch competition at the World Frisbee Championships for three consecutive years at the Rose Bowl.

Later he starred in *Floating Free,* a documentary nominated for an Academy Award, and in a television commercial for Cycle dog food; performed for Amy Carter at the White House and at halftime at Super Bowl XII; and appeared as a guest on such television programs as *The Tonight Show, Good Morning America,* the *Today* show, the *Merv Griffin Show,* and *Hour Magazine.*

This great canine athlete was honored by having the Gaines Ashley Whippet Invitational for disc-catching dogs named after him. Sponsored by the Gaines dog food company, the invitational is probably Ashley's greatest legacy.

In February 1981, I brought Ashley Whippet onto the TV show *Hour Magazine,* where I did the animal spots. The dog was a fabulous guest. He, Gary Collins, and I had a wonderful time as Ashley delighted the audience with his tremendous talent for leaping and catching. *Hour Magazine* was taped in Hollywood before a live audience. At the end of the segment, Gary and I hurled dozens of Frisbees into the audience. It took Alex Stein all he had to restrain the dog from leaping into the crowd to snap them up. What a delight he was.

The best part was the day before we taped the show. I had gotten off the plane from New York at noon and met Ashley, Alex, and their mentor, Irv Lander, along with a photographer, by three that afternoon. We gathered in a beautiful Los Angeles park, where I learned the proper way to throw a Frisbee. Both Stein and Ashley Whippet were my teachers and I had as enjoyable a time with them as I ever had anywhere in my life.

The death of Ashley Whippet is a sad loss. It is especially hard on Alex Stein, who claimed him for his "best friend." I'll never watch a pennant game again without imagining at least one spectacular leap from that brilliant Whippet who stole our hearts and captured our imagination. We'll miss you, Ashley Whippet. But we'll be watching for your offspring, Lady Ashley and Ashley Whippet, Jr., who have great paw prints to fill.

• • •

*It is fatal to let any dog know she is funny, for she immediately
loses her head and starts hamming it up.*
—P. G. Wodehouse

a dog's best friend

anonymous

O Lord, don't let me once forget,
How I love my trusty pet—
Help me learn to disregard
Canine craters in my yard.
Show me how to be a buddy
Even when my sofa's muddy.
Don't allow my pooch to munch
Postal carriers for lunch.
Shield my neighbor's cat from view,
Guide my steps around the doo.
Train me not to curse and scowl
When it's puppy's night to howl.
Grant I shan't awake in fear
With a cold nose in my ear.
Give me patience without end—
Help me be "A DOG'S BEST FRIEND."

a prayer for animals

albert schweitzer

Hear our humble prayer, O God,
for our friends the animals,
especially for animals who are suffering;
for any that are hunted or lost or deserted
or frightened or hungry;
for all that must be put to death.
We entreat for them all Thy mercy and pity,
and for those who deal with them
we ask a heart of compassions and gentle hands and kindly
words.
Make us, ourselves, to be true friends to animals
and so to share the blessings of the merciful.

part eight

litter-ature

If you eliminate smoking and gambling, you will be amazed
to find that almost all an Englishman's pleasures can
be, and mostly are, shared by his dog.
—George Barnard Shaw

peter pan

j. m. barrie

Author and playwright James Barrie (1860–1937) was the creator of Peter Pan, the boy who refused to grow up. No literary figure knows in advance, if ever, that a particular work will live on past his or her lifetime. Barrie, however, lived long enough to see his story grow in popularity and in stature as Peter entered the culture permanently as an iconic character representing boys who resist growing up and refuse to leave childhood. The tale of Peter Pan had its genesis in the games and stories that Barrie shared with the Llewelyn Davies boys. Barrie's novel, *The Little White Bird* (1902), draws on some of these experiences. Already established as a London dramatist, Barrie transformed the stories of Peter into a complete stage play, produced in 1904, and it became a huge success. Among his works of fiction are *Auld Licht Idylls* (1888) and *A Window in Thrums* (1889). Barrie's reputation was largely based on his work for the London stage beginning in 1889 with a dramatization of his novel *A Window in Thrums*. Other plays include *The Little Minister* (1891), *Quality Street* (1901), *The Admirable Crichton* (1902), *What Every Woman Knows* (1908), *The Twelve-Pound Look* (1910), *The Will* (1913), and *Dear Brutus* (1917).

The story of Peter Pan is about a fantastic, whimsical character who enters into the London bedroom of three children, Wendy, John, and Michael Darling, and entices them to fly with him to Neverland where they have many adventures with Peter's Lost Boys, Tinker Bell, and Peter's nemesis, Captain Hook. What makes this story appropriate for this book is the character of Nana, a dedicated Newfoundland dog that is "employed" by the children's father as a nurse to take care of them, an economic measure. In this story, the dog, although silent, is drawn in almost human terms.

from chapter one: peter breaks through

All children, except one, grow up. They soon know that they will grow up, and the way Wendy knew was this. One day when she was two years old she was playing in a garden, and she plucked another flower and ran with it to her mother. I suppose she must have looked rather delightful, for Mrs. Darling put her hand to her heart and cried, "Oh, why can't you remain like this for ever!" This was all that passed between them on the subject, but henceforth Wendy knew that she must grow up. You always know after you are two. Two is the beginning of the end.

Of course they lived at 14, and until Wendy came her mother was the chief one. She was a lovely lady, with a romantic mind and such a sweet mocking mouth. Her romantic mind was like the tiny boxes, one within the other, that come from the puzzling East, however many you discover there is always one more; and her sweet mocking mouth had one kiss on it that Wendy could never get, though there it was, perfectly conspicuous in the right-hand corner.

The way Mr. Darling won her was this: the many gentlemen who had been boys when she was a girl discovered simultaneously that they loved her, and they all ran to her house to propose to her except Mr. Darling, who took a cab and nipped in first, and so he got her. He got all of her, except the innermost box and the kiss. He never knew about the box, and in time he gave up trying for the kiss. Wendy thought Napoleon could have got it, but I can picture him trying, and then going off in a passion, slamming the door.

Mr. Darling used to boast to Wendy that her mother not only loved him but respected him. He was one of those deep ones who know about stocks and shares. Of course no one really knows, but he quite seemed to know, and he often said stocks were up and shares were down in a way that would have made any woman respect him.

Mrs. Darling was married in white, and at first she kept the books perfectly, almost gleefully, as if it were a game, not so much as a Brussels sprout was missing; but by and by whole cauliflowers dropped out, and instead of them there were pictures of babies without faces. She drew them when she should have been totting up. They were Mrs. Darling's guesses.

Wendy came first, then John, then Michael.

For a week or two after Wendy came it was doubtful whether they would be able to keep her, as she was another mouth to feed. Mr. Darling was frightfully proud of her, but he was very honourable, and he sat on the edge of Mrs. Darling's bed, holding her hand and calculating expenses, while she looked at him imploringly. She wanted to risk it, come what might, but that was not his way; his way was with a pencil and a piece of paper, and if she confused him with suggestions he had to begin at the beginning again.

"Now don't interrupt," he would beg of her. "I have one

. . . Mr. Darling had a passion for being exactly like his neighbours; so of course, they had a nurse. As they were poor, owing to the amount of milk the children drank, this nurse was a prim Newfoundland dog, called Nana, who had belonged to no one in particular until the Darlings engaged her.

pound seventeen here, and two and six at the office; I can cut off my coffee at the office, say ten shillings, making two nine and six, with your eighteen and three makes three nine seven, with five naught naught in my cheque-book makes eight nine seven—who is that moving?—eight nine seven, dot and carry seven—don't speak, my own—and the pound you lent to that man who came to the door—quiet, child—dot and carry child—there, you've done it!—did I say nine nine seven? yes, I said nine nine seven; the question is, can we try it for a year on nine nine seven?"

"Of course we can, George," she cried. But she was prejudiced in Wendy's favour, and he was really the grander character of the two.

"Remember mumps," he warned her almost threateningly, and off he went again. "Mumps one pound, that is what I have put down, but I daresay it will be more like thirty shillings—don't speak—measles one five, German measles half a guinea, makes two fifteen six—don't waggle your finger—whooping-cough, say fifteen shillings"—and so on it went, and it added up differently each time; but at last Wendy just got through, with mumps reduced to twelve six, and the two kinds of measles treated as one.

There was the same excitement over John, and Michael had even a narrower squeak; but both were kept, and soon you might have seen the three of them going in a row to Miss Fulsom's Kindergarten school, accompanied by their nurse.

Mrs. Darling loved to have everything just so, and Mr. Darling had a passion for being exactly like his neighbours; so of course, they had a nurse. As they were poor, owing to the amount of milk the children drank, this nurse was a prim Newfoundland dog, called Nana, who had belonged to no one in particular until the Darlings engaged her. She had always thought children important, however, and the Darlings had become acquainted with her in Kensington Gardens, where she spent most of her spare time peeping into perambulators, and was much hated by careless nurse-maids, whom she followed to their homes and complained of to their mistresses. She proved to be quite a treasure of a nurse. How thorough she was at bath-time; and up at any moment of the night if one of her charges made the slightest cry. Of course, her kennel was in the nursery. She had a genius for knowing when a cough is a thing to have patience with and when it needs a stocking around your throat. She believed to her last day in old-fashioned remedies like rhubarb leaf, and made sounds of contempt over all this new-fangled talk about germs, and so on. It was a lesson in propriety to see her escorting the children to school, walking sedately by their side when they were well behaved, and butting them back into line if they strayed. On John's soccer days she never once forgot his sweater, and she usually carried an umbrella in her mouth in case of rain. There is a room in the basement of Miss Fulsom's school where the nurses wait. They sat on forms, while Nana lay on the floor, but that was the only difference. They affected to ignore her as if an inferior social status to themselves, and she despised their light talk. She resented visits to the nursery from Mrs. Darling's friends, but if they did come she first whipped off Michael's pinafore and put him into the one with blue braiding, and smoothed out Wendy and made a dash at John's hair.

No nursery could possibly have been conducted more correctly, and Mr. Darling knew it, yet he sometimes wondered uneasily whether the neighbours talked.

He had his position in the city to consider.

Nana also troubled him in another way. He had sometimes a feeling that she did not admire him. "I know she admires you tremendously, George," Mrs. Darling would assure him, and then she would sign to the children to be specially nice to father. Lovely dances followed, in which the only other servant, Liza, was some-times allowed to join. Such a midget she looked in her long skirt and maid's cap, though she had sworn, when engaged, that she would never see ten again. The gaiety of these romps! And gayest of all was Mrs. Darling, who would pirouette so wildly that all you could see of her was the kiss, and then if you had dashed at her you might have got it. There never was a simpler happier fam-ily until the coming of Peter Pan.

Mrs. Darling first heard of Peter when she was tidying up her children's minds. It is the nightly custom of every good mother af-ter her children are asleep to rummage in their minds and put things straight for next morning, repacking into their proper places the many articles that have wandered during the day. If you could keep awake (but of course you can't) you would see your own mother doing this, and you would find it very interesting to

watch her. It is quite like tidying up drawers. You would see her on
her knees, I expect, lingering humorously over some of your contents, wondering where on earth you had picked this thing up,
making discoveries sweet and not so sweet, pressing this to her
cheek as if it were as nice as a kitten, and hurriedly stowing that
out of sight. When you wake in the morning, the naughtiness and
evil passions with which you went to bed have been folded up
small and placed at the bottom of your mind; and on the top,
beautifully aired, are spread out your prettier thoughts, ready for
you to put on.

I don't know whether you have ever seen a map of a person's
mind. Doctors sometimes draw maps of other parts of you, and
your own map can become intensely interesting, but catch them
trying to draw a map of a child's mind, which is not only confused, but keeps going round all the time. There are zigzag lines on
it, just like your temperature on a card, and these are probably
roads in the island; for the Neverland is always more or less an island, with astonishing splashes of colour here and there, and
coral reefs and rakish-looking craft in the offing, and savages and
lonely lairs, and gnomes who are mostly tailors, and caves through
which a river runs, and princes with six elder brothers, and a hut
fast going to decay, and one very small old lady with a hooked
nose. It would be an easy map if that were all, but there is also first
day at school, religion, fathers, the round pond, needle-work, mur-
ders, hangings, verbs that take the dative, chocolate pudding day,
getting into braces, say ninety-nine, three-pence for pulling out
your tooth yourself and so on, and either these are part of the
island or they are another map showing through, and it is all
rather confusing, especially as nothing will stand still.

Mrs. Darling consulted Mr. Darling, but he smiled pooh-pooh.
"Mark my words," he said, "it is
some nonsense Nana has been
putting into their heads; just the
sort of idea a dog would have.
Leave it alone, and it will blow
over."

Of course the Neverlands vary a good deal. John's, for instance, had a lagoon with flamingoes flying over it at which John was shooting, while Michael, who was very small, had a flamingo with lagoons flying over it. John lived in a boat turned upside down on the sands, Michael in a wigwam, Wendy in a house of leaves deftly sewn together. John had no friends, Michael had friends at night, Wendy had a pet wolf forsaken by its parents, but on the whole the Neverlands have a family resemblance, and if they stood still in a row you could say of them that they have each other's nose, and so forth. On these magic shores children at play are forever beaching their coracles. We too have been there; we can still hear the sound of the surf, though we shall land no more.

Of all delectable islands the Neverland is the snuggest and most compact, not large and sprawly, you know, with tedious distances between one adventure and another, but nicely crammed. When you play at it by day with the chairs and table-cloth, it is not in the least alarming, but in the two minutes before you go to sleep it becomes very real. That is why there are night-lights.

Occasionally in her travels through her children's minds Mrs. Darling found things she could not understand and of these quite the most perplexing was the word Peter. She knew of no Peter, and yet he was here and there in John and Michael's minds, while Wendy's began to be scrawled all over with him. The name stood out in bolder letters than any of the other words, and as Mrs. Darling gazed she felt that it had an oddly cocky appearance.

"Yes, he is rather cocky," Wendy admitted with regret. Her mother had been questioning her.

"But who is he, my pet?"

"He is Peter Pan, you know, mother."

At first Mrs. Darling did not know, but after thinking back into her childhood she just remembered a Peter Pan who was said to live with the fairies. There were odd stories about him, as that when children died he went part of the way with them, so that they should not be frightened. She had believed in him at the time, but now that she was married and full of sense she quite doubted whether there was any such person.

"Besides," she said to Wendy, "he would be grown up by this time."

"Oh no, he isn't grown up," Wendy assured her confidently, "and he is just my size." She meant that he was her size in both mind and body; she didn't know how she knew, she just knew it.

Mrs. Darling consulted Mr. Darling, but he smiled pooh-pooh. "Mark my words," he said, "it is some nonsense Nana has been putting into their heads; just the sort of idea a dog would have. Leave it alone, and it will blow over."

from chapter two: the shadow

. . . It was dreadful the way all the three were looking at him, just as if they did not admire him. "Look here, all of you," he said entreatingly, as soon as Nana had gone into the bathroom, "I have just thought of a splendid joke. I shall pour my medicine into Nan's bowl, and she will drink it, thinking it is milk!"

It was the colour of milk; but the children did not have their father's sense of humour, and they looked at him reproachfully as he poured the medicine into Nana's bowl. "What fun," he said doubtfully, and they did not dare expose him when Mrs. Darling and Nana returned.

"Nana, good dog," he said, patting her, "I have put a little milk into your bowl, Nana."

Nana wagged her tail, ran to the medicine, and began lapping it. Then she gave Mr. Darling such a look, not an angry look: she showed him the great red tear that makes us so sorry for noble dogs, and crept into her kennel.

Mr. Darling was frightfully ashamed of himself, but he would not give in. In a horrid silence Mrs. Darling smelt the bowl. "O George," she said, "it's your medicine!"

"It was only a joke," he roared, while she comforted her boys, and Wendy hugged Nana. "Much good," he said bitterly, "my wearing myself to the bone trying to be funny in this house."

And still Wendy hugged Nana. "That's right," he shouted. "Coddle her! Nobody coddles me. Oh dear no! I am only the bread-winner, why should I be coddled—why, why, why!"

"George," Mrs. Darling entreated him, "not so loud; the servants will hear you." Somehow they had got into the way of calling Liza the servants.

"Let them," he answered recklessly. "Bring in the whole world. But I refuse to allow that dog to lord it in my nursery for an hour longer."

The children wept, and Nana ran to him beseechingly, but he waved her back. He felt he was a strong man again.

"In vain, in vain," he cried; "the proper place for you is the yard, and there you go to be tied up this instant."

"George, George," Mrs. Darling whispered, "remember what I told you about that boy."

Alas, he would not listen. He was determined to show who was master in that house, and when commands would not draw Nana from the kennel, he lured her out of it with honeyed words, and seizing her roughly, dragged her from the nursery. He was ashamed of himself, and yet he did it. It was all owing to his too affectionate nature which craved for admiration. When he had tied her up in the back-yard, the wretched father went and sat in the passage, with his knuckles to his eyes.

In the meantime Mrs. Darling had put the children to bed in unwonted silence and lit their night-lights. They could hear Nana barking, and John whimpered, "It's because he is chaining her up in the yard," but Wendy was wiser.

"That is not Nana's unhappy bark," she said, little guessing what was about to happen; "that is her bark when she smells danger."

Danger!

"Are you sure, Wendy?"

"Oh yes."

Mrs. Darling quivered and went to the window. It was securely fastened. She looked out, and the night was peppered with stars. They were crowding round the house, as if curious to see what was to take place there, but she did not notice this, nor that one or two of the smaller ones winked at her. Yet a nameless fear clutched at her heart and made her cry, "Oh, how I wish that I wasn't going to a party to-night!"

Even Michael, already half asleep, knew that she was perturbed, and he asked, "Can anything harm us, mother, after the night-lights are lit?"

"Nothing, precious," she said; "they are the eyes a mother leaves behind her to guard her children."

She went from bed to bed singing enchantments over them and little Michael flung his arms round her. "Mother," he cried, "I'm glad of you." They were the last words she was to hear from him for a long time.

No. 27 was only a few yards distant, but there had been a slight fall of snow, and Father and Mother Darling picked their way over it deftly not to soil their shoes. They were already the only persons in the street, and all the stars were watching them. Stars are beautiful, but they may not take an active part in anything, they must just look on for ever. It is a punishment put on them for something they did so long ago that no star now knows what it was. So the older ones have become glassy-eyed and seldom speak (winking is the star language), but the little ones still wonder. They are not really friendly to Peter, who has a mischievous way of stealing up behind them and trying to blow them out; but they are so fond of fun that they were on his side to-night, and anxious to get the grown-ups out of the way. So as soon as the door of 27 closed on Mr. and Mrs. Darling there was a commotion in the firmament, and the smallest of all the stars in the Milky Way screamed out:

"Now, Peter!"

• • •

Blessed is the person who has earned the love of an old dog.
—Sidney Jeanne Seward

that spot

jack london

I don't think much of Stephen Mackaye any more, though I used to swear by him. I know that in those days I loved him more than my own brother. If ever I meet Stephen Mackaye again, I shall not be responsible for my actions. It passes beyond me that a man with whom I shared food and blanket, and with whom I mushed over the Chilcoot Trail, should turn out the way he did. I always sized Steve up as a square man, a kindly comrade, without an iota of anything vindictive or malicious in his nature. I shall never trust my judgment in men again. Why, I nursed that man through typhoid fever; we starved together on the headwaters of the Stewart; and he saved my life on the Little Salmon. And now, after the years we were together, all I can say of Stephen Mackaye is that he is the meanest man I ever knew.

We started for the Klondike in the fall rush of 1897, and we started too late to get over Chilcoot Pass before the freeze-up. We packed our outfit on our backs part way over, when the snow began to fly, and then we had to buy dogs in order to sled it the rest of the way. That was how we came to get that Spot. Dogs were high, and we paid one hundred and ten dollars for him. He looked worth it. I say looked, because he was one of the finest-appearing dogs I ever saw. He weighed sixty pounds, and he had all the lines of a good sled animal. We never could make out his breed. He wasn't husky, nor Malemute, nor Hudson Bay; he looked like all of them and he didn't look like any of them; and on top of it all he had some of the white man's dog in him, for on one side, in the thick of the mixed yellow-brown-red-and-dirty-white that was his prevailing color, there was a spot of coal-black as big as a water-bucket. That was why we called him Spot.

He was a good looker all right. When he was in condition his muscles stood out in bunches all over him. And he was the strongest-looking brute I ever saw in Alaska, also the most intelligent-looking. To run your eyes over him, you'd think he could outpull three dogs of his own weight. Maybe he could, but I never saw it. His intelligence didn't run that way. He could steal and forage to perfection; he had an instinct that was positively grewsome for divining when work was to be done and for making a sneak accordingly; and for getting lost and not staying lost he was nothing short of inspired. But when it came to work, the way that intelligence dribbled out of him and left him a mere clot of wobbling, stupid jelly would make your heart bleed.

There are times when I think it wasn't stupidity. Maybe, like some men I know, he was too wise to work. I shouldn't wonder if he put it all over us with that intelligence of his. Maybe he figured it all out and decided that a licking now and again and no work was a whole lot better than work all the time and no licking. He was intelligent enough for such a computation. I tell you, I've sat and looked into that dog's eyes till the shivers ran up and down my spine and the marrow crawled like yeast, what of the intelligence I saw shining out. I can't express myself about that intelligence. It is beyond mere words. I saw it, that's all. At times it was like gazing into a human soul, to look into his eyes; and what I saw there frightened me and started all sorts of ideas in my own mind of reincarnation and all the rest. I tell you I sensed something big in that brute's eyes; there was a message there, but I wasn't big enough myself to catch it. Whatever it was (I know I'm making a

fool of myself)—whatever it was, it baffled me. I can't give an
inkling of what I saw in that brute's eyes; it wasn't light, it wasn't
color; it was something that moved, away back, when the eyes
themselves weren't moving. And I guess I didn't see it move, either;
I only sensed that it moved. It was an expression,—that's what it
was,—and I got an impression of it. No; it was different from a
mere expression; it was more than that. I don't know what it was,
but it gave me a feeling of kinship just the same. Oh, no, not sentimental kinship. It was, rather, a kinship of equality. Those eyes
never pleaded like a deer's eyes. They challenged. No, it wasn't de-
fiance. It was just a calm assumption of equality. And I don't think
it was deliberate. My belief is that it was unconscious on his part.
It was there because it was there, and it couldn't help shining out.
No, I don't mean shine. It didn't shine; it moved. I know I'm talking rot, but if you'd looked into that animal's eyes the way I have,
you'd understand. Steve was affected the same way I was. Why, I
tried to kill that Spot once—he was no good for anything; and
I fell down on it. I led him out into the brush, and he came along
slow and unwilling. He knew what was going on. I stopped in a
likely place, put my foot on the rope, and pulled my big Colt's.
And that dog sat down and looked at me. I tell you he didn't plead.
He just looked. And I saw all kinds of incomprehensible things
moving, yes, moving, in those eyes of his. I didn't really see them
move; I thought I saw them, for, as I said before, I guess I only
sensed them. And I want to tell you right now that it got beyond
me. It was like killing a man, a conscious, brave man who looked
calmly into your gun as much as to say, "Who's afraid?" Then, too,
the message seemed so near that, instead of pulling the trigger
quick, I stopped to see if I could catch the message. There it was,
right before me, glimmering all around in those eyes of his. And
then it was too late. I got scared. I was trembly all over, and my
stomach generated a nervous palpitation that made me seasick. I
just sat down and looked at that dog, and he looked at me, till
I thought I was going crazy. Do you want to know what I did?

I threw down the gun and ran back to camp with the fear of God in my heart. Steve laughed at me. But I notice that Steve led Spot into the woods, a week later, for the same purpose, and that Steve came back alone, and a little later Spot drifted back, too.

At any rate, Spot wouldn't work. We paid a hundred and ten dollars for him from the bottom of our sack, and he wouldn't work. He wouldn't even tighten the traces. Steve spoke to him the first time we put him in harness, and he sort of shivered, that was all. Not an ounce on the traces. He just stood still and wobbled, like so much jelly. Steve touched him with the whip. He yelped, but not an ounce. Steve touched him again, a bit harder, and he howled—the regular long wolf howl. Then Steve got mad and gave him half a dozen, and I came on the run from the tent.

I told Steve he was brutal with the animal, and we had some words—the first we'd ever had. He threw the whip down in the snow and walked away mad. I picked it up and went to it. That Spot trembled and wobbled and cowered before ever I swung the lash, and with the first bite of it he howled like a lost soul. Next he lay down in the snow. I started the rest of the dogs, and they dragged him along while I threw the whip into him. He rolled over on his back and bumped along, his four legs waving in the air, himself howling as though he was going through a sausage machine. Steve came back and laughed at me, and I apologized for what I'd said.

There was no getting any work out of that Spot; and to make up for it, he was the biggest pig-glutton of a dog I ever saw. On top of that, he was the cleverest thief. There was no circumventing him. Many a breakfast we went without our bacon because Spot had been there first. And it was because of him that we nearly starved to death up the Stewart.

We made money out of Spot. If we sold him once, we sold him twenty times. He always came back, and no one asked for their money. We didn't want the money. We'd have paid handsomely for any one to take him off our hands for keeps.

He figured out the way to break into our meat-cache, and what he didn't eat, the rest of the team did. But he was impartial. He stole from everybody. He was a restless dog, always very busy snooping around or going somewhere. And there was never a camp within five miles that he didn't raid. The worst of it was that they always came back on us to pay his board bill, which was just, being the law of the land; but it was mighty hard on us, especially that first winter on the Chilcoot, when we were busted, paying for whole hams and sides of bacon that we never ate. He could fight, too, that Spot. He could do everything but work. He never pulled a pound, but he was the boss of the whole team. The way he made those dogs stand around was an education. He bullied them, and there was always one or more of them fresh-marked with his fangs. But he was more than a bully. He wasn't afraid of anything that walked on four legs; and I've seen him march, single-handed, into a strange team, without any provocation whatever, and put the kibosh on the whole outfit. Did I say he could eat? I caught him eating the whip once. That's straight. He started in at the lash, and when I caught him he was down to the handle, and still going.

But he was a good looker. At the end of the first week we sold him for seventy-five dollars to the Mounted Police. They had experienced dog-drivers, and we knew that by the time he'd covered the six hundred I miles to Dawson he'd be a good sled-dog. I say we knew, for we were just getting acquainted with that Spot. A little later we were not brash enough to know anything where he was concerned. A week later we woke up in the morning to the dangdest dog-fight we'd ever heard. It was that Spot come back and knocking the team into shape. We ate a pretty depressing breakfast, I can tell you; but cheered up two hours afterward when we sold him to an official courier, bound in to Dawson with government despatches. That Spot

> "What that dog needs is space," Steve said the second day. "Let's maroon him."

was only three days in coming back, and, as usual, celebrated his arrival with a rough-house.

We spent the winter and spring, after our own outfit was across the pass, freighting other people's outfits; and we made a fat stake. Also, we made money out of Spot. If we sold him once, we sold him twenty times. He always came back, and no one asked for their money. We didn't want the money. We'd have paid handsomely for any one to take him off our hands for keeps. We had to get rid of him, and we couldn't give him away, for that would have been suspicious. But he was such a fine looker that we never had any difficulty in selling him. "Unbroke," we'd say, and they'd pay any old price for him. We sold him as low as twenty-five dollars, and once we got a hundred and fifty for him. That particular party returned him in person, refused to take his money back, and the way he abused us was something awful. He said it was cheap at the price to tell us what he thought of us; and we felt he was so justified that we never talked back. But to this day I've never quite regained all the old self-respect that was mine before that man talked to me.

When the ice cleared out of the lakes and river, we put our outfit in a Lake Bennett boat and started for Dawson. We had a good team of dogs, and of course we piled them on top the outfit. That Spot was along—there was no losing him; and a dozen times, the first day, he knocked one or another of the dogs overboard in the course of fighting with them. It was close quarters, and he didn't like being crowded.

"What that dog needs is space," Steve said the second day. "Let's maroon him."

We did, running the boat in at Caribou Crossing for him to jump ashore. Two of the other dogs, good dogs, followed him; and we lost two whole days trying to find them. We never saw those two dogs again; but the quietness and relief we enjoyed made us decide, like the man who refused his hundred and fifty, that it was cheap at the price. For the first time in months Steve and I laughed and whistled and sang. We were as happy as clams. The dark days were over. The nightmare had been lifted. That Spot was gone.

Three weeks later, one morning, Steve and I were standing on the river-bank at Dawson. A small boat was just arriving from Lake Bennett. I saw Steve give a start, and heard him say something that was not nice and that was not under his breath. Then I looked; and there, in the bow of the boat, with ears pricked up, sat Spot. Steve and I sneaked immediately, like beaten curs, like cowards, like absconders from justice. It was this last that the lieutenant of police thought when he saw us sneaking. He surmised that there were law-officers in the boat who were after us. He didn't wait to find out, but kept us in sight, and in the M. &. M. saloon got us in a corner. We had a merry time explaining, for we refused to go back to the boat and meet Spot; and finally he held us under guard of another policeman while he went to the boat. After we got clear of him, we started for the cabin, and when we arrived, there was that Spot sitting on the stoop waiting for us. Now how did he know we lived there? There were forty thousand people in Dawson that summer, and how did he savve our cabin out of all the cabins ? How did he know we were in Dawson, anyway? I leave it to you. But don't forget what I have said about his intelligence and that immortal something I have seen glimmering in his eyes.

There was no getting rid of him any more. There were too many people in Dawson who had bought him up on Chilcoot, and the story got around. Half a dozen times we put him on board steamboats going down the Yukon; but he merely went ashore at the first landing and trotted back up the bank. We couldn't sell him, we couldn't kill him (both Steve and I had tried), and nobody else was able to kill him. He bore a charmed life. I've seen him go down in a dog-fight on the main street with fifty dogs on top of him, and when they were separated, he'd appear on all his four legs, unharmed, while two of the dogs that had been on top of him would be lying dead.

I saw him steal a chunk of moose-meat from Major Dinwiddie's cache so heavy that he could just keep one jump ahead of Mrs. Dinwiddie's squaw cook, who was after him with an axe. As he went up the hill, after the squaw gave up, Major Dinwiddie himself came out and pumped his Winchester into the landscape. He emptied his magazine twice, and never touched that Spot. Then a policeman came along and arrested him for discharging firearms inside the city limits. Major Dinwiddie paid his fine, and Steve and I paid him for the moose-meat at the rate of a dollar a pound, bones and all. That was what he paid for it. Meat was high that year.

I am only telling what I saw with my own eyes. And now I'll tell you something, also. I saw that Spot fall through a water-hole. The ice was three and a half feet thick, and the current sucked him under like a straw. Three hundred yards below was the big water-hole used by the hospital. Spot crawled out of the hospital water-hole, licked off the water, bit out the ice that had formed between his toes, trotted up the bank, and whipped a big Newfoundland belonging to the Gold Commissioner.

In the fall of 1898, Steve and I poled up the Yukon on the last water, bound for Stewart River. We took the dogs along, all except Spot. We figured we'd been feeding him long enough. He'd cost us more time and trouble and money and grub than we'd got by selling him on the Chilcoot—especially grub. So Steve and I tied him down in the cabin and pulled our freight. We camped that night at the mouth of Indian River, and Steve and I were pretty facetious over having shaken him. Steve was a funny cuss, and I was just sitting up in the blankets and laughing when a tornado hit camp. The way that Spot walked into those dogs and gave them what-for was hair-raising. Now how did he get loose? It's up to you. I haven't any theory. And how did he get across the Klondike River? That's another lacer. And anyway, how did he know we had gone up the Yukon? You see, we went by water, and he couldn't smell our tracks. Steve and I began to get superstitious about that dog. He got on our nerves, too; and, between you and me, we were just a mite afraid of him.

The freeze-up came on when we were at the mouth of Henderson Creek, and we traded him off for two sacks of flour to an outfit that was bound up White River after copper. Now that whole outfit was lost. Never trace nor hide nor hair of men, dogs, sleds, or anything was ever found. They dropped clean out of sight. It became one of the mysteries of the country. Steve and I plugged away up the Stewart, and six weeks afterward that Spot crawled into camp. He was a perambulating skeleton, and could just drag along; but he got there. And what I want to know is who told him we were up the Stewart? We could have gone a thousand other places. How did he know? You tell me, and I'll tell you.

No losing him. At the Mayo he started a row with an Indian dog. The buck who owned the dog took a swing at Spot with an axe, missed him, and killed his own dog. Talk about magic and turning bullets aside—I, for one, consider it a blamed sight harder to turn an axe aside with a big buck at the other end of it. And I saw him do it with my own eyes. That buck didn't want to kill his own dog. You've got to show me.

I told you about Spot breaking into our meat-cache. It was nearly the death of us. There wasn't any more meat to be killed, and meat was all we had to live on. The moose had gone back several hundred miles and the Indians with them. There we were. Spring was on, and we had to wait for the river to break. We got pretty thin before we decided to eat the dogs, and we decided to eat Spot first. Do you know what that dog did? He sneaked. Now how did he know our minds were made up to eat him? We sat up nights laying for him, but he never came back, and we ate the other dogs. We ate the whole team.

And now for the sequel. You know what it is when a big river breaks up and a few billion tons of ice go out, jamming and milling and grinding. Just in the thick of it, when the Stewart went out, rumbling and roaring, we sighted Spot out in the middle. He'd got caught as he was trying to cross up above somewhere. Steve and I yelled and shouted and ran up and down the bank, tossing our hats in the air. Sometimes we'd stop and hug each other, we were that boisterous, for we saw Spot's finish. He didn't have a chance in a million. He didn't have any chance at all. After the ice-run, we got into a canoe and paddled down to the Yukon, and down the Yukon to Dawson, stopping to feed up for a week at the cabins at the mouth of Henderson Creek. And as we came in to the bank at Dawson, there sat that Spot, waiting for us, his ears pricked up, his tail wagging, his mouth smiling, extending a hearty welcome to us. Now how did he get out of that ice? How did he know we were coming to Dawson, to the very hour and minute, to be out there on the bank waiting for us?

The more I think of that Spot, the more I am convinced that there are things in this world that go beyond science. On no scientific grounds can that Spot be explained. It's psychic phenomena, or mysticism, or something of that sort, I guess, with a lot of Theosophy thrown in. The Klondike is a good country. I might have been there yet, and become a millionaire, if it hadn't been for Spot. He got on my nerves. I stood him for two years all together, and then I guess my stamina broke. It was the summer of 1899 when I pulled out. I didn't say anything to Steve. I just sneaked. But I fixed it up all right. I wrote Steve a note, and enclosed a package of "rough-on-rats," telling him what to do with it. I was worn down to skin and bone by that Spot, and I was that nervous that I'd jump and look around when there wasn't anybody within hailing distance. But it was astonishing the way I recuperated when I got quit of him. I got back twenty pounds before I arrived in San Francisco, and by the time I'd crossed the ferry to Oakland I was my old self again, so that even my wife looked in vain for any change in me.

Steve wrote to me once, and his letter seemed irritated. He took it kind of hard because I'd left him with Spot. Also, he said he'd used the "rough-on-rats," per directions, and that there was nothing doing. A year went by. I was back in the office and prospering in all ways—even getting a bit fat. And then Steve arrived. He didn't look me up. I read his name in the steamer list, and wondered why. But I didn't wonder long. I got up one morning and found that Spot chained to the gate-post and holding up the milkman. Steve went north to Seattle, I learned, that very morning. I didn't put on any more weight. My wife made me buy him a collar and tag, and within an hour he showed his gratitude by killing her pet Persian cat. There is no getting rid of that Spot. He will be with me until I die, for he'll never die. My appetite is not so good since he arrived, and my wife says I am looking peaked. Last night that Spot got into Mr. Harvey's hen-house (Harvey is my next door neighbor) and killed nineteen of his fancy-bred chickens. I shall have to pay for them. My neighbors on the other side quarreled with my wife and then moved out. Spot was the cause of it. And that is why I am disappointed in Stephen Mackaye. I had no idea he was so mean a man.

• • •

Don't accept your dog's admiration as conclusive
evidence that you are wonderful.
—Ann Landers

underdog

mordecai siegal

No dogs allowed without proper papers,
No cure for the common cur.
"No mutts, if you please," said the let- 'em-eat-cakers,
"Can't stand that mixed colored fur."

But Darwin still haunts us with graven glee,
He smirks in the ghostly fog.
"Bananas and trees are man's pedigree,
He's just one more underdog!"

dandy: the story of a dog

w. h. hudson

"Dandy" is one of many stories, essays, and sketches that first appeared in various magazines before being published in the collection *A Traveller in Little Things*, in 1921. Author William Henry Hudson (1841–1922), a prolific writer, naturalist, and ornithologist, was born in Buenos Aires, Argentina, to Anglo-American parents and spent his childhood wandering on the pampas among gauchos, shepherds, and flocks of wildlife. His was a childhood filled with adventure and wonder until he was stricken by typhus and a few years afterward by rheumatic fever, which weakened his heart. Eventually, he emigrated to England in 1870, where he struggled as a writer for a number of years. His first book was published as *The Purple Land That England Lost* in 1885 and is now known simply as *The Purple Land*. It was very popular and launched his long, successful literary career first in nonfiction and then fiction. His books on ornithology are still available in print and much of his writing is filled with colorful and fascinating descriptions of birds and plant life. Hudson was honored by both the British and Argentinean governments, who each have claimed him for one of their own.

He was of mixed breed, and was supposed to have a strain of Dandy Dinmont blood, which gave him his name. A big ungainly animal with a rough shaggy coat of blue-gray hair and white on his neck and clumsy paws, he looked like a Sussex sheep dog with legs reduced to half their proper length. He was, when I first knew him, getting old and increasingly deaf and dim of sight, otherwise in the best of health and spirits, or at all events very good tempered.

Until I knew Dandy I had always supposed that the story of Ludlam's dog was pure invention, and I dare say that is the general opinion about it; but Dandy made me reconsider the subject, and eventually I came to believe that Ludlam's dog did exist once upon a time, centuries ago perhaps, and that if he had been the laziest dog in the world Dandy was not far behind him in that respect. It is true he did not lean his head against a wall to bark; he exhibited his laziness in other ways. He barked often, though never at strangers; he welcomed every visitor, even the tax-collector, with tail-waggings and a smile. He spent a good deal of his time in the large kitchen, where he had a sofa to sleep on, and when the two cats of the house wanted an hour's rest they would coil themselves up on Dandy's broad shaggy side, preferring that bed to cushion or rug. They were like a warm blanket over him, and it was a sort of mutual benefit society. After an hour's sleep Dandy would go out for a short constitutional as far as the neighboring thoroughfare, where he would blunder against people, wag his tail to everybody, and then come back. He had six or eight or more outings each day, and, owing to doors and gates being closed and to his lazy disposition, he had much trouble in getting out and in. First he would sit down in the hall and bark, bark, bark, until some one would come to open the door for him, whereupon he would slowly waddle down the garden path, and if he found the gate closed he would again sit down and start barking. And the bark, bark would go on until some one came to let him out. But if after he had barked about twenty or thirty times no one came, he would deliberately open the gate himself, which he could do perfectly well, and let himself out. In twenty minutes or so he would be back at the gate and barking for admission once more, and finally, if no one paid any attention, letting himself in.

Dandy always had something to eat at meal-times, but he too liked a snack between meals once or twice a day. The dog-biscuits were kept in an open box on the lower dresser shelf, so that he could get one "whenever he felt so disposed," but he didn't like the trouble this arrangement gave him, so he would sit down and start barking, and as he had a bark which was both deep and loud, after it had been repeated a dozen times at intervals of five seconds, any person who happened to be in or near the kitchen was glad to give him his biscuit for the sake of peace and quietness. If no one gave it him, he would then take it out himself and eat it.

Now it came to pass that during the last year of the war dog-biscuits, like many other articles of food for man and beast, grew scarce, and were finally not to be had at all. At all events, that was what happened in Dandy's town of Penzance. He missed his biscuits greatly and often reminded us of it by barking; then, lest we should think he was barking about something else, he would go and sniff and paw at the empty box. He perhaps thought it was pure forgetfulness on the part of those of the house who went every morning to do the marketing and had fallen into the habit of returning without any dog-biscuits in the basket. One day during that last winter of scarcity and anxiety I went to the kitchen and found the floor strewn all over with the fragments of Dandy's biscuit-box. Dandy himself had done it; he had dragged the box from its place out into the middle of the floor, and then deliberately set himself to bite and tear it into small pieces and scatter them about. He was caught at it just as he was finishing the job, and the kindly person who surprised him in the act suggested that the reason of his breaking up the box in that way was that he got something of the biscuit flavor by biting the pieces. My own theory was that as the box was there to hold biscuits and now held none, he had come to regard it as useless—as having lost its function, so to speak—also that its presence there was an insult to his intelligence, a constant temptation to make a fool of himself by visiting it half a dozen times a day only to find it empty as usual. Better, then, to get rid of it altogether, and no doubt when he did it he put a little temper into the business!

Dandy, from the time I first knew him, was strictly teetotal, but in former and distant days he had been rather fond of his glass. If a person held up a glass of beer before him, I was told, he wagged his tail in joyful anticipation, and a little beer was always given him at mealtime. Then he had an experience, which, after a little hesitation, I have thought it best to relate, as it is perhaps the most curious incident in Dandy's somewhat uneventful life.

One day Dandy, who after the manner of his kind, had attached himself to the person who was always willing to take him out for a stroll, followed his friend to a neighboring public-house, where the said friend had to discuss some business matter with the landlord. They went into the taproom, and Dandy, finding that the business was going to be a rather long affair, settled himself down to have a nap. Now it chanced that a barrel of beer which had just been broached had a leaky tap, and the landlord had set a basin on the floor to catch the waste. Dandy, waking from his nap and hearing the trickling sound, got up, and going to the basin quenched his thirst, after which he resumed his nap. By-and-by he woke again and had a second drink, and altogether he woke and had a drink five or six times; then, the business being concluded, they went out together, but no sooner were they in the fresh air than Dandy began to exhibit signs of inebriation. He swerved from side to side, colliding with the passers-by, and finally fell off the pavement into the swift stream of water which at that point runs in the gutter at one side of the street. Getting out of the water, he started again, trying to keep close to the wall to save himself from another ducking. People looked curiously at him, and by-and-by they began to ask what the matter was. "Is your dog going to have a fit—or what is it?" they asked. Dandy's friend said he didn't know; something was the matter no doubt, and he would take him home as quickly as possible and see to it.

When they finally got to the house Dandy staggered to his sofa, and succeeded in climbing on to it and, throwing himself on his cushion, went fast asleep, and slept on without a break until the following morning. Then he rose quite refreshed and appeared to have forgotten all about it; but that day when at dinner-time some one said "Dandy" and held up a glass of beer, instead of wagging his tail as usual he dropped it between his legs and turned away in evident disgust. And from that time onward he would never touch it with his tongue, and it was plain that when they tried to tempt him, setting beer before him and smilingly inviting him to drink, he knew they were mocking him, and before turning away he would emit a low growl and show his teeth. It was the one thing that put him out and would make him angry with his friends and life companions.

I should not have related this incident if Dandy had been alive. But he is no longer with us. He was old—half-way between fifteen and sixteen: it seemed as though he had waited to see the end of the war, since no sooner was the armistice proclaimed than he began to decline rapidly. Gone deaf and blind, he still insisted on taking several constitutionals every day, and would bark as usual at the gate, and if no one came to let him out or admit him, he would open it for himself as before. This went on till January, 1919, when some of the boys he knew were coming back to Penzance and to the house. Then he established himself on his sofa, and we knew that his end was near, for there he would sleep all day and all night, declining food. It is customary in this country to chloroform a dog and give him a dose of strychnine to "put him out of his misery." But it was not necessary in this case, as he was not in misery; not a groan did he ever emit, waking or sleeping; and if you put a hand on him he would look up and wag his tail just to let you know that it was well with him. And in his sleep he passed away—a perfect case of euthanasia—and was buried in the large garden near the second apple-tree.

Animals are people too ya know.
—Radar O'Reilly in M*A*S*H

part nine

heavenly days

*Among God's creatures two—the dog and the guitar—have
taken all the sizes and all the shapes in order not
to be separated from the man.*
—*Andrés Segovia*

the bonding

roger caras

Roger A. Caras (1928–2001) was born in Methuen, Massachusetts. An author, animal-news reporter, animal activist, humane organizational administrator, he referred to himself as a naturalist. He first worked for NBC's *Today* show and later as a featured reporter on ABC's *World News Tonight* with Peter Jennings, as well as a contributing pets and wildlife reporter for *Nightline, 20/20,* and *Good Morning America.* He also hosted a nationally syndicated CBS radio program, "Pets and Wildlife." As a broadcaster, he exercised his vast knowledge of biology and zoology. The Walt Disney organization engaged his services as a consultant for their theme park Animal Kingdom at Disney World in Florida. He had worked for Walt Disney himself as a publicist when he was a young man starting out.

Although he was the author of more than sixty published books, he is still best known in the animal world for his groundbreaking work as the fourteenth president of the ASPCA. He was an active member of the exclusive Westminster Kennel Club and, during his tenure, was "the voice of Westminster" at Madison Square Garden, announcing their annual dog show. A portion of *A Celebration of Dogs* involves Caras's youthful passion for animals. The following selection from Chapter 3 of that book concerns his early experience as a young worker at the Angell Memorial Animal Hospital, a part of the Massachusetts SPCA, when his young man's dream was to become a veterinarian.

The first assignment given to the eager and somewhat brash new boy was, of course, cage cleaning. After my initial trial period, I graduated to the waist-high bathtubs in the grooming section, watching my hands and forearms turn into prunes as I worked. I bathed, clipped, and deburred dogs all day long. I seriously questioned if my back would ever be right again. A slight forward tilt for eight hours a day can do one heck of a job, even on a teenager's sacroiliac.

Promotions came in proper order, and after passing through some less rewarding departments (like the euthanasia room) I ended up in a white jacket in the clinic helping the staff veterinarians, or at least doing menial chores that made their lives a little easier. I hoisted animals on and off examining tables (after first lathering the stainless-steel surfaces with antiseptic solutions), held animals while they were examined and treated, guided clients in and out, and took dogs and cats back and logged them in if they had to be hospitalized. It was a rich experience for a boy just turning fifteen. Heading for work after school and on weekends didn't seem a chore, really. I was beginning to focus on a career. At that point I was determined to become a veterinarian.

One day the veterinarian on duty groaned as he pulled a card from the wooden holder on the wall. It was a familiar card, one side completely filled in with very little room left on the reverse.

"O.K., ask Mr. Jones to come in." (Jones was not his name, but that hardly matters.)

The client was a tired man with gray skin. He gave the impression that life had not been an unmixed blessing. His weariness hung on him like an ill-fitting shawl. In his arms, wrapped in an old but obviously frequently laundered blanket, was a positively ancient Boston terrier. The old man put his old dog on the table gently, obviously with love, and looked up at the tall young veterinarian, who towered over him. There was some hope in the old man's eyes, a little, but not really very much.

The veterinarian had seen this dog before, often, but he went through the gestures of examining him: stethoscope to heart, palpation of the abdomen, a look in the mouth and down the throat, a quick glance in the ears.

"The new medicine doesn't seem to be helping very much," the old man fairly croaked. "It's hard to tell, but there doesn't seem to be much change."

The veterinarian looked down at the floor for a moment, then put his foot on the rung of the examining table. He took a deep breath and leaned forward, prepared to make the speech he had made so many times before.

"You know there is never going to be any change, Mr. Jones. You know very well I am giving you medication for . . ." The veterinarian glanced over at the record card. ". . . for Gutsy to humor you. I can't be any blunter than that. Your dog is eighteen years old. He is blind, deaf, incontinent, he can't walk, he is frightened and in pain, and you are not being nice to him by keeping him alive this long. In nature he would have died long ago."

The young doctor was really being as kind as he knew how to be, but he had been begging Mr. Jones to have his dog put to sleep for over six months. Mr. Jones, however, was back every week trying new medication, always with the faintest hint of hope in his eyes. We all knew him. We all understood his plight, or at least we thought we did. There wasn't a veterinarian or a kennel helper at Angell who hadn't been through the same scene many times before.

"You don't think there is anything you can do?" The same question was asked every week.

"No, I *know* there is nothing we can do. We can't turn back the clock, and time has run out on Gutsy. You are not being kind to him by prolonging this very bad period for him."

The old man thought for a moment, then shook his head. He had come to a decision.

"Well, if it must be it must be. I'll take him home and do it now."

The veterinarian reached out and took the old man's elbow as he bent forward to wrap his old dog up and carry him away.

"Don't do that, please. It is a very difficult thing to do at home. You won't have the right materials, and you will be cruel to him even though you are trying to be kind. Let me do it here. I have a drug that will work very quickly. You can stay and help me if you want. You hold him and I will give him an injection. He won't even feel it and it will be over instantly. You will be able to see that for yourself. Please, don't try it yourself."

The old man thought again for a moment, then looked up into the veterinarian's eyes. Having finally decided to put his dog to death, the old man was finding new strengths, strengths that obviously had been eluding him for a long time.

"My wife died almost twenty years ago. I never wanted to re-marry. We had just one son, and he married a girl in China. They have three children, but I have never been able to go there and they can't afford to come here. We're half a world apart. I don't know why God worked it out this way for me, but Gutsy is all the family I have had for a long, long time. If he has to be killed, I'll do it. It is up to me. Thank you, doctor."

The veterinarian started to protest again, but the old man had gathered his dog up in his arms and was at the door. I was in the process of opening it for him when he turned back.

"Gutsy and I really do appreciate everything you have tried to do. We understand, truly we do."

The old man was gone, and the doctor was shaking his head as he reached for the next card in the wall rack.

We read about it the next day. It wasn't front-page news, by any means, but it did make most of the Boston dailies. The old man had gone home, stuffed paper under the door, sealed the windows, and placed his rocking chair in front of the stove. He turned the oven on, but he didn't light it. I am sure he was rocking slowly, perhaps hum-ming reassuringly to Gutsy, as they both went to sleep. I cried. I think the veterinarian did, too. I know some of the other kennel kids did, and I resented those who didn't.

• • •

So many get reformed through religion. I got
reformed through dogs.
—Lina Basquette

going home

stephen and patti thompson

Stephen and Patti Thompson have written several plays and a book dedicated to their many friends-in-fur, and they invite you to visit them at www.cathymns.com. They have written words and music for *Cat Hymns,* both a book and a CD song collection. The lyrics for "Going Home" are by the Thompsons; the melody is that of "Amazing Grace."

My time has come, now I must go,
My time on Earth is done.
Angelic voices call to me,
"Come home. Good dog. Well done!"

I feel your hands, I see your face,
I taste the tears you leave.
But I must go, I can not stay,
Please master do not grieve.

Dogs have been here ten thousand years,
E'r since man first was born,
To guard and guide and with him live,
'Till Gabriel blows his horn.

And when, my master, you're called home,
On that bright glorious day,
I'll meet you at your Master's throne,
We'll walk heaven's gold highway.

My time has come and I must go,
For now my work is done.
Angelic voices call to me,
"Come home. Good dog. Well done!"

Did you hear about the dyslexic agnostic insomniac who stays up
all night wondering if there really is a dog?
—Anonymous

• • •

Every dog has its day, and I have had mine.
—George Bernard Shaw

to my dog

john galsworthy

My dear! When I leave you
I always drop a bit of me—
A holy glove or sainted shoe—
Your wistful corse I leave it to,
For all your soul has followed me—
How could I have the stony heart
So to abandon you!

My dear! When you leave me
You drop no glove, no sainted shoe;
And yet you know what humans be—
Mere blocks of dull monstrosity!
My spirit cannot follow you
When you're away, with all its heart
As yours can follow me.

My dear! Since we must leave
(One sorry day) I you, you me;
I'll learn your wistful way to grieve;
Then through the ages we'll retrieve
Each other's scent and company;
And longing shall not pull my heart—
As now you pull my sleeve!

• • •

In dog years I'm dead!
—Anonymous

enter tarzan

mordecai siegal

This story concerns the impact that a young dog has on a lonely, with-drawn child, and its profound influence on his life. "Enter Tarzan" is a true story, one that reflects everything expressed in the writings within these pages. It is included to show how a dog bursting into one's life can profoundly change it for the better.

The first time I saw him was when my father came through the front door and set him loose on the floor. He was lightning out of a bottle as he tore across the living room, sliding over the Sunday comics, which I always spread out in a neat and orderly pile. I was lying on my stomach at the time, holding my chin in my hands, my elbows on the floor, lost in a four-colored paper fantasy, one of several avenues of escape. The big puppy's hind legs loped ahead of his front legs like those of a kangaroo chasing bubbles. It happened so fast, there was no time to escape. Paws over ass, he scattered the newspaper into a sliding mishmash, with no regard for the neat pile or the page count. Flash Gordon crumbled into the leg of the couch and Mandrake the Magician slid on top of Dick Tracy. The pages scattered everywhere. The phantasmagoria behind my eyes shut off like a light switch. My heart stopped, he scared me so much. I was ten and my inner boat was capsized. I lost the page count, for better or worse, and I never recovered it, not ever. Something out there with a motorboat tongue had just crashed through the invisible bricks that shielded me. When a dashing young dog suddenly and without warning bursts into the life of a kid, he tears through solid emotional walls, brick by brick, and slurps his way to the unsuspecting heart.

The orangy blur quickly panted in and out and squeaked out a bark—at least I thought it was a bark—with his tongue hanging out the side of his mouth. My bones turned to milk and I could hardly move as he sprinted back and forth from my face to my father's shoes, then off the baseboards and around again, quick-licking my nose as he dashed by. He was a comet burning into six directions at the same time. It was a frenzy that I had never seen before. The puppy was happy to be there and I was overwhelmed.

I tried to duck my head into my armpit, but he wouldn't allow it. He wrapped his belly around the back of my neck like a hairy inner tube, stuck his tongue in my ear, and rubbed a bit of fur and saliva and leaking droplets on my ticklish skin, and for the first time that I could remember, I laughed deeply from the gut, laughed again until my stomach hurt. It was an unfamiliar sensation, and my face stretched in new directions as my shoulders smoothed out the protective semicolon that was my chest. Suddenly, I had a puppy dog, and the first quiet ten years just washed away in a riptide of unexpected pleasure and laughter. I looked at the scattered newspaper, and staring up at me was my absolute favorite hero, Tarzan, with Jane clinging to his back and Boy in his arms as he swung from a vine. They were the family I always dreamed about, even though I never could find a vine on the streets of Philadelphia. Sitting in front of me was my new dog, my everlasting pal, and I could give him no greater honor than to name him after my jungle dad. Like all miracles, he was completely unexpected.

South Philadelphia was a very gray place in 1938, crowded with people out of work, who had nothing to do but pitch pennies against brick walls and look for the ketchup bus that came in

There was no doubt that Tarzan was my dog. He sought me out from the beginning and decided that we were brothers and that he would go on scattering the Sunday comics no matter what.

July to take them to New Jersey to pick tomatoes for a day's work. Before Tarzan dashed into my life, all I could muster was a set of one-word answers when questioned. I just wanted to be left alone so I could pretend that I was invisible. That helped me transport myself into a world of my own creation. Sometimes I smiled, not often, and only as a way of avoiding attention. I was a quiet kid with nothing to say as I looked for the corner of a room where I could sit quietly and successfully go unnoticed and where no one would bother me. Sanctuary was to be invisible. Although I rarely spoke, my speech was not impaired, only my trust.

Our food was as gray as the neighborhood once my father lost his job. He was caught stealing a carton of cigarettes off the truck he loaded and unloaded. I don't know how long he was out of work, because I was only four when it happened, but I remember being cold and hungry that winter. I wore my pants out at the knees and my coat was too thin for the frigid weather.

My mom was upset most of the time and yelled at my father a lot, and when she did, he yelled back. Their combat was about money and being out of work. He shouted, he threatened, and one day he grabbed his hat and coat and disappeared. I remember hiding under the bed and peeing in my pants.

He was gone for two years. Those were the years I developed my disappearing act. There was more, a lot more, but I didn't think about it. I was invisible.

Then in the blink of an eye, everything changed. The streets emptied and the men went back to work, and some went into the army. My father came home. He had a job. Just before the war with Japan, they rented a nice house with a porch and a yard. It was six blocks away on a quiet tree-lined street and was quite simply another world. Everything changed and nothing changed. We were still a bunch of broken eggs. My mother and father never stopped arguing about money and things I didn't understand. I stayed quietly in my own world until that orange-haired surge of energy jumped onto my lap and into my life as only a dog can.

Try hiding from a young dog. It can't be done. It was a heavenly gift.

There was no doubt that Tarzan was *my* dog. He sought me out from the beginning and decided that we were brothers and that he would go on scattering the Sunday comics no matter what. If I got up to leave the room, he would follow me. Where I walked, he walked. When it was time to go to bed, he would stretch his long front legs, raise his rear end, and trot upstairs with me. Unlike most dogs, he enjoyed the stairs. He always ran ahead of me and hopped on the bed before I got there, standing with his tongue hanging out, proclaiming that he had won the race. Tarzan was my teddy bear and my protector and my friend all rolled into one loving person that made life available with every sweet breath he took. My arms clutched his thick furry neck and I slept well knowing he was there. I have a dreamy memory of my mother coming into my room each night and shooing him off the bed. He reluctantly curled up on the floor next to me, then jumped right back up after she'd left the room.

He grew to be a big dog—at least he seemed big to me, because I was such a puny kid—and his red-orange coat was profuse and lionlike. I loved burying my head in it. He smelled like my father's hairbrush, and when I hugged him, I would try to duplicate each breath he took. I could never catch his rhythm, though. It was a game we played as we lay quietly on the living room floor, on top of the papers. His legs were long and thick and I could barely close my fingers around them. His paws were soft as velvet. He had the brightest eyes I have ever seen and they had the look of smartness, but more than that. When he looked into my eyes, he could see the deepest part of me and know all my secrets as if by magic. He knew everything and there was no place to hide from him. Much to everyone's surprise, I even began talking—first to Tarzan and then to everyone else. As I remember it, I jabbered a lot about what I was going to do that day or about what I had done the day before. My plans always involved the dog. I finally had a brother that loved me. I finally had plans.

A year had passed and life was much brighter and happier as we grew together. A few kids in the neighborhood quickly made friends, if only to be around Tarzan. He was a magnet for people we passed on the street. Everyone stopped to pet him, talk to him, and tell me what a lucky boy I was to have such a dog. It felt good.

One warm day in May, I heard Tarzan barking in the yard. I went out and found him hovering over a large turtle, maybe seven inches square, that had waddled in from a hole at the bottom of the fence. It was larger than a cocoa tin and had the most unusual design on its shell—black-and-yellow blotches, with shades of dark green in between. I had never seen a turtle that didn't come from Atlantic City and have its tiny back painted blue and yellow for Easter. I held the exotic creature with both hands. It had heft. It stuck its head out of the shell, nipped my finger, and went back in. I was awestruck. I set him down and immediately named him Mandrake. The three of us became a family that summer. He stayed outside in the yard, where I fed him a spoonful of tuna fish on a lettuce leaf every day. After that, he never nipped me again.

Mandrake appeared the same day as my grandmother. She managed to bring her own dark clouds with her. My mom's father had died and so now her mother had come to live with us. She was a stern woman, who did not smile and who never doubted or questioned anything she said. She dispensed opinions and gave orders at least a dozen times a day. She spoke in Russian when she didn't want me to understand her. Despite this, her tone of voice, the expression on her face, and her gestures allowed me to understand what she was saying anyway. I quickly understood that she thought my mother was wasting money feeding a dog. She also criticized her for allowing Tarzan to live in the house, believing that dogs were dirty and had filthy habits. She constantly

I kissed her on the cheek as she got into the taxi with her suitcases and told her that Tarzan would miss her at breakfast time. She ignored me and slammed the car door. I waved good-bye with a big grin on my face . . .

told my mother what she was doing wrong in a cosmic monotone coming from someplace around her deadpan face. I became very cautious around her from the first day she marched in with her suit-cases, complaining about the furniture not being covered with sheets. I kept Tarzan with me all the time, as though she was going to snatch him away, and I also thought it was a good idea to keep Mandrake outside. I walked the dog early in the morning and late in the evening because she made me nervous. She hardly ever saw him.

Off the kitchen, there was a small pantry, where my mother kept canned food, a snow shovel, my father's tools, and an assort-ment of things that would have gone in a garage if we'd had one. One warm morning, the old lady came downstairs earlier than usual and went looking for her breakfast. Tarzan was in the living room. She walked around him, muttering her disapproval at his presence on the carpet. He had his chin on the floor and followed her with swiveling eyes. Like everyone else, he was subdued around her. She went into the pantry and found a box of cereal, sat down at the table, and filled a bowl with the crunchy flakes and drenched them in milk and sugar. She stared at the dog coldly and shook her head with every spoonful she put in her mouth. He stared back with innocent caution. Dogs do not have to be rocket scientists to grasp disapproval when it comes their way, especially from a person with a pickle puss.

My mom and I came downstairs at the same time and were horrified to see the two of them eyeballing each other. Then we noticed the box on the table. My grandmother said she was hun-gry and had found the cereal, which she loved. She said the flakes were large and very crunchy, and she wondered why we'd hidden the box from her. My mom grinned and I looked down at the floor. And then the dam burst and we started to laugh uncontrollably. I hadn't laughed that hard since the day Tarzan came. The old woman demanded to know why we were laughing. Mom told her that she was eating dog food. It was called Grow Pup and was for Tarzan. She wouldn't believe it until we showed her a drawing of a smiling puppy face on the box. She slammed her hand on the table, rose from her chair, and said she didn't care, that the cereal was delicious and too good for a dog. With a red face, she walked upstairs, where she stayed all day, sulking. We never mentioned her taste for dog food again, at least not in front of her, and like a gift from heaven, she stopped complaining about the dog. As a matter of fact, she stopped complaining about everything and soon after went to live with my aunt. I kissed her on the cheek as she got into the taxi with her suitcases and told her that Tarzan would miss her at breakfast time. She ignored me and slammed the car door. I waved good-bye with a big grin on my face, knowing everything was about to get better.

It was a Tom Sawyer summer, and Tarzan, Mandrake, and I were having a great time. All that was missing was Becky Thatcher. I liked playing in the backyard with them, but Tarzan preferred the front of the house, where he could see the kids in the neighborhood and watch the cars go by. He kept pulling at the leash whenever another kid appeared or anyone else who wanted to give him a pet or a hug. I guess I made more friends that summer because of him than I ever had before. In the mornings, we would squat under the big tree in front of my house and watch the ants create mounds of sand or carry grains of bread into their tunnels. Occasionally, I brought Mandrake outside to eat his fill of ants, and that made a big hit with the kids in the neighborhood.

August was grasshopper and lightning bug time. A small swarm of the green jumpers overran our street. They were everywhere. You could catch them by the dozens and save them in a cigar box, then let them go after you were finished looking at them. If you put one on your finger and rubbed the top of its head, it would spit out a brownish fluid that we called "tobacco juice." It was boy stuff, although there wasn't a merit badge for tobacco juice. Tarzan got very excited by them and tried to catch them as they jumped everywhere. He kept all the kids doubled up with laughter.

After supper, we sat on the front steps of the porch to watch the show from dozens of tiny green lights glowing on and off in midair. It was a midsummer night's dream, with fireflies and grasshoppers, breezy leaves, and a box turtle and a dog with a heart as great as a mom's. Across the street and down the block, Mr. Luchowski was on his porch, gently strumming on his mandolin. I would give anything now to know what that soft, haunting song was that gave everyone in the neighborhood a sweet reverie and a break from the war news.

Tarzan ran as far as he could on his leash when the lightning bugs flashed, and he snapped them into his mouth when he could. They were easy because they flew so slowly. We all caught them. I put mine in an empty jelly jar with holes punched into the lid for air, but the dog swallowed his. I looked down his throat and could see the light still flashing as he gulped them out of sight. My mom looked away with distaste, but I was amazed.

Autumn came and there were crunchy leaves all over the sidewalk and along the curb stones. It was jacket and apples weather and the streets got dark earlier. Traffic was noisier and busier. School began, and homework ended the leisurely rhythm of summer.

It was darker outside now when I walked the dog. I remember the night I closed my black-and-white-marbled copybook and went downstairs, looked for the leash, and called for Tarzan. My mom told me my father had already gone out with the dog. I went back up the stairs and flopped on my bed. My eyes began to close and my copybook slid to the floor. I was drifting to sleep when I heard the front door open with a fury and then slam shut with a bang. My father was agitated and shouting. My eyes opened quickly as I tried to understand what was happening. I heard him say something about Tarzan, but he was so upset that he could hardly utter a clear sentence. He was shaken and out of control. Suddenly, like a stab in the heart, I heard him say Tarzan was dead.

I barely heard the rest. My ears started to close down. There was something about unhooking the leash and teaching him to walk without it. They ponderously climbed the stairs to tell me, but they were too late. I had flown away, turned invisible, and clinched my lips shut. When they opened the door and came into the room, I was lying on my back, staring at the wall, my head turned away from them. My mother sat on the bed and took my hand, but I could hardly feel it. They both tried to talk to me, but I didn't answer, because I couldn't hear them. I simply wasn't there. They turned out the light, left the room, and shut the door.

In the end, hunger won out. It always does. I was twelve and I was hungry. I went down to breakfast and to my mom. From that time on, I couldn't look my father in the eyes. I hated him. As weeks passed into months, the echoes of summertime laughter and the bark of an orange dog would make me ache with sadness and then suddenly make me laugh. It was a deep wound that itched when the weather changed. The kids in the neighborhood kept coming around. They liked to hear stories about Tarzan and the grasshoppers or Tarzan and the lightning bugs and Tarzan and the wicked grandmother. On occasion, I would let them rap their knuckles on Mandrake's shell and offer him a bit of tuna fish.

It is rare to be able to pinpoint with absolute certainty when the pain stops or when you are no longer a little boy. One day, you simply discover that the child you once were is gone, along with your Captain Midnight decoder ring and your baseball cards. I went to school, I served my country, I got married, I raised three children, and I devoted the better part of my adult life to writing books about dogs. A memory of a big orange sweetheart with huge chocolate eyes would not allow me to remain invisible or refuse to talk. My dog Tarzan, my first dog, my first friend, is as dear to me now as he was so long ago. When I go quiet, as I sometimes do, I think of him swallowing a lightning bug or scattering my Sunday comics all over the floor, and I laugh quietly to myself. He was the dog of my life and I was blessed to have had him.

Like a lot of kids, I remembered only the bad stuff and hardly asked about the good things. It's not fair, but I guess it's part of growing up. Many decades later, under a chilly rain and a canvas canopy bounded by tears and black clothing, I whispered under my breath, "Thanks for getting me Tarzan, Dad," and the iron anvil inside my chest fell away as I licked away the one drop that ran down my cheek. It could have been rain. "Good-bye, Dad. Say hello to Tarzan for me."

• • •

I am I because my little dog knows me.
—*Gertrude Stein*

erica's song

arlene klein

From Arlene Klein's collection of poems *I Never Wanted To Say Goodbye*, "Erica's Song" offers gentle words to comfort those who mourn the loss of a pet.

"MomMom! Dusty and Casey are not old and sick anymore.
They are in heaven. They are happy and they play."
The words I will cling to forevermore
About the little dogs she still looks for.

Her gentle voice trails on soft as silk.
She takes a bite of a cookie and a sip of milk.
She continues to gaze at the photos on the wall
Of the dogs she loves and their names she calls.
RJ, DD and Kody come and sit at her feet.
She hugs and kisses them and she repeats,

"MomMom! Dusty and Casey are not old and sick anymore.
They are in heaven. They are happy and they play."

Words so profound from one so small,
One so young with no experience at all
Except the love and kindness she gives
To the animals she knows, who with me live.
A myriad of visions before my eyes pass
Of years shared with the dogs that flew by so fast.
The last haunting memory that I try to erase
Of the stare in their eyes, the look on their face.
At last, those thoughts I can finally replace
With pleasant dreams of them in a faraway place.

Summer and autumn quickly passed by,
The cold winter is here and spring draws nigh.
Time has healed the pain and now I clearly see
The dogs where Erica wants them to be.
The genuine love of a child only three,
She takes my hand and utters to me,
"MomMom! Dusty and Casey are not old and sick anymore.
They are in heaven. They are happy and they play."

• • •

He seemed neither old nor young. His strength lay in his eyes.
They looked as old as the hills, and as young and as
wild. I never tired looking into them.
                                        —John Muir

old dogs, old friends:

enjoying your older dog

bonnie wilcox, d.v.m., and chris walkowicz

Chris Walkowicz, a president emeritus of the Dog Writers Association of America, is an established author of numerous books and articles about dogs and an accredited American Kennel Club show judge, a major accomplishment. Although the recipient of many awards, including the DWAA's Best Book Award, the Communicator Award, and a Fido Award for Woman of the Year, she hasn't changed her philosophy: "If I can save just one dog's life, my work will be worthwhile."

Bonnie Wilcox is a retired veterinarian. She has owned and shown German Shorthaired Pointers for most of her life. A Field Spaniel is now enjoying her free time. Bonnie has coauthored four books with Chris Walkowicz: *Old Dogs, Old Friends*, two editions of *Successful Dog Breeding* (a DWAA Best Book Award winner), the *Atlas of Dog Breeds of the World*, and *The Complete Question and Answer Book on Dogs*.

from chapter 1: memories are forever

Old dogs, like old shoes, are comfortable. They might be a bit out of shape and a little worn around the edges, but they fit well.

Old friends know and accept our idiosyncrasies and our imperfections. And old dogs are the best of friends. They not only accept us as we are, they don't offer advice or criticism. The elderly pet makes few demands upon us and is usually happy to simply curl up by our feet. Pets don't carry tales to others when we fail at a task or behave in a less-than-sterling manner. No wonder some people say, "The more I know about people, the more I like my dog."

As you stroke your old guy's head and think about the secrets you have shared over the years, the flood of memories is as soothing as a cool creek on a hot summer day. Memories such as the puppy ecstasy whenever you returned home and the steamy day you shared an ice cream cone. Or the day he ran his first sled race, squinting into the wind, snow and ice coating his face, his inheritance exuberantly urging him on despite bitter cold and inexperience.

A teenager might remember feeding Sheba those detested carrots under the table so Mom would consent to dessert—and that even Sheba wouldn't eat the broccoli!

Or the walk around the block when Alf tried to make friends with a kitten; his puzzled look when his overtures brought only a hiss and a swat on the nose.

"When the mother duck introduced her nine little ones to Spicey," recalls Tommie, "she watched us as intently as we watched her. Spicey, you were so still, I thought you were holding your breath."

. . . We, the owners of aging pets, are actually the lucky ones. We've had time to build memories, and—until the last moment— there's always time to create more.

. . . How old is old? Due to the differences in various breeds, old age cannot be generalized. Small dogs tend to live longer than their giant counterparts whose life expectancy is about nine years. Toys often live to be fifteen years old, and medium-sized dogs are in the middle of the age range (about twelve years). The American Kennel Club classifies dogs seven and older as senior citizens in the breed ring, where they may be entered in the Veterans class. Competition in Veterans Obedience classes begins at eight years of age.

As we all know, there is no fountain of youth. From the moment of birth, aging begins. No one travels in the other direction, but as the well-worn saw has it, "It's better than the alternative."

Our canine friends have advantages over us in this aging process. They don't remember what youth was like nor lament wasted time or long-gone svelte figures and physical abilities. They don't fear growing older or dying. No sighing over wrinkles or gray hair. Animals have no concept of yesterday or tomorrow; they live only for today. Thus they're perfectly content being a bit slower, a bit grayer, a bit less active.

Dogs don't grieve when their children grow up or leave home and couldn't care less why they don't come to visit. They don't mope if no one sends a card or brings a present. There's no urge to see the world or to dangle a granddog on their knees. And there's no depression when they see the number of candles on the cake or if they fail to reach a goal set when they were younger. Dogs have no mid-life crises or disappointment when sexual activity decreases or when reproductive organs are surgically removed. Their owners find them increasingly easy to live with as they age.

Mature, healthy dogs are extremely tolerant with the young, whether canine or human. They allow youngsters many liberties. Dogs sometimes grit their teeth or sigh, but when the youthful attention becomes too much, they simply rise and move to another spot.

In the world of dogs, growing older is peaceful. It means gaining privileges pups don't have or more time to sleep in the sun. Maturity often brings free access to the entire house rather than confinement to one or two rooms.

When Satin was young, she lived the life of a show dog: training classes, shampoos and blow drys, long hours in crates traveling, laborious labors and demanding whelps. Now the Afghan sleeps beside her beloved owners' bed on a soft carpet. She takes naps on the couch; no other dog is allowed on the furniture. When "Mom" first noticed the old gal creeping up to rest her bones, "Dad" said, "Aw, let her be, she deserves it."

Now Satin rides in the car whenever she wants, but only when she wants to. If she'd rather stay home to snooze on the couch, she is free to do so. This grandma can visit the kennel's puppies, play a bit, then leave any time she wishes. Once a year she is gussied up, taken to a local show and fussed over by everyone.

Someone said to her owner, "Do you think Satin misses her old glamorous life?" and was answered, "Are you kidding?"

Whether or not they have memories is unknown to us; perhaps they have vague recollections known only to them. . . .

from chapter 2: grow old with me

Grow old with me!
The best is yet to be . . .
—Robert Browning

When people first consider adding a dog to their family, most tend to think of puppies. As with human adoptions, the expectant family wishes to share everything from the beginning. They want to experience the joy of cuddling a tiny, perfect, adorable infant.

Canine—like human—infants aren't always perfect, however. They drool, they piddle (a lot), they spill their food and then sit in it or smash it into their hair. When teething, they sink their needle-sharp teeth into soft parts of your body. Babies sleep when you want to play with them, and they wake when you want to sleep. Young people and dogs both experience an inexplicable attraction to mud, rain puddles and other messy things. The sloppier the better.

They behave their worst just when you want to show them off. At times they are frightened, and you must comfort them. At other times their escapades frighten you and there is little comfort.

Once a person has endured all of these joys (especially two or three or five times), she may wish to cherish and remember them in her heart rather than underfoot. Not all people want to tread that path again.

Parents sometimes admit they enjoy their children more when the kids are a bit older—as preteens, teenagers or even adults.

Veteran dog owners also might prefer the age of reason, the time when the animal becomes that best friend they were looking for. They, unlike new parents, have a choice and can skip right over the frustrations of housebreaking, cutting teeth and middle-of-the-night yowls by adopting an older dog.

Life-styles change. When your schedule demands concentration or long hours, it's not easy to train a pup in the social amenities. An adult dog won't be as likely to cut his teeth on antique chair legs or electrical cords. He's able to last several hours without answering nature's call. He might even protect your property once he decides that's his job.

The same qualities you might seek in a puppy should be apparent in an older dog: a personality that suits you and the capability to be a good companion. Basic mental and physical soundness (allowing for temporary problems perhaps induced by stress) are important. It does no one any good to adopt a dog who is doomed to a life of terror, instability, or illness.

If you decide to look for an older dog, he will stick out like a petunia in an onion patch. Search the shelters in your area and ask your veterinarian to keep an eye out. Hard as it is to believe, animals are sometimes abandoned at veterinary clinics or boarding kennels. You'll know when you see the right dog. An invisible bond is there from the start and remains forever.

When Glenda first saw Laddie, he was tied in the backyard of a young, harassed mother. What was Glenda even doing there? She'd always had smooth-coated little dogs, Chihuahuas, and here she was, at a friend's suggestion, looking at the sad eyes of a middle-aged Sheltie who'd been dubbed "King" when he'd been adopted less than a month before.

She wrote, "There at the end of a stretch of knotted string, looking downcast and decidedly miserable, sat a sable Sheltie. Larger than some, but with breeding apparent in the refined head and well-proportioned body, he did indeed present a regal appearance. But there was something else: an aura of weariness, a tangible acknowledgment of having lived an existence that did not exactly coincide with the stately title he had so recently acquired. My friend was right—I could not abandon him. Something between us clicked and our lives were to be united for the next five years.

First she renamed him, then he retrained her: how to bathe a "large" dog, how to groom (turning patiently from side to side), an introduction to obedience classes. Glenda's job required extended travel, and Laddie joined her on the trips. She says he adapted so well that one day she left a meeting, still wrapped up in her thoughts, when she realized somebody was missing. "When I returned to claim him, he nonchalantly appeared, stretching languidly as he emerged from under the conference table . . . confident that I would return."

from the appendix

HUMAN VS. DOG AGES

DOG	HUMAN
6 months	10 years
8 months	13 years
10 months	14 years
12 months	15 years
18 months	20 years
2 years	24 years
4 years	32 years
6 years	40 years
8 years	48 years
10 years	56 years
11 years	60 years
12 years	64 years
13 years	68 years

14 years	72 years
15 years	76 years
16 years	80 years
18 years	88 years
20 years	96 years
21 years	100 years

copyright acknowledgments